Official MFC Publication

The light at the end of the tunnel

a potted history of Morecambe Football Club

by Lawrence Bland and Derek Quinn

We would like to thank the following Sponsors:
Jack Baxter, D Boustead, Brian Carford, Richard Craig, Allen Crossley,
Mick Dennison, David Firth, Alan Freear, Jack Fretwell, Fretwell Meat Technicians,
Andy Hammond, Kevin Hobbs, Peter Howard, Daniel Logan, Ian Lyon,
Philip Markham, Ian McNicholas, Jonathan Metcalfe Alan Metcalfe, Ian Monk,
Ian Murphy, Ken Ormrod, Keith Perry, Mr. and Mrs. J. Preston,
Mark Proctor and family, Lionel Proctor, Stephen Porter, Lionel Procter,
Neil Roebuck, Mike Saban, Mrs Saban, Janet Sutcliffe, Jonty Tarbuck,
Rod Taylor, Trevor Taylor, Tim Traynor, Jeff Udall, Tony Wade, Roger Walker.

MINUTES
the total football solution

THE LIGHT AT THE END OF THE TUNNEL -
A POTTED HISTORY OF MORECAMBE FOOTBALL CLUB
by Lawrence Bland and Derek Quinn
Published by 90 Minutes Publications, Darwen
Text copyright © Derek Quinn 2004
Printed in the UK by Mercer Print, Accrington.
Design, page layout & cover montage by Darren Brown.
Cover photography by Kimberley Harper.
Photographs courtesy of Mike Williamson and 'The Visitor'
(compiled by Mercer Print / 90 Minutes Publications).
ISBN 0-9546251-2-9

FOREWORD
By Peter McGuigan

I am delighted to have been asked to
write the foreword to this exciting new
book detailing the history of the club.
Since that first team was chosen in
August 1920 the club has been at the
heart of the local sporting community.
There have been a huge number of
highs, and a few lows as well, along
the way but nobody can say life at
Morecambe Football Club has ever
been dull.

Lawrence and Derek have delved into
that history and produced a book that
charts in detail those highs and lows,
and brings to life the careers of a
host of individuals who have helped
the club get where it is today.

Every single person in this book has
played his part in that success and

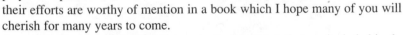

their efforts are worthy of mention in a book which I hope many of you will
cherish for many years to come.

As a club we can look back and savour the successes that are included in the
book. But we are also looking to write some exciting new chapters in the
years to come.

Our goal is to reach the Football League as soon as possible. We have made
massive strides in the last few years and we want to continue to reach new
heights and rewrite the history books once more.

Peter McGuigan
Morecambe FC Chairman.

the
shr⚽mps
the official matchday magazine of morecambe football club

Nationwide
NATIONWIDE CONFERENCE

£2

OFFICIAL CLUB SPONSORS

THURNHAM LEISURE GROUP

LCR

UMBRO

MATCH SPONSOR

Beaufort Road Post Office

MATCH BALL SPONSOR

Motor Move On Line Car Sales

PROGRAMME SPONSOR

CAPITAL BANK
LEISURE

WIRRAL PROGRAMME CLUB
NATIONWIDE CONFERENCE
PROGRAMME OF THE YEAR '02-'03

MORECAMBE v NORTHWICH VICTORIA

Saturday 7th February 2004
Issue 16

A

ABANDONED HOME MATCHES
October 29, 1932 v Chorley, 0-0, FA Cup 3rd Qualif. Rd, 32 minutes (waterlogged pitch).
November 25, 1939 v Hustle-Rite, 3-2, North Lancs League, 77 minutes.
April 9, 1958 v Bacup Borough, 0-2, league, 80 minutes (bad light and late start).
December 24, 1960 v Lancaster City, 0-0, league, 20 minutes (fog).
November 23, 1963 v Horwich RMI, 0-0, league, 10 minutes (fog).
January 1, 1982 v Lancaster City, 0-1, league, 60 minutes (fog).
January 1, 1997 v Southport, 2-2, league, 45 minutes (icy pitch).
January 28, 1997 v Stalybridge Celtic, 0-0, League Cup 3rd Rd, 17 minutes (fog).
August 26, 2000 v Northwich Victoria, 1-0, 41 minutes (waterlogged pitch).

ACCRINGTON STANLEY. Morecambe first met the original Stanley in the Lancashire
Combination in 1920/21. The first game at Peel Park on February 12, 1921 saw a crowd
of 8,000 see Stanley win 6-1. The two sides met in the FA Cup 1st Rd at Peel Park on
November 17, 1956, with Stanley winning 4-1.
After Stanley withdrew from the league, Accrington joined the Lancashire Combination
during the 1963/64 season. Their first meeting ended in a 5-1 win for Morecambe at Peel
Park on October 24. In the return at Christie Park on March 6, 1965, Morecambe won 7-1.
After the club was reformed in 1968 they met in an FA Cup 1st Qualifying Rd tie at
Christie Park on September 18, 1971. Morecambe won 2-0 with goals from Richmond
and Lancaster.

ADAMS, BILLY. 1947-50. Left-back 24 (2 cup) apps. Ex-PNE.

ADAMS PARK: Home ground of Wycombe Wanderers, then managed by Martin
O'Neill. The Shrimps' only trip was on February 2, 1993, in a FA Trophy 2nd Rd replay
which ended with a 2-0 defeat watched by 4,492.

ADLINGTON: Just 1 meeting, a 2-1 win in the 2nd Rd of the Lancashire Junior Cup on
November 2, 1929 at Christie Park, Att: 723.

AGGBOROUGH STADIUM: Home of Kidderminster Harriers and the venue of the
club's first away game in the Conference. Morecambe lost 4-2, their 1st defeat in 22 games.

AIREY, ALBERT: 1952-54. Outside-left 43 (8 cup) apps; 12 goals. Ex-Horwich RMI
and Fleetwood player who was a member of the Lancashire Junior Cup final team of
1947/48.

AIREY, JOHN (JACK): 1963-66. Outside-left 32 (9 cup) apps; 12 (3 cup) goals. Ex-
professional with Blackburn Rovers from January 1959 to June 1963 where he made 3
apps, scoring 1 goal. Joined in August 1963 but suffered a badly broken leg.

ALDCLIFFE ROAD: Morecambe played one game there beating Lancaster Lads Club in the wartime 1940-41 season in the North Lancashire League, winning 6-2 on September 28, 1940.

ALDERSHOT TOWN: First met the 'Shots' in the Conference at Christie Park on September 6, 2003, winning 2-0. Att: 1,948.

ALDRED: 1920-22. Centre-forward 36 (2 cup) apps; 19 goals. Morecambe's first deaf player who joined in November 1920. A league player with Oldham Athletic where he made 69 apps and scored 16 goals between 1916 and 1919.

ALDREN, JACK: 1938-39 and 1945-46. Goalkeeper 2 apps. He may only have played two games but Jack conceded 20 goals. He played in a pre-war 6-0 defeat at Darwen on April 25, 1939 and was then between the sticks seven years later for the Shrimps' record defeat, a 14-1 reverse at Chorley on Good Friday, 1946.

ALFORD, CARL: 1990-91. Centre-forward 5 apps. One that got away in many ways. Carl had two short spells at Morecambe in 1990 and 1991 but failed to impress and was allowed to leave. In hindsight it was a big mistake as he became a prolific non-league goalscorer with clubs like Witton Albion, Macclesfield Town, Kettering, Rushden & Diamonds and Yeovil. In March 1996 he became non-league's most expensive player when Rushden & Diamonds bought him from Kettering Town for £85,000. After scoring 50 goals in 78 league appearances for Stevenage Borough he had another big money move, joining Doncaster Rovers for £55,000 in May 2000. Won 2 England semi-professional caps.

ALFRETON TOWN: The 'Reds' knocked Morecambe out of the FA Cup in the 1st Qualifying Rd at Christie Park on Sept 15, 1984, in the only meeting between the sides. Att: 298.

ALI, MARVIN: 1989-1991. Forward 21+2 (14+1 cup) apps; 7 (7 cup) goals. Maltese-born Ali was brought to the club from Mossley by manager Bryan Griffiths in the 1989/90 season and soon proved a great crowd favourite. His mazey runs, pace and ability to score spectacular goals brought scouts flocking to Christie Park. In his first season he scored 12 goals in 31 games.

ALL-STAR XI: The club's floodlights were switched-on on October 27, 1960 as Morecambe beat an All-Star XI 4-3, Att: 3,500. Sir Tom Finney *(right)* played in the game and returned to Christie Park for another All-Stars XI team on December 7, 1960, for the opening of the new £10,000 Auxiliary Supporters' Club.

ALLEN, ADRIAN: 1956-58. Outside-right 34 (7 cup) app; 9 (2 cup) goals. A junior with PNE before being called up for National Service where he played football for the Royal Navy and Combined Services. Joined Southport as an amateur in May 1954 making 6 appearances before moving to Morecambe in August 1956. Later played for Lancaster City, Netherfield and Darwen.

ALLEN, SHAUN: 1987-88 and 1991-92. Midfield 31 (16 cup) apps. Former PNE apprentice who joined Morecambe for the first time in August 1987. He then moved to Chorley where he made 65 appearances between 1988-91 before rejoining the Shrimps for a short spell. Went on to play for Lancaster City and St Gregory's in Preston.

ALLISON, MIKE: 1991-94. Goalkeeper 88 (45 cup) apps. Joined in May 1991 from Chesterfield where he made 16 appearances. A consistent goalkeeper who played in some big games in the early 90s. Left Morecambe for Witton Albion and later played for Horwich RMI, St Helens Town, Rossendale Utd, Warrington Town and Fulwood Amateurs. President's Cup winner 1991-92.

ALT PARK: Troubled and vandalised home of the now defunct Knowsley United and formerly the home of Huyton Rugby League club. Morecambe played four matches there. The first game was a friendly on August 17, 1991, which ended in a 1-1 draw. Morecambe won 3-2, on May 7, 1994, in a league game in front of 102 people but lost 2-1 in a cup game on November 1, 1994. The final encounter was a league clash on January 14, 1995, which ended 1-1.

ALTRINCHAM: Morecambe first met the Robins in a Christmas friendly at Woodhill Lane on December 27, 1920. Altrincham arrived short of players so Morecambe's Aldred and Anderson played for the visitors who won 3-0.
The two sides have met on many occasions, since with perhaps the most memorable being the Shrimps' record Conference victory, a 7-0 win on February 17, 1996. Att: 983.

ALTY, COLIN: 1970-73. Midfield 30 (5 cup) apps; 13 goals. Spent four years at PNE between 1960 and 1964 but despite making 65 appearances in the reserves did not feature in the first team. He finally made his Football League debut with Southport where he spent six successful years between 1964 and 1970, making 184 league and six cup appearances, scoring 22 goals. His best season was in 1966-67 when he was the player of the year as Southport took the runners-up spot in Division Four.
He joined Morecambe in August 1970 but tragically broke his leg on three separate occasions and was released in April 1973, moving on to Skelmersdale Utd.

ALVECHURCH: The 2 sides met in a pre-season friendly on August 2, 1980 with Morecambe winning 3-1 with two goals from Parry and one from Gibson.

AMERICAN FOOTBALL: Fylde Falcons played 2 games at Christie Park in 1987. On July 12 the Falcons beat Manchester Spartans 60-0 and 7 days later lost 40-27 to Manchester All-Stars.

ANCHOR GROUND: The home ground of Darwen FC was first visited on September 13, 1920. A crowd of 5,000 watched a 2-2 draw.

ANDERSON, STEWART: 1992-93. Midfield 18 (11 cup) apps; 3 goals. A member of the successful Colne Dynamoes and Witton Albion sides of the late 80s and early 90s who was signed by Bryan Griffiths in October 1992 for £2,000 after a successful loan period. His spell was a short one however, as he left to join Stalybridge Celtic for £2,500 in February 1993. Later moved to Accrington Stanley, Ashton Utd, Mossley and Chadderton where he was assistant manager in 2002-03.

ANFIELD: Morecambe Reserves visited Liverpool's home ground for the club's only visit on January 8, 1938, for a West Lancashire League clash with Liverpool Reserves. A crowd of 6,500 watched a 1-1 draw. The club should have returned to Anfield on December 14, 1989 for a Lancashire League KO Cup, 1st round tie but Morecambe could not raise a team.

ANNAN, RICHARD: 1996-97. Defender 17+1 (11+1 cup) apps. A member of the Crewe Alexandra team that won promotion to Division Two in the 1993/94 season the former Leeds apprentice joined the Shrimps after spells at Farsley Celtic, Guiseley and Halifax Town. Joined Morecambe in July 1996 but was released in May 1997. Moved on to Stalybridge Celtic, Hyde Utd and Guiseley.

APPLEBY PARK: Former home of North Shields where Morecambe played three times in the 1983/84 season in cup competitions. The Shrimps played there in the FA Cup 2nd Qualifying Rd and at the same stage in the FA Trophy. Unfortunately, the Shrimps were knocked out on both occasions.

ARBORIES MEMORIAL GROUND: Home of Padiham. Just one visit with a 2-0 win in the Lancashire Combination League on November 11, 1961.

ARBROATH: Only one meeting with the 'Red Lichties' which was a pre-season friendly on July 19, 1999. The game, at Christie Park, ended 0-0.

ARMISTEAD, JIMMY: 1934-40. Left-back 188 (31 cup) apps; 2 goals. Local player who was a regular for six years after impressing in the reserves.

ARMSTRONG, DEREK: 1962-64. Outside-left 76 (16 cup) apps; 39 (6 cup) goals. Signed for the club in the summer of 1962, Carlisle-born Derek made one full appearance for Blackpool in 1958 and one for Carlisle in 1961, before being released and signing for the Shrimps. In his first season, Derek made 42 league and eight cup appearances, scoring 28 league and two cup goals. He opened his account with a goal in a 7-1 home win over Bacup Borough and became a regular scorer during the season. The following season, saw Derek make 34 league and seven cup appearances, scoring 11 league and four cup goals. His final goal for the club was in a 2-1 win at Barrow reserves on February 17, 1964. Later joined a string of clubs as both player and manager including Fleetwood, Netherfield, Lancaster City and Lytham. Was last known to be coaching in America.

ARMSTRONG, ROBBIE: 1989-96. Midfield/Left-back 193+1 (76 cup) apps; 7 (1 cup) goals. Signed by Bryan Griffiths in January 1990, Robbie originally played in midfield but was switched to left back where he starred in the promotion winning side. The former Kirkby Town, Southport and Rhyl player was almost ever present for two seasons but unfortunately sustained a serious injury in the FA Trophy game v Southport in 1994, which kept him out of the side for the best part of a year. He was released by the club during the first term in the Conference but was granted a well earned testimonial along with Gary Dullaghan and Paul Tomlinson. Moved to Lancaster. President's Cup winner 1991-92. Unused sub in Lancashire Cup win of 1995-96.

ARNOLD, IAN: 2001-03. Forward 23+4 (4 cup) apps; 7 goals. A former Middlesbrough trainee who played for a host of Conference clubs before joining the Shrimps from Southport in May 2001. Was released in October 2002 and joined Barrow. Had a loan spell with Workington.

ASHINGTON: Morecambe's first opponents in the Northern Premier League visited Christie Park for the one and only time on August 10, 1968 when a crowd of 2,000 watched a 0-0 draw.
The reverse fixture on March 15, 1969, ended in a 2-0 win for Morecambe with goals from Derek Varcoe and Derek Lancaster. Ashington finished third from bottom of the table in that season and withdrew from the NPL.

ASHTON PARK: Home of Dick Kerr's, a Preston works team Morecambe played against in the Lancashire Combination from 1920 to 1935. The first visit was a 5-3 defeat in November 6, 1920. It was a memorable game as Peel became the first Morecambe player to be sent off! The last meeting, at Ashton Park on November 23, 1935, was declared void as Dick Kerr's later withdrew from the league. Morecambe had won the game 1-0 with a goal from Hall.

ASHTON TOWN: Just 1 meeting against the team from Ashton-in-Makerfield in the 1st Rd of the Lancashire Junior Cup on November 2, 1974, winning 6-1 at Christie Park. Att: 425.

ASHTON UNITED: Formerly known as Hurst until 1947. Morecambe first met the 'Robins' in 1920-21 losing 4-1 away on March 12, 1921. Att: 2,000. Morecambe won the return game at Woodhill Lane, on March 19, with goals from Gornall (2) and Gradwell.

ASHWORTH, JIMMY: 1946-49. Centre-forward 90 (18 cup) apps; 73 (9 cup) goals. Jimmy will always be remembered by Morecambe fans for the eight goals he scored in a game. In a record shared with Arnold Timmins, Jimmy scored eight in the club's 12-0 away win at Great Harwood Town on December 28, 1946.
Jimmy was born in Ireland but was brought up in Morecambe and played for local junior sides, before being signed by Blackpool in the 1936/37 season. He enjoyed a good start to his career and scored a hatful of goals for Blackpool's reserves and A team before making his first team debut in the 1938/39 season, where he made four appearances in the season.

The 1939/40 season saw him score three goals in four games but then came the war which put a block on his career. He first came to the attention of Morecambe officials when on April 26, 1939, he scored seven goals for Blackpool in a 9-1 victory over the Shrimps in a benefit match. He made his first appearance for the Shrimps in a friendly 2-0 win over the RAF on January 27, 1940 when he scored both goals.

After the war, Jimmy played in two friendlies for the Shrimps, before being signed for £150 from Blackpool at the start of the 1946/47 season. He made his debut at Fleetwood on August 31, 1946, in what must have been an enthralling 5-5 draw.

He went on to be the club's leading scored for three successive seasons – 1946/47, 1947/48 and 1948/49. His last game for the Shrimps was at home to Prescot Cables on May 8, 1949 when he scored in a 2-1 win before leaving to join Netherfield as player manager. He died on December 17, 1990, aged 72.

ASPIN, JIMMY: 1972-76. Defender 76+2 (14+1 cup) apps; 2 goals. Popular local player born in 1951 who progressed from the Reserves. Played locally for clubs such as Lansil and was Lancaster City Reserve team coach in 1985-86.

ATHERTON: Morecambe played Atherton in the Lancashire Combination from 1920-21 to 1930-31. First meeting was at Atherton on October 9, 1920, with the home side winning 4-0. On April 30, 1927, Morecambe recorded one of their biggest ever wins with a 10-3 victory.

ATHERTON COLLIERIES: The sides have met only twice. The first game was on December 7, 1985 at Christie Park with Morecambe winning a Lancashire Junior Cup 1st Rd game 4-0, Att: 318.

The two sides met again in the 2nd round of the same competition on January 30, 1988, with Morecambe winning 2-1, with goals from Andy Edwards and Dave Lancaster. Att: 268.

ATHLETIC GROUNDS: The home of Hindley Green Athletic who were opponents in the Lancashire Combination between 1925-26 and 1927-28.

The first meeting ended in a 6-3 win for Morecambe on January 30, 1926.

ATHLETIC GROUND: The home of Scarborough before the ground was renamed the McCain Stadium. The two seaside resorts have clashed on a regular basis over the years in the NPL and Conference. The club's first visit to Scarborough was on January 18, 1969, in a 0-0 draw watched by 1,600.

ATKINS, ERNIE: 1933-40 and 1946-48. Left-half/Right-half/Inside-right 242 (41 cup) apps; 27 (12 cup) goals. Long serving player who joined Morecambe in August 1933 after playing for Dick Kerr's. He rejoined in August 1946. Ernie's brother Harry played in the pre-season trial matches in 1939-40 and may have played two Combination games.

ATKINSON, PETER: 1972-76. Goalkeeper 32 (9 cup) apps. Joined in January 1973, aged 19. Released in May 1986, he moved to Carnforth Rangers.

B

BABBAGE WAY: Home of Worksop Town where Morecambe travelled for an FA Cup 2nd Qualifying Rd tie on September 23, 1995, winning 3-2. Att: 529.

BACUP BOROUGH: Opponents in the Lancashire Combination from 1920 to 1968. The first meeting was in Morecambe's third ever game on August 31, 1920, which ended in a 2-1 defeat.

BAILEY, F: 1934-35. Right-back. 45 (9 cup) apps; 2 goals. Joined Morecambe October, 1946.

BAINES, HARRY: 1949-57. Right-back 237 (38 cup) apps. One of the most influential individuals in the club's history, Morecambe-born Harry was a long serving player who went on to become chairman. Harry made a record 237 consecutive appearances for the club. The sequence began on August 18, 1951, and ended on April 21, 1956, when the Shrimps beat South Liverpool 2-0 at Christie Park. The record run was ended with an injury and he decided to retire from playing, though he did go on to make one first team appearance in the 1956-57 season. Harry was a late starter for Morecambe largely due to the intervention of the war. Born in Bolton-le-Sands he played for Lancaster Schoolboys and then Brookhouse Rangers in the North Lancashire League before joining the Grenadier Guards and serving in Germany and the south of England where he made several appearances for Slough Town. After the war he returned to Morecambe and signed for the Shrimps in 1949. His first team debut came as inside-left in a 1-0 defeat at Rossendale United on March 25, 1950. The following season he established himself as the club's regular right-back and was soon labelled 'long ball Baines'. After hanging up his boots after 275 appearances (and no goals) Harry became financial secretary in 1957, a position he held until 1959. He then had a break from the club before joining the board of directors in 1964. Seven years later he became chairman, replacing Robert Altham in July 1971. Altham had been chairman for 21 years. His biggest achievement was leading the club to its FA Trophy win in 1974. Ill health forced him to stand down as chairman in 1976 and he left the board in 1977. Harry died, aged 64, on November 7, 1991.

BALDWIN, BOB: 1967-76. Defender 307+4 (108+3 cup) apps. The captain of FA Trophy winning side of 1974 joined the Shrimps for the princely sum of £90 from Fleetwood in August, 1967. Baldwin, a junior with PNE from 1958-59, the Preston-born player also had spells at Netherfield and Horwich RMI, before spending five years at Fleetwood. Described by the Visitor as an 'Outstanding defender who reads the game well and acts as a strong tackling sweeper,' Bob was eventually released in April 1976 after an outstanding Christie Park career which, apart from the Trophy win, saw him pick up a Lancashire Combination League and cup winner's medal in 1967-68, a Lancashire Senior Cup winner's medal in 1967-68, and a Lancashire Junior Cup winner's medal in 1968-69. He moved on to become player manager with BAC Preston.

BALLAM ROAD: Former home of Lytham who Morecambe first met in the FA Cup on October 3, 1925. Lytham surprisingly won 2-1 in a season where Morecambe were runners-up in the Combination and winners of the Lancashire Junior Cup.

BALM, JON: 1984-88. Midfielder 57+4 (22+3 cup) apps; 4 (2 cup) goals. Joined Morecambe in March 1985 after making 148 appearances for Barrow. A former Everton apprentice he moved to Vickers Sports Club in 1988-89.

BAMBER BRIDGE: Surprisingly no league meetings between the sides.
The first meeting was a big one – an ATS Lancashire Trophy final at Deepdale on April 10, 1995. Bamber Bridge won 2-1. Att: 2,180. Morecambe's first team have never visited Irongate although the Reserves have played there.

BANGOR CITY: Rivals in the Lancashire Combination between 1938-39 and 1949-50. The first match between the sides was at Christie Park on December 10, 1963, with a 1-1 draw watched by 1,245. The teams became rivals again in the NPL with 2 games standing out. The first was a 3-2 1st round FA Cup win at Bangor on November 16, 1968. The other game was memorable for the wrong reasons – a 9-0 league defeat on September 21, 1981.

BANKS, ANDY: 1995-2001. Goalkeeper 85+3 (32+1 cup) apps. A former PNE (1990-94) and Bury (1994-95) keeper who joined in August 1995. Made his mark as being the only Conference goalkeeper to save a Clive Walker penalty. Was loaned to Squires Gate and Chorley in 1998 and Leek Town in 2000 before being released in May 2001. Later played for Lancaster City and Fleetwood Town. Unused sub in Lancashire Cup final 1998-99.

BARCELONA UNIVERSITY U22s: Played at Christie Park in a friendly on November 4, 1987 with Morecambe winning 6-3.

BARLOW, STUART: 1989-90. Forward *(right)* one cup app . Made just one appearance as a loan signing from Everton in March 1990. Later made his mark in the Football League as a regular goalscorer with Everton, Oldham Athletic, Wigan, Tranmere Rovers and Stockport County.

BARNES, DAVE: 1984-85. Forward 34+4 (9 cup) apps; 13 (5 cup) goals. The former Netherfield, Fleetwood Town and Lancaster City striker joined in July 1984 and had one season before rejoining Fleetwood Town. Later had a second spell at Lancaster City before moving on to Blackpool Mechanics, Poulton Town and Wyre Villa.

BARNES, DONALD: 1950-54. Forward 28 (9 cup) apps; 10 (2 cup) goals. Local player who later moved to Ingleborough and Lancaster City.

BARNET: First meeting against the Bees was on September 11, 2001 with a 1-0 Conference victory at Christie Park. Att: 1,283.

BARNOLDSWICK TOWN: First met in the Lancashire Combination from 1924-25 to 1933-34. First meeting was a 2-0 defeat on November 1, 1924 on May 2, 1925 at Christie Park. The second game was more memorable as the Shrimps sealed the win they needed to lift the Combination title. Morecambe won 4-0 at Rosebery Park (Christie Park) on May 2, 1925.

BARNOLDSWICK PARK VILLA: Just one meeting in the Lancashire Junior Cup 3rd Rd at Christie Park on November 23, 1929, in a game which Morecambe won 2-1. Att: 740.

BARNSLEY: The Tykes visited Christie Park for a pre-season friendly on August 3, 1974, winning 4-2, Att: 500.

BARON, BILLY: 1954-56. Right-back and Outside-right 52 (4 cup) apps; 5 goals. Former PNE and Lancaster City player, who joined in October 1954. Later played for Leyland Motors and Lytham before emigrating to Australia where he played and coached for several clubs.

BARON, MARK: 1982-86. Midfield/Forward 93+4 (31+1 cup) apps; 14 (2 cup) goals. Ex-Lancaster City and Wren Rovers player who joined Morecambe in August 1982. After being released in September, 1985, moved on to Fleetwood Town, Lancaster City and Wren Rovers.

BARROW: The club first met the Bluebirds in the Lancashire Combination before Barrow joined the Football League. Morecambe's first ever away game was at Barrow on August 30, 1920, losing 4-0. Long serving player Jackie Farnworth made his debut in the game. One memorable game for Barrow was a 7-3 win at Christie Park on October 16, 1974 when the Visitor reporter wrote: *"You really wondered whether you were watching Morecambe or the Marx Brothers at Christie Park."* Att: 405.

BARROW RESERVES: The two sides used to meet regularly during Barrow's Football League days. The first meeting was a 1-1 draw at Holker Street on October 10, 1931.

BARTON STADIUM: Home of Winsford United where Morecambe lost 2-0 on their first visit on September 26, 1992. Att: 541.

BARTON, PETER: 1969-71. Goalkeeper 19 (3 cup) apps. Ex-Barrow apprentice who made his debut for the reserves aged just 15, in November 1966. Joined Morecambe in October, 1969.

BASEBALL: Played at Christie Park on July 14, 1944, when the 2nd US Air Force beat the Canadian Army Pay Corps 5-2.

BATES. 1921-22. Outside-right 21 (3 cup) apps. Joined in September 1921.

BATH CITY: First met the Romans in a Conference game at Christie Park on November 11, 1995, winning 1-0. Att: 1,007.

BAXTER, JAMES CUNNINGHAM: 1961-62. Inside-left 3 apps; 1 goal. Veteran, Scottish forward who made a brief comeback with Morecambe in August 1961. Was a leading professional in the 40s and 50s, scoring 55 goals in 224 games for Barnsley between 1945-52, and 65 goals for Preston North End in 245 apps between 1952-57. At North End he was a member of the FA Cup final squad of 1953-54. Someone once wrote of Jimmy, who died in May 1994, aged 69: *"Cigarette smoking Jimmy was no great athlete. You could say he didn't have the look of a footballer but he was an instinctive inside-forward who could spot the telling pass."*

BAXTER, STUART: 1975-76. Defender 1 app in 1975 v Altrincham.
Did not make much of a mark at Christie Park but forged himself a great career in coaching culminating in his appointment as national coach of South Africa in March 2004. He moved into management with Orebro and AIK Solna in Sweden before coaching spells in Norway, Portugal, USA and Japan before joining the England Youth coaching staff in January 2001, managing England U19s.

BEANLAND, TONY: 1972-73. Left-half/Left-back 28+2 (12 cup) apps; 1 goal. A pro who made 143 apps for Southport between 1962-66 before moving on to Southend Utd, Wrexham and Bradford Park Avenue, playing in their final game in the Football League. Joined Morecambe in August 1972. Released in April 1973.

BEARD, GEOFF: 1967-68. Defender 4 cup apps. Former Skerton Old Boys and Lancaster City player who was in the club's Reserves between 1965-68. Played at Trimpell from 1972-78 and became Morecambe Reserve team manager in October 1979, replacing Don Cubbage.

BEARDWOOD, GEOFFREY: 1947-48. Centre-forward 31 (7 cup) apps; 18 (1 cup) goals. Ex-PNE, Accrington Stanley and Chorley player who joined Morecambe in November 1947. Moved to Darwen in 1949-50.

BEBBINGTON, PETER: 1970-72. Full-back 44 (5 cup) apps; 1 goal. Former Oswestry Town, Leicester City, Barrow and Stockport County player who joined Morecambe in September 1970. Moved to Winsford Utd where he played from 1972-80.

BEDFORD, FRED: 1928-30 and 1931-32. Outside-right/Centre-forward 25 (7 cup) apps; 23 (4 cup) goals. Came out of retirement to play for Morecambe after spells with Blackburn Rovers, Accrington Stanley, Barnsley, Lancaster Town and Tranmere Rovers.

Made an immediate impact with three hat-tricks in his first three games, chalking up 16 goals in his first 10 games and being transferred to Bradford City for £500 on October 9, 1928. He scored a hat-trick on his debut for them as well in an 8-2 win at Ashington. He returned to Morecambe for 2 games in September 1931.

BEDFORD TOWN: The team Morecambe beat 1-0 in the quarter-final of the FA Trophy in the year they won it. The match was interrupted at half time by the Shrimps' first ever streaker. Att: 2,515.

BEDFORD TERRACE: Home of Billingham Town where Morecambe played twice in seven days in two cup competitions. The first game was a 5-0 win in the FA Cup on September 28, 1985. Att: 174. Returned on October 5 and drew 1-1 in the FA Trophy with Thornton scoring. Att: 108.

BEDLINGTON TERRIERS: Only one meeting which was a 4th Qualifying Rd FA Cup tie at Welfare Park on October 28, 2000, with Morecambe winning 3-1. Att: 918. Morecambe: M Smith, Fensome, A Lyons, McKearney, Hardiker (1), Walters (Knowles), Black (1), Drummond, Thompson (1) (Heald); Rigoglioso (Norman), Eastwood.

BEESLEY, JOHN: 1982-84. Forward 32+1 (13 cup) apps; 20 (10 cup) goals. Former Burscough and Southport striker who joined the Shrimps in January 1983. Returned to Southport for a fourth spell in January 1984. Later played for Skelmersdale Utd.

BELL, NORMAN: 1946-47. Goalkeeper 19 (3 cup) apps. First played a handful of games for Morecambe in the North Lancashire League in 1939-40 before joining again in September 1946. Played for Lancaster Town/City between 1934-46. Died in Lancaster on October 12, 1988, aged 81.

BELLE VUE, DONCASTER: First played there against Bridlington Town in the NPL on December 4, 1993, winning 4-0 in a game watched by only 44 people.

BELLE VUE, MANCHESTER: The former home of Manchester Central who the club played in the Lancashire Combination from 1928-29 to 1930-31.
First visit was on September 8, 1928, a 1-1 draw.

BELLE VUE, RHYL: First visit to Rhyl was a bad one, losing 6-1 on April 7, 1984, in the NPL. Att: 322.

BENISTON, STEVE: 1978-81. Forward 11+5 (1 cup) apps; 2 goals. Born in Nottingham in 1962 and had trials with Nottingham Forest and Notts County before signing for Morecambe in August 1978, after his family moved here.
Father Eric and Steve both played for the Reserves at Wrexham on May 11, 1979 in a 3-0 defeat. Released in April 1981 and later played for Lansil and Ingleton.

BENNETT, JOHN: 1973-75. Defender 48 (27 cup) apps; 3 cup goals. A former apprentice and pro with Liverpool between 1963-66 who moved to Chester, where he played 72 games between 1966-69. One of only a few players to win the FA Trophy with two different clubs.
First picked up a winner's medal with Macclesfield in the 1969-70 season before being a part of the Morecambe team that lifted the Trophy in 1974. The full-back was released by the Shrimps in April 1975, moving to Stalybridge Celtic.

BENSON, JACK: 1939-40. 3 (1 cup) app in August 1930. Also played regularly for Morecambe in the North Lancashire League in 1939-40 and 1940-41. He rejoined in August 1945 and was at the club until 1951, making 73 (20 cup) appearances at Right-half scoring 3 (3 cup) goals. Moved to Bolton-le-Sands in 1951-52. Combination Cup winner in 1945-46. Jack later became a director at Christie Park in the 1960s. He died on October 23, 1983, aged 62.

BENTLEY, JAMES (JIM): 2002-2004. Defender 59 (14+2 cup) apps; 7 (2 cup) goals. Born Liverpool, June 11, 1976. Signed from Telford United in July 2002 where he made 141+1 appearances, scoring 23 goals in five years. A former YTS player with Manchester City who had trials with Walsall and Grimsby Town. Skipper for the 2004/05 season. Lancashire Cup winner 2003-04.

BENYON, JOSEPH (JOE): 1928-29. Outside-left 29 (7 cup) apps; 6 goals. Joined in August 1928 and released in May 1929. Former Atherton, Chorley, Runcorn and Accrington Stanley player who had a trial with Norwich City in 1925.

BERRY, F: 1920-22. Goalkeeper 36 (2 cup) apps. Former Altrincham player who joined in September 1920.

BETTS, MICHAEL (MIKE): 1980-82. Defender 27 (2 cup) apps. Son of former Manchester City player Barry Betts who joined in December 1980. Born in Barnsley on September 21, 1956, he made 4+3 appearances for Blackpool and played for a host of clubs including Barrow, Northwich Victoria and a spell in Sweden and America.

BIGNALL, MIKE: 1997-98. Forward 19+3 (2+1 cup) apps; 11 (1 cup) goals. Signed for £6,000 from Stevenage Borough on March 24, 1997. A regular goalscorer, he played for the England semi-professional side against the Highland League at Cove on May 10, 1997, while at the club. The former Wrexham schoolboy was sold to Kidderminster Harriers for £10,000 on November 21, 1997, where he scored 11 goals in 27+4 apps. After a loan spell at Hednesford Town joined Aylesbury Utd for £5,000 in March 1999. Despite his goals, failed to settle at any one club and moved on to Boreham Wood, Harrow Borough and St Albans City *(pictured in action - right)*.

BILLINGHAM SYNTHONIA: Met in the FA Trophy with a 2-0 win on November 2, 1985, in the club's only meeting. Att: 116.

BILLINGHAM TOWN: Met Billingham three times in the 1985-86 season – all within 11 days! Won 5-0 at Billingham in the FA Cup on September 28, 1985, and drew 1-1 in the FA Trophy on October, 5. The replay at Christie Park was won 2-0 on October, 8.

BIRCH, RAY: 1987-88. Forward 9 (2+1 cup) apps; 1 goal. Much travelled player who joined in October, 1987, before moving on to Rhyl in January, 1988. His full list of clubs is: Halifax Town, Bradford City, Stamford, Rushden Town, Corby Town, Southport, Tranmere Rovers, Kettering Town, Fleetwood Town, Morecambe, Rhyl, Fleetwood Town, Caernarfon Town, Bangor City, Newtown, Accrington Stanley, Droylsden, Knowsley Utd, Burscough, Warrington Town, Droylsden, Warrington Town, Congleton Town and Burscough.

BIRCHALL, JOHN: 1981-82. Defender/Midfielder 21 (3 cup) apps. Joined Morecambe as player coach in October, 1981, aged 31.

BIRTWISTLE, EDDIE: 1935-40 and 1945-46. Inside-left 88 (8 cup) apps; 25 (2 cup) goals. Born, 1909 he joined Morecambe in November, 1935 and rejoined in January, 1946. Well know locally for being a leading official with Westgate Cricket Club.

BIRTLES, JACKIE: 1947-48. Right-back 27 (5 cup) apps. Joined in September 1947.

BIRTLES, NEIL: 1979-81. Defender 22 (7 cup) apps; 1 goal. Born in Morecambe in 1960 Neil played for Trimpell and Lancaster City (1978-79) before joining the Shrimps in October, 1979. Released in January, 1981, and moved on to Trimpell. Played for the West Lancashire League XI in 1981-82.

BISHOP AUCKLAND: One forgettable visit was in the FA Cup for a first round tie on November 23, 1974, which Morecambe lost 5-0. Att: 1,250. Morecambe returned the same season winning 1-0 in the FA Trophy on January 11, 1975. Met later in the NPL and numerous cup matches.

BLACK, RYAN-ZICO: 1999-2004. Forward 46+54 (19+3 cup) apps; 15 (4 cup) goals. Born Guernsey, August 4, 1981, the youngster was one of the first to come through the new Academy system which he joined in the summer of 1998. Was selected for the Northern Ireland Under 21 squad before being released in September, 2003. He joined Northwich Victoria but was released in December, 2003.
Later moved to play in the League of Ireland.

BLACKBURN, CHRIS: 2003-04. Midfield 4+1 apps. Joined from Northwich Victoria in February 2004 for £3,000. Previously played for Chester City where he made 70+12 apps, scoring seven goals.

BLACKBURN ROVERS: Morecambe beat Rovers 2-1 in the Lancashire Senior Cup 1st Rd on December 5, 1967, at Christie Park. Att: 1,600. Rovers played 10 of their regular first team players.
Morecambe: Millard, Varcoe, Baldwin, Halstead, Irving, Porter (1), Holding, Crompton, Borrowdale, Timmins (Hough (1)), Lea.
Rovers: Blacklaw, Coxon, Wilson, Clayton, Coddington, Hole, Ferguson (1), Rodgers, Gilliver, Darling, Connelly. The Visitor wrote: *"It was a superb win and was gained by soccer skill coupled with a determination to succeed."*
Rovers reserves team currently play their home games at Christie Park.

BLACKPOOL: Blackpool visited Christie Park on April 1926, 1939 for Arthur Thompson's benefit match. Blackpool won 9-1 with Jimmy Ashworth scoring seven goals.

BLACKPOOL 'B': Morecambe faced them in the Lancashire Combination between 1950-53 and 1954-55, playing at Lytham or Squires Gate. The first meeting was away on September 23, 1950, losing 3-1.

BLACKPOOL MECHANICS: The reserves regularly played Mechanics in the Lancashire Combination with Mechanics record crowd of 1,200 for a game in August 1968, at Common Edge Road. Heavyweight boxing champion, Brian London, once played for Mechanics at Christie Park. The first teams have met only once in the ATS Lancashire Challenge Trophy 3rd Rd, at Christie Park, on February 20, 1990, with Morecambe winning 4-0. Att: 339.

Pre-season friendlies versus Blackburn Rovers (above) and Blackpool (below).

BLACKPOOL RESERVES: The two sides met in the Lancashire Senior Cup 1st Rd on September 24, 1968, with Morecambe winning 2-0. Att: 2,000.

BLAKENALL: One disastrous meeting against the now defunct club in the FA Trophy 3rd Rd at the Red Lion Ground on January 15, 2000. Att: 376. Hot favourites Morecambe lost 2-1.

BLACKWELL, ERNEST: 1930-31. Left-back 4 apps. Born July 19, 1897 and died in 1964. Was a goalkeeper with Scunthorpe Utd, Sheffield Utd, Sheffield Wednesday and Aberdeen. Switched to defence when he joined Morecambe in August, 1930.

BLONDEL, FRED: 1945-46, 1946-48 and 1950-51. Inside-left 44 (17 cup) apps; 28 (6 cup) goals. Born Lancaster on October 31, 1923. Died May 24, 1987.
Joined the Shrimps in August 1945 and moved to Bury for £350 in July 1946 where he made one app. Moved on to Witton Albion before moving back to Morecambe in March 1947. Left again to join Netherfield for £50 in October 1947. Spent three seasons there and spells at Lancaster City and Rossendale Utd before joining Morecambe for a third time. Later played for Netherfield again and Lansil.

BLYTH SPARTANS: Several big cup matches between the two sides, the first two being in the FA Cup 1st Rd. The first clash was on November 15, 1958, which Blyth won 2-1 at a foggy Christie Park. Att: 6,500. The second was at Croft Park on November 3, 1962, where Morecambe again lost 2-1. Att: 4,490.

BOLDON COLLIERY WELFARE: Only one meeting at the Boldon Sports Park on November 13, 1971, in the 2nd Qualifying Rd of the FA Trophy. Morecambe won 2-1. Att: 516. The club is now known as Bolden Community Association.

BOLTON WANDERERS: The Trotters brought a first team to Christie Park for a pre-season friendly on August 9, 1982. Bolton won 2-0. Att: 500.

BOLTON WANDERERS B: The clubs met in the Lancashire Combination in 1953-54 and 1954-55. First meeting was at Christie Park on August 19, 1953, with a 1-1 draw.

BOLTON WANDERERS RES: Morecambe lost 3-1 at home on November 12, 1921, in a friendly. Att: 500.

BOND, ERIC (BUSTER): 1950-51 and 1956-57. Outside-left 2 (1 cup) apps. Born Morecambe on July 7, 1931. Started with Sion Baptist Church as a goalkeeper in 1946-47 before moving to outside-left. Made his debut for Morecambe Reserves in January 1949. Moved to Ingleton 1951. After army service with the King's Own in the Korean War he returned to play for Ingleton, Caton Utd and Bolton-le-Sands. Played one game for Morecambe in April 1957. Later helped coach Morecambe's A team in the 1960s and was groundsman at Morecambe in the 1970s. Played for the North Lancashire League XI in 1955-56. Eric died on April 28, 2004, aged 72.

BOND, JACK: 1927-32. Left-Half 27 (4 cup) apps; 1 goal. Uncle of Eric Bond who joined Morecambe in September 1927. Played locally for Morecambe Park Villa and Carnforth Rangers. Moved to Morecambe Victoria in 1931-32.

BOOTH, BILLY: 1946-48. Outside-Left 40 (10 cup) apps; 14 (3 cup) goals. Former Lancaster City, Manchester City and Wigan Athletic player who joined in May 1947. Later played for Lancaster City 1952-53.

BOOTH STREET: Home of Congleton Town. Only one visit to date, a 3-0 FA Cup 3rd Qualifying Rd victory on October 8, 1994. Att: 308.

BOOTHAM CRESCENT: Home of York City and scene of many epic FA Cup games. The first came on November 26, 1966, with a 1st Rd tie ending 0-0. Att: 5,596. The Shrimps travelled there again for a 2nd Rd tie on December 7, 1968, a game which ended in a 2-0 defeat. Att: 5,071. A third cup tie, another 1st Rd game at the same venue, ended 0-0. Att: 3,692.

BOOTLE: A former Football League club that has been reformed on several occasions. Morecambe met the second reformed club in the Lancashire Combination between 1949-50 and 1953-54. The first meeting was at Christie Park on January 28, 1950, a 1-1 draw. Bootle withdrew from the league at the end of the 1953-54 season. The Bucks were reformed again and Morecambe faced them in a pre-season friendly on August 5, 1997. A weakened Morecambe lost 4-1.

BOROUGH PARK: Home of Workington with the club's first visit being in the NPL on December 10, 1977. A crowd of 486 watched Workington win 4-1.

BOROUGH PARK STADIUM: The second ground of Blackpool Borough Rugby League club on Princess Street which was used by Blackpool (Wren) Rovers in 1989-90. Met in a Lancashire Junior Cup 1st Rd tie on December 9, 1989, with 150 watching the Shrimps win 4-3 in Morecambe manager Bryan Griffiths's first game.

BOROUGH SPORTS GROUND: Home of Sutton Utd where Morecambe won 1-0 on their only visit on April 22, 2000. Att: 659.

BORROWDALE, KEITH: 1958-68 and 1978-79. Centre-forward 344+1 (109 cup) apps; 230 (59 cup) goals. The club's record goalscorer was probably one of the bargain buys of the century. Keith was signed from Chorley for the princely sum of £40 in 1958. The club had been looking for a goalscorer to replace the legendary Ray Charnley who had moved to Blackpool and came across Bowness-born Keith while playing for Chorley Reserves against our own second string. He scored four goals in a 7-1 Chorley win on March 29, 1958, and the club acted quickly. It proved to be a wise move, as he went on to score 289 goals for the club, with a record 52 in the 1961/62 season alone. A player who caught the eye of a host of league clubs Keith was happy to stay part-time and continue working as an accountant with Lakeland Laundry.

Their loss was Morecambe's gain, as he scored 18 hat-tricks while at the club, another record. His debut came in a 1-0 win at Droylsden on August 23, 1958, and although national service limited his appearances in the early years he soon became a prominent member of the successful teams of the 1960s. His last game came at the end of the 1967/68 season though almost 10 years later he was back in a Morecambe shirt. By now he was the club coach under the reign of manager Mick Hogarth and an injury crisis forced him to name himself as a substitute for four games. He only came off the bench once, however, and his final run out came at the age of 42 against Bangor City on May 5, 1979. Unfortunately for the romantics, he failed to get his name on the scoresheet. Keith made a total of 451 league and cup appearances in his 10 seasons with the club. The Borrowdale name returned to Christie Park in the 1990s when his son Peter joined the club before going on to enjoy a fruitful spell at Lancaster City. Lancashire Combination League winner in 1961-62, 1962-63, 1966-67, 1967-68. Combination Cup winner in 1964-65, 1966-67 and 1967-68. Lancashire Cup winner in 1961-62, 1962-63 and Lancashire Senior Cup winner 1967-68.

BOSTON UTD: There have been many meetings with the Pilgrims in the Northern Premier League, Conference and cup ties. The first meeting was in the NPL at Christie Park on August 24, 1968, a 1-1 draw which saw Steve Done score on his debut. Att: 2,000.

BOUNDARY PARK: Home of Oldham Athletic. Morecambe used to play Oldham's Reserves in the Lancashire Combination. The club's first visit on December 18, 1937, was abandoned after 70 minutes due to fog with Morecambe losing 1-0.
Best result was on April 22, 1968, when Morecambe beat the Oldham Athletic first team 1-0 in the semi-final of the Lancashire Cup.

BOWER FOLD: Home of Stalybridge Celtic. First visit was on December 12, 1988, in the NPL which ended in a 1-1 draw. Att: 359.

BOWKER, ALAN: 1945-47. Left-back 24 (10 cup) apps. Joined Morecambe in August 1945. Moved to Lancaster City and Heysham.

BOYD, GEORGE: 1933-36. Centre-half 85 (10 cup) apps; 13 goals. Joined Morecambe in November, 1933, from Bradford.

BRABIN, GARY: 1991-92. Midfielder 1 cup app. Could be classed as one that got away after playing just one game – a pre-season cup game against Lancaster City in August 1991. Joined Runcorn instead and helped them to the FA Trophy final in both the 1992-93 and 1993-94 seasons. He was then picked up by Doncaster Rovers and went on to have a long league career with Bury, Blackpool, Lincoln City and Hull City before moving into the League of Wales.

BRADFORD CITY: Played the Bantams in a friendly on September 20, 1922, at Rosebery Park, winning 4-1. Att: 2,000.

BRADFORD PARK AVENUE: After Bradford dropped out of the Football League the clubs met in the NPL. The first meeting was at Christie Park on September 5, 1970, with Don Cubbage being sent off in a 2-0 defeat. Att: 1,326. Bradford PA was reformed in 1988. Morecambe first met the new club in the FA Trophy 2nd Rd at their new ground, the Horsfall Stadium, on February 8, 1997. A crowd of 915 watched Morecambe win 1-0.

BRADLEY, WILLIAM (BILL): 1950-52 and 1953-54. Goalkeeper 10 (1 cup) apps. Joined Morecambe in September, 1950, and made his debut at the age of just 16 as a Lancaster Royal Grammar School pupil. Signed amateur forms for PNE in August, 1951, but continued to play for Morecambe before joining the RAF in 1952-53. Returned to Morecambe and later played for Morecambe Grammar School Old Boys from 1958-62.

BRAITHWAITE, BOB: 1956-57. Left-half 22 (10 cup) apps; 3 goals. Born in Sedbergh on February 8, 1934. Died on August 4, 2003. A former Windermere and Netherfield player who signed in August 1956. Later played for Staveley and Sedbergh.

BRANDON UTD: Just one visit, a 6-0 win in the 1st Qualifying Rd of the FA Cup on September 14, 1996. Att: 267.

BREIGHTMET UTD: This Bolton & District side were the club's first opponents in the FA Cup on September 25, 1920, at Woodhill Lane. A 1-1 draw. The 2 sides met again in the FA Cup in the 1922-23 season, with Morecambe winning 4-0 after a 2-2 draw.

BRENNAN, MARK: 1991-92. Midfield 9+1 (3+1 cup) apps; 1 goal. Joined in August, 1991, from South Liverpool where he made more than 200 appearances. Released in December, 1991, and later played for Southport, Chorley, Ashton Utd, Marine, Bangor City, Bamber Bridge, Accrington Stanley and St Helen's Town.

BREARTON, TERRY: 1959-61. Right-back 26 (4 cup) apps. The ex-Bradford City player joined in August, 1959.

BRENTFORD: Just 1 meeting with the Bees which came at Griffin Park in the FA Cup 1st Rd on November 17, 2001. A crowd of 4,026 watched Morecambe lose 1-0.

BREWERY FIELD: Home of Spennymoor Utd. First visit was for an FA Cup 4th Qualifying Rd tie on October 28, 1967. A crowd of 2,500 watched Spennymoor win 1-0.

BRIDLINGTON TOWN: First meeting was an away trip for an FA Cup 2nd Qualifying Rd game on September 27, 1986. A crowd of 186 watched Morecambe win 1-0. Bridlington gained promotion to the Premier Division of the NPL but had to play at Doncaster Rovers. Just 64 people watched Morecambe win 4-0 on December 4, 1993. The return game at Christie Park was won 7-1. The present club was reformed in 1994.

BRIGG TOWN: Just one meeting with the Zebras at the Hawthorns on September 10, 1994. Morecambe won a FA Cup 1st Qualifying Rd tie 4-0. Att: 145.

BRINDLE, KEITH: 1984-85. Defender/Midfielder 40 (7 cup) apps; 1 (1 cup) goal. An experienced defender who had played more than 500 games for Lancaster City and been the subject of a £7,000 move to Stafford Rangers before joining in August, 1984. Released in May 1985 and returned to Lancaster City. Managed Thame Utd in the South Midlands and after a spell as assistant, was Lancaster City boss from November, 1991, to November, 1992. Has also had two spells as manager of Garstang in the West Lancs League.

BRITISH POLICE: Just one game, a 3-2 defeat in a friendly at Christie Park on February 23, 1993.

BRITTON, JAMES (JIMMY): 1937-38 and 1938-39. Right-half/Centre-forward/Outside-left 16 (2 cup) apps; 1 goal. Played largely for the reserves, Standfast and Lancaster City before becoming a professional after the war with Bradford PA (8 apps) and Rochdale (20 apps). Finished his career playing for Rossendale Utd, Dry Dock Utd and Ingleborough. Still playing for Standfast in his 40s.

BRITTON, IAN: 1989-90. Midfield/Forward 6+1 (3 cup) apps. A top player who made 263 appearances for Chelsea before moving on to Dundee Utd, Arbroath, Blackpool (106 apps), Burnley (108 apps). Joined in August, 1989, for a short spell, Later managed at Burnley Bank Hall and Nelson and was assistant boss at Accrington Stanley.

BROAD, JAMES (JIMMY): 1931-32 Inside-left 1 (1 cup) apps; 1 goal. May have made only two appearances for the Shrimps, but was one of the most remarkable players ever to have put on a Morecambe shirt. Played for a string of clubs in England and all over Europe, and was even a coach at Barcelona in 1924.
Played for Manchester City (November 1909), Manchester Utd (October 1910), Royal Club Coruna of Spain (until September 1911), Manchester City (September 1912), Oldham Athletic (August 1913-18). Was a wartime guest with Blackburn Rovers, Manchester City, Morton and Millwall. Helped Millwall to reach the Football League, with 32 goals in 39 games in the Southern League. Moved to coach Las Palmas in Spain in October, 1920, before switching to Stoke City for £2,000 in June, 1921, making 111 apps and scoring 60 goals. Barcelona was the next step in August, 1924, before returning to play for Sittingbourne, Everton, New Brighton, Geneva (Switzerland), Fleetwood and Morecambe. Later coached in Turkey, South America, the Netherlands and Norway.

BROADHALL WAY: Home of Stevenage Borough. Morecambe's first visit, on April 27, 1996, saw Stevenage crowned Conference champions after a 1-1 draw. Att: 2,556.

BROADHEAD, JAMES (JIMMY): 1930-31 Right-half/Left-half 33 (4 cup) apps; 1 goal. Born Rotherham August 25, 1894. Died 1955. Joined from Horwich RMI in July, 1930, and was captain for the 1930-31 season. Previous clubs included Norwich City (Southern League), South Shields, Nelson and Barnoldswick Town.

BROCKLEHURST, JOHN: 1958-61. Right-half 92 (30 cup) apps; 3 (1 cup) goals.

Joined in August, 1958, after spells as Stalybridge Celtic, Accrington Stanley, Heywood, Bradford Park Avenue, Wigan Athletic and Horwich RMI. Later played for Fleetwood and Darwen, retiring in April, 1964.

BROMSGROVE ROVERS: First played 'The Greens' in a GMAC Cup 3rd Rd tie at Christie Park on February 2, 1988. Morecambe won 3-0. Att: 421.

BROOKE, MICKY: 1981-82. Defender 13+3 (2 cup) apps; 1 goal. Joined in December 1981 after spells with Ellesmere Port Town, Altrincham, Winsford Utd and Stalybridge Celtic.

BROOKS, STEVE: 1985-87. Defender 37 (22 cup) apps; 1 cup goal. Joined in August, 1985, from Halifax Town. Was a professional with Hartlepool Utd where he made 62+1 apps, scoring two goals. Badly injured his left elbow while playing for Morecambe in September, 1986, which ended his career. He officially retired in December, 1986.

BROWELL, TOMMY: 1933-34. Centre-forward 3 apps; 1 goal. Born Walbottle October 19, 1892. Died October, 1955. Was a respected professional with a great goalscoring record. Began his career with Hull City, scoring 32 goals in 48 apps between 1910-12, and moved on to Everton for a fee of £1,650 in December, 1911. Scored 26 goals in 50 apps for the Toffeemen, before switching to Manchester City. In 13 years at Maine Road he scored 122 goals in 222 apps and was a member of the FA Cup final team of 1925-26. He is still City's sixth highest goalscorer to this day.
Moved to Blackpool, making 67 apps between 1930-33, scoring 27 goals. Joined Morecambe from Lytham in December 1933.

BROWN, ARTHUR: 1924-30 and 1932-34. Inside-left/Centre-half. 214 (57 cup) apps; 74 (19 cup) goals. Born Preston, 1896. Died Lancaster, January, 16, 1974, aged 79. One of the stars of the great team of the 1920s, he joined in August, 1924, before moving on to coach Lancaster Town in June, 1930. Was player-coach at Morecambe Victoria from 1931-32 before rejoining the Shrimps in November, 1932. Retired in October, 1933 before re-joining briefly again in April, 1934. Combination League winner in 1924-25 and Lancashire Cup winner in 1924-25 and 1925-26.

BROWN, CLARENCE: 1932-33. Outside-left. 2 apps in December, 1932.

BROWN, GORDON: 1963-64. Inside-left 4 apps; 4 goals. A former England Youth international who joined in March, 1964, on a month trial. Played in the Football League with Scunthorpe Utd, Derby County, Southampton and Barrow.

BROWN, GREG: 1998-99 (loan) and 1999-2001. Defender 27+8 (4+1 cup) apps; 1 goal. Signed in January, 2000, after two impressive loan spells when with Macclesfield Town. Joined Bangor City at the end of the 2000-01 season.

BROWN, JIMMY: 1990-93. Midfielder 67+4 (27 cup) apps; 9 (4 cup) goals. Joined from Vauxhall Motors and proved to be a competitive midfield player. Loaned to Skelmersdale Utd in September, 1992, before joining Burscough. Was a member of the Runcorn side that reached the FA Trophy final in the 1992-93 season. Later played for Caernarfon Town, Stalybridge Celtic, Witton Albion, Barrow, Lancaster City, Droylsden, Accrington Stanley and Altrincham. President's Cup winner in 1991-92.

BROWNBILL, DEREK: 1982-84. Forward 60+1 (24+1 cup) apps; 19 (9 cup) goals. A former Liverpool player who made one first team appearance, Derek was signed by Les Rigby at the start of the 1982/83 season. He proved to be a useful acquisition as he finished the season as top scorer with 13 league and eight cup goals from 48 appearances. The 1983/84 campaign was not as fruitful however as he scored just 6 league and 1 cup goal in 36 appearances. After Rigby was sacked Derek was released by new manager Sean Gallagher. He joined South Liverpool and then Warrington Town where he played in the 1986/87 FA Vase final at Wembley.

BROWS LANE: Former home of Formby, first visited for a pre-season friendly, on August 12, 1974, in a 2-0 win.

BRUCE PARK: Home of Wren Rovers. First visit was a 7-1 Lancashire Cup replay win on February 9, 1980. This was the first match in which the Jones twins played together for Morecambe.

BUCHANAN, WILLIAM. 1956-58: Right-back 57 (20 cup) apps; 1 cup goal. The Glasgow-born defender, joined in August 1955 after playing for Motherwell, Carlisle Utd and Barrow (where he made 242 appearances in six years).

BUCKLEY, TED: 1954-55. Right-Half 21 (5 cup) apps; 1 goal. A former PNE reserve team player, who later joined BAC Preston.

BUCKLEY, GARY: 1988-89. Midfield/Forward 6 (1 cup) apps; 1 goal. Manchester-born player who made 4+2 appearances for Man City before a £25,000 move to PNE in October 1981. Made 27+2 apps, scoring two goals at Deepdale before spells at Hull City, Chorley and a return to the Football League with Bury, 23+8 appearances, one goal; where he picked up an injury that forced him to quit the game for two years. Joined Morecambe in June 1988, after a comeback with Chorley and was player-coach for a short spell, before being released in October, 1988. Later played for Chorley, Leyland Motors, Salford and Radcliffe Borough.

BUCKS HEAD: Home of Telford Utd. First visit was a GMAC Cup 4th Rd replay game on Sunday, March 13, 1988, which Morecambe won 2-0. Att: 1,300.

BUCKS PARK: Home of Bootle but also the temporary home of South Liverpool just prior to them folding. Morecambe played there on April 27, 1991, beating South Liverpool 4-0 in the last meeting with the club.

BURDON, CARL: 1988-89. Forward 13 (3+1 cup) apps; 5 (1 cup) goals. Former Stoke City apprentice who joined in July, 1988. Moved to Penrith and Carlisle Utd.

BURGESS, FRED: 1945-46. Outside-right 18 (3 cup) apps; 8 goals. Born in Morecambe, 1915, and joined the club in September, 1945. Moved to Lancaster City, 1947-49.

BURKE, MARSHALL: 1986-87. Midfield/Forward 10+2 (1+3 cup) apps; 3 (1 cup) goals. Scottish, schoolboy international, who joined from Colne Dynamoes in February, 1987. Returned to Colne and later played for Clitheroe. Had Football League experience with Burnley (22+2 apps, 5 goals), Blackburn Rovers (34+5 apps, 7 goals), Lincoln City 49+1 apps; 6 goals), Cardiff City (3 apps), Scarborough 54+1 apps, 17 goals) and Tranmere Rovers (3 apps).

BURNDEN PARK: Former home of Bolton Wanderers where Morecambe have visited for numerous Lancashire Junior Cup finals. The first visit was for one such final replay with Chorley on March 6, 1926, which resulted in a 1-1 draw watched by 12,891.

BURNLEY FC: One of the greatest nights in Morecambe's history came on May 13, 1968, when the Shrimps beat a strong Burnley side, then in Division 1, 2-1 in front of a crowd of 4,230 at Christie Park to become the first non-league side to win the Lancashire Senior Cup. Only two days previously, five of the Burnley team had been in the side that beat the mighty Leeds 3-0 and the Morecambe victory was the stuff footballing dreams are made of. On the way to the final, the Shrimps had beaten Blackburn Rovers, Bury and Oldham Athletic, but few thought Ken Waterhouse's side would have a chance in the final. Morecambe beat the odds with Arnold Timmins the hero. Timmins scored the opening goal on 12 minutes after a Gerry Irving through ball. Burnley levelled through Martin Dobson eight minutes later and the game then went from end to end in an enthralling contest. Clear cut chances were few and far between however, and the game looked to be heading for a draw until with just seven minutes left Morecambe were awarded a penalty which Timmins stroked home to give Morecambe a celebrated win. MORECAMBE: Millard, Varcoe, Halstead, Irving, Baldwin, Porter, Martin, Crompton, Borrowdale, Timmins (2), Lea. Sub: Holden.
BURNLEY: Jones, Smith, Buxton, Bellamy, Merington, Kinsella, Coates, Casper, Dobson (1), Thomas, Kindon. Sub: Ternant.
Burnley also provided the opposition when Morecambe officially opened their new floodlights on Wednesday, August 4, 1993.

BURNS, PAUL: 1993-2000. Defender 195+26 (68+7 cup) apps; 23 (6 cup) goals.
The former Grimsby Town, Burscough, Southport, Prescot, Caernarfon Town, Southport and Accrington Stanley player joined in exchange for Paul Byron in November, 1993, and was to be a regular for almost five seasons. He was the club's player of the year in 1994-95 and picked up three Lancashire Cup winners medals. He was part of the team that won promotion to the Conference and also helped the side win the Spalding Cup Final in the 1997-98 season. Maintained his success with Accrington Stanley, winning the

Lancashire Cup again. At Burscough, he was part of the team that surprised everyone to win the FA Trophy in 2002-03. Lancashire Cup winner in 1993-94, 1995-96 and 1989-90. Spalding Cup winner in 1997-98 *(pictured below taking a penalty v Runcorn 1995).*

BURROWS, GREN: 1949-57. Goalkeeper 173 (30 cup) apps. Former Bolton-le-Sands player who became a regular with the Shrimps after joining in April 1950. While with the club played for a Lancashire Combination XI against a Dutch XI, the Lancashire FA and the England Amateur XI v Northern Nomads at Macclesfield on January 1, 1954.

BURSCOUGH RANGERS: First met away in the Lancashire Combination on September 14, 1927, winning 2-1. Rangers folded during the 1934-35 season.

BURSCOUGH: The Linnets were reformed in 1946-47 and dropped the Rangers. They played in the Liverpool Combination before joining the Lancashire Combination in 1953-54. First meeting was in the FA Cup, losing 1-0 in a replay at Christie Park on October 3, 1951, after drawing 2-2 at Burscough on September 29.
The club's best result at Burscough was in the FA Cup on October 7, 1961, with an 8-1 win. Att: 2,250.

BURTON: Morecambe faced Burton twice in the North Lancashire League during 1939-40. Won 3-2 at Christie Park on December 16, 1939. The return match ended 3-3.

BURTON ALBION: Morecambe have played the Brewers for several seasons in the NPL and latterly the Conference. The first meeting was at Christie Park on December 15, 1979, with Morecambe losing 3-1. Att: 280.

BURY: Strangely there have been few meetings with the Shakers, although Morecambe did beat them 1-0 in the quarter-final of the Lancashire Senior Cup at Christie Park on March, 12, 1968. Att: 3,000. Saile scored an own goal. Bury included Alec Lindsey and Alex Dawson in their side. Only Morecambe reserves have played at Gigg Lane.

BUTCHERS ARMS: Home of Droylsden. The first visit was on April 7, 1937, with a 3-3 draw in the Lancashire Combination League.

BUTLER, ROBERT (BOBBIE): 1920-21 and 1926-30. Inside-forward 11 (5 cup) apps; 3 (1 cup) goals. Joined in August, 1920. Moved to Halton in October, 1920. Returned in January, 1927. Moved to Morecambe Victoria 1931-32.

BUXTON: Played Morecambe in their first game in the NPL on August 11, 1973. Morecambe won 4-1. Att: 1,010.

BYRAM, GRAHAM: 1976-82 and 1987-89. Goalkeeper 177 (44 cup) apps. Born in Morecambe on May 9, 1960, and made his debut as a 16-year-old after playing for the reserves in the 1975-76 season. Had trials with West Ham Utd in January, 1978. Left Morecambe for Penrith 1982-84, Workington 1984-85, Penrith 1986-87 and Lancaster City before returning to Christie Park in June, 1987. Was Morecambe's player of the year in the 1978-79 season. Later played for Colne Dynamoes, Netherfield and Penrith again. Played for the FA XI v UAU in 1978-79.

BYRON, PAUL: 1992-94. Defender 36+3 (12 cup) apps; 5 (1 cup) goals. Signed in December, 1991, but played no games and joined Bamber Bridge. Signed again in July, 1992, and moved to Accrington Stanley in November, 1993, in a swap move with Paul Burns. Later played for Lancaster City, Netherfield and Bamber Bridge, becoming manager of the latter in January, 2002.

C

CAERNARFON TOWN: The Canaries had a spell in the NPL with the first meeting between the sides coming at the Oval in the League Cup 1st Rd, 1st leg, on December, 9, 1985. A crowd of 116 watched a 2-2 draw.

CAIN, IAN: 1989-97. Forward 261+12 (101+5 cup) apps; 75 (21 cup) goals. A then record transfer fee, of £7,500, was paid for the player from Fleetwood Town in August, 1989. Cain had played a starring role as Fleetwood reached the FA Vase final in the 1984-85 season and 25 goals in the 1988-89 season persuaded Larry Milligan to pay a big fee. Cain *(pictured right)* didn't let anyone down. He was the leading goalscorer and player of the season in 1989-90 and was also chosen as the NPL's player of the season. He was an integral part of the team that helped Morecambe win promotion to the Conference. Was eventually released in May, 1997, after a spell on loan at Lancaster City. Joined Chorley and later played for Wyre Villa and Kirkham & Wesham.

CALVER, REGINALD JOHN: 1967-68. Left-back 4 cup apps. Joined in September, 1967, but moved to Runcorn and Witton Albion. Became Clitheroe player-manager in 1970-71.

CAMBRIAN CUP: A pre-season cup competition that took place in 1982-83 and 1983-84 with little interest or success.

CAMBRIDGE UTD: The U's became Morecambe's second Football League scalp in the FA Cup when a Mark Quayle goal gave the Shrimps a 2-1, 2nd Rd, win at Christie Park on December 9, 2000. Att: 3,427.

CAMPBELL, JOSEPH (JOE): 1928-29. Outside-right 12 (1 cup) app. Joined in November, 1928, after playing for Oldham Athletic, Wigan Borough, Blackburn Rovers, Rochdale and Stalybridge Celtic. Released in May, 1929.

CANAL STREET: Former home of Runcorn. Morecambe's first visit was on March 10, 1969, which ended 1-1. Runcorn FC Halton now play at the Halton Stadium in Widnes.

CAPPER, BRIAN: 1957-67. Left-half 163 (41 cup) apps; 1 (2 cup) goals. Former Everton junior who joined in August, 1957. Later became club trainer and Reserve team manager, 1966-68. After three years out of football, became Reserve team trainer at Lancaster City.

CAPSTICK, CHARLES: 1938-39. Centre-forward 1 app in February, 1939. Trialist from Caton, who later became Lancaster City chairman. Died April 13, 1989, aged 79.

CAPSTICK, JAMES (JIMMY): 1988-90 and 1990-91. Defender/Midfield 26+1 (8 cup) apps; 2 goals. Joined in February, 1989, from Barrow. Returned to Holker Street in October, 1989, and made a further 31+2 apps with 5 goals before rejoining the Shrimps in March, 1990. Returned to Barrow again in October, 1990, and moved to Lancaster City in July, 1991. He became assistant manager at Holker Old Boys between 1993-2001.

CARLISLE CITY: Played the junior club in Carlisle in a pre-season friendly at Christie Park on August 8, 1979, winning 2-1.

CARLISLE UTD: Morecambe first met the Cumbrians in a pre-season friendly at Christie Park on July 17, 1997, with Carlisle winning 2-0. Morecambe reserves have played at Brunton Park in the Lancashire League.

CARLISLE, RICHARD TUSAN (DICK): 1922-30. Centre-half 244 (69 cup) apps; 32 (6 cup) goals. Joined in August, 1922, and later became coach and captain of Morecambe's 1924-25, championship winning side. Joined from Wigan Borough where he was captain during the side's first season in the Football League. Retired aged 39 and became a coach for Preston North End A team. Combination League winner in 1924-25. Lancashire Junior Cup winner in 1925-26 and 1926-27. Combination Cup winner in 1926-27.

CARLTON, DANNY: 2001-2004. 39+36 (9+11 cup) apps, 25 (6 cup) goals. Born Leeds, December 22, 1983. Came to the club on trial in May, 2001, and signed full forms in January, 2002. Soon began to shine up front with his pace and eye for goal and finished the 2003/04 season as the top scorer, with 17 league goals from 28 starts and 4 cup goals. His form earned him a call up for the England semi-professional squad in May, 2004, when he played against Iraq. Signed a new contract in May, 2004.
Lancashire Cup winner 2003-04.

CARPENTER, MARK: 1981-83. Defender 26 (8 cup) apps; 1 (1 cup) goals. Joined from Chorley in March 1982, aged 21.

CARR, D: 1922-24. Outside-left 22 (5 cup) apps; 1 (2 cup) goals. Joined in February, 1923.

CARRIGAN, JOE: 1948-50. Centre-half 45 (7 cup) apps. Former New Brighton player who joined in October, 1948.

CARROLL, JOSEPH (JOE): 1981-82 and 1982-83. Forward/Midfield 27 (3 cup) apps; 15 (2 cup) goals. Well travelled player who had played for Oldham Athletic, Halifax Town and Barrow before spells in Australia, Finland, USA and Hong Kong. Signed in February, 1982, but moved to Australia in April, 1982. Returned in November, 1982, but went back to Australia again in March, 1983.

CARRUTHERS, ALLAN: 1986-88. Midfield 58 (25 cup) apps; 3 goals. Former Coventry City apprentice who joined in July, 1986, from Workington. Moved to Gretna in 1988 and later played for Penrith and Gretna again.

CARTER, ARTHUR: 1935-39 and 1945-47. Goalkeeper 47 (15 cup) apps. Born Leeds 1918. Died, July 7, 1995, aged 77. Joined in December, 1935, before moving to Manchester City 1938-39 season. Rejoined in August, 1945, before moving to Lancaster City for the 1947-48 season.

CARTER, DAVID: 1978-79 and 1983-85. Defender 15+2 apps. Former Everton player who joined in August, 1978. Moved to Lancaster City, 1979-82, before returning to Morecambe in March, 1984. Now a prominent local estate agent.

CATON ROAD: Home of Lansil where Morecambe first played in the North Lancashire League during 1939-40. First game saw a 2-1 win on October 7, 1939. The 1940-41 season opened at Caton Road with a 6-2 win.

CATON UTD: Morecambe reserves played Caton Utd in the second match of the 1939-40 season in the North Lancashire League, losing 5-1. The return fixture at Christie Park on January 20, 1940, was drawn 2-2. The clubs have since met in some practice friendlies. On October 12, 1993, the teams had a practice match at Christie Park which Morecambe won 14-1 with Steve Holden scoring eight, Ian Cain five and Jim McCluskie one.

CATTERAL: 1946-47. Left-back 11 (2 cup) apps. Joined in November 1946 and was briefly the club captain before moving to Clitheroe.

CAUSEWAY LANE: Home of Matlock Town where Morecambe lost 3-0 on their first visit on October 11, 1969. Att: 862.

CELTIC: A Celtic Youth team played a Christie Park on Sunday, September 23, 1973 in a friendly with Lancaster Celtic. Celtic won 8-1 with, future first team regular, George McCluskie the star of the show.

CENTRAL AVENUE: Former home of Worksop Town. First visit on April 12, 1969, ended in a 4-1 defeat. Att: 491.

CENTRAL GROUND: Former home of Witton Albion. First visit on March 18, 1980, ended in a 3-0 defeat. Att: 623.

CERAOLO, MARK: 1995-99. Forward 37+46 (19+19 cup) apps; 26 (17 cup) goals. The former Crewe trainee *(pictured right)* joined in July 1995, after a spell of summer football for Sarpsborg in Norway.

The light at the end of the tunnel

Good goal record but his time at Christie Park was blighted by a string of injuries. Loaned to Chorley in February 1999 and moved to Ashton Utd in March 1999. Played for Accrington Stanley.

CHADWICK, EDGAR: 1928-29. Inside-left/Outside-right 20 (2 cup) apps; 18 (1 cup) goals. Joined in November, 1928, after spells at Nelson (38 apps, 19 goals in Division Three North), Lancaster City and Barnoldswick. Moved to Bacup Borough, 1931-32.

CHAIRMEN: Club chairmen include:

F Moss: 1922-24.
Arthur Holt: 1924-29.
William Curwen: 1929-34 and 1945-46.
A Ashton, Ernest Kershaw: 1934-39 and 1946-49.
Peter Wareing: 1939.

George Brown: 1949-53.
Robert Altham: 1953-71.
Miles Taylor (acting chairman April to August 1971)
Harry Baines: 1971-75.
John Dixon: 1975-81.
Eric Fisher: 1981.

Geoff Gill: 1982-84.
Eddie Weldrake: 1984-94.
Ken Parker: 1994-97.
Rod Taylor: 1997-2000.
Peter McGuigan: 2000 – present.

CHAMBERS, ROBERT (BOB): 1930-32. Centre-half 43 (9 cup) apps; 5 (2 cup) goals. Born Newcastle-upon-Tyne, December 11, 1899. Died 1972.
Vastly experienced defender who joined in July, 1930. Began his professional career with Lincoln City (23 apps, 12 goals); Burnley (4 apps); Rotherham County (100 apps, 6 goals), Torquay Utd, Carlisle, Exeter City, New Brighton, Colwyn Bay, Hurst.

CHARLES STREET: Home of New Cross (later Manchester North End). Morecambe's first visit was a 4-1 defeat in the Combination on April 11, 1923.

CHARNLEY, RAY: 1954-57 and 1970-72. Centre-forward 137+3 (36+1 cup) apps; 76 (22 cup) goals. A local lad who went on to play for England, Ray's story is a real local hero tale. Born on May 29, 1935. Ray, who had failed to impress in a trial at Preston North End, joined Morecambe from Bolton-le-Sands for just £15 in September, 1954. His debut was a 2-5 away defeat at Lancaster City in a Combination Cup game on September 29, 1954, but things got much better from there. He had three excellent seasons at Christie Park and scored regularly. In the 1956/57 season, he scored 31 league goals in 37 apps, and also added 12 cup goals in 15 games, helping the Shrimps to reach the Combination Cup final where they lost to Horwich. Shortly after that game he was signed by Blackpool, for £750, in May, 1957, and became a Bloomfield Road favourite. He was Blackpool's top scorer for seven out of the next 10 seasons, the best being in 1961/62 when he scored 30 goals. His eye for goal saw him earn his one and only England cap on October 3, 1962, in a 1-1 draw against France at Hillsborough, in a game watched by a crowd of 35,380. In December, 1967, after scoring 193 goals in 363 league games for Blackpool, Ray joined Preston North End, where he scored 4 times in 23 games. He then moved to Wrexham in July, 1968, before ending his Football League career at Bradford Park Avenue. Ray returned to Christie Park in 1970 under Ronnie Clayton who was sacked after a

3-1 home defeat by Stafford Rangers on August 15, 1970. When Ken Waterhouse returned as manager in December, 1970, Ray did not fit in with his plans and although he only made 24 league starts, he still finished the season as top scorer, with 13 goals. He was released after 14 games of the 1971/72 season with his last game being on Good Friday, 1972, when he scored in a 3-0 home win over Chorley.

CHELTENHAM TOWN: The first meeting against the Robins was in the Conference away on December 13, 1997, losing 2-1. Att: 1,717.

CHERRY, JAMES: 1929-30. Forward 31 (3 cup) apps; 10 goals. Joined in August 1929. Later moved to Prescot Cables.

CHERRYWOOD ROAD: Home of Farnborough Town. Morecambe's first visit was in the Conference on January 6, 1996, losing 3-1. Att: 729. The ground was then officially known as the John Roberts Ground, becoming the Aimita Stadium 2000-03, before returning to Cherrywood Road 2003-04.

CHESHIRE LEAGUE & LANCASHIRE COMBINATION INTER-LEAGUE CUP: The two leagues joined forces for two seasons. In 1961-62, Morecambe beat Tranmere Rovers Reserves 4-1 at home before losing 2-1 to Congleton Town at Christie Park. The next season saw a 4-0 defeat at Chester Reserves.

CHESTER: Met in the FA Cup 2nd Rd, at Sealand Road, on November 25, 1961, when a crowd of 7,965 watched Morecambe clinch their first FA Cup victory over a Football League club, winning 1-0. When Chester became Chester City the clubs met in a pre-season friendly at Christie Park on August 2, 1991.
Another memorable FA Cup tie came in the FA Cup 2nd Rd at Christie Park on December 7, 2002. A crowd of 4,296 watched Morecambe win 3-2.

CHESTER, KEVIN: 1981-82. Forward 16 (4 cup) apps; 3 goals. Joined in August 1981. Moved to Vickers SC in November 1981. Played for Lancaster City between 1982-85.

CHESTERFIELD: The Spireites were beaten in the memorable FA Cup run of 2002/03. After beating Chester, Morecambe travelled to Saltergate and won 2-1 on November 16, 2000, thanks to an injury time goal from Garry Thompson. Att: 3,703.

CHESTER-LE-STREET: Morecambe visited Moor Park on October 2, 1982, in the 2nd Qualifying Rd of the FA Cup winning 5-1.

CHORLEY: Morecambe have played the Magpies in the Lancashire Combination and NPL since the first meeting at Woodhill Lane on October 23, 1920 which Chorley won 2-1. Att: 1,200. Morecambe's record defeat was at Chorley with a 14-1 defeat on Good Friday, 1946, in the Lancashire Combination. Morecambe rested the first team because of an important cup tie and fielded a squad made up of trialists. Morecambe's best win over Chorley was a 7-1 victory on February 28, 1967. Att: 1,500.

CHRISTIE CUP: The cup was presented by J B Christie in the 1920s for an end of season local knockout competition.

CHRISTIE, JOSEPH BARNES: Born in Accrington on May 17, 1863, the legendary J B Christie was a businessman with the firm of Messrs Myrtle, Burt & Co exporters and merchants of Manchester who had a large trade in the Dutch West Indies. He moved to Morecambe from his home in Southport when he retired and lived in the town for 10 years. A generous benefactor for many good causes in Morecambe, is best remembered for his association with the football club where he was club president. Starting as president of the supporters club he helped arrange the lease of Rosebery Park. In March 1926 the ground was renamed Christie Park.
A man with great foresight he was intent on getting the Shrimps on a better financial footing and formed the club into a limited company at a meeting on May 9, 1927.
Mr Christie died on June 1, 1929, aged 76.

CHRISTIE PARK: The first game of football played at Christie Park was on Saturday, August 3, 1921, when the club held its first trial match. Just over 200 people saw the Reds lose 3-1 to the Whites. The first league game at the club's current home was played on August 27, 1921 when Fleetwood beat the Shrimps 4-0. The crowd was a superb 3,500 with the steamship Greyhound of Blackpool bringing 900 spectators form the Fylde coast. It must have been a great sight as the boat linked up with a special electric train to the old Promenade station and charabancs which ferried supporters to the ground.

After the club was formed in 1920 its base was at Woodhill Lane, a ground it shared with the town's cricket club. The arrangement was far from perfect however, and the FA told the club it would have to find its own ground for the next season.

After looking at some land behind the horse tram depot on Lancaster Road, now the site of a Netto store, the club finally decided on a spot of rough pasture further down Lancaster Road. With the financial backing of retired businessman Joseph Barnes Christie who was the president of the supporters club, the land was acquired with Mr Christie paying the rent. The ground was originally designed to be in an oval shape similar to that of Lancaster City's ground at Giant Axe with stands on all four sides and a capacity of between 8-10,000. The plans were altered however, and the ground constructed normally with a wooden stand built to hold 700 that lasted until the main stand was built in 1962. There was a covered area, known as the 'Scratching Shed' at the Lancaster Road end of the ground and with a number of repairs down the years lasted until 1967. The ground was originally called Rosebery Park presumably after the nearby Rosebery Avenue which sources say was named after Lord Rosebery, the Liberal Prime Minister from 1894 to 1895. In January 1928, Mr Christie, by now the club president, bought the ground and gave it to the Corporation of Morecambe with a condition that it should be used by Morecambe Football Club. If the club disbanded it should then become a playground for the children of the resort. It was at this time that the ground was named Christie Park in his honour.

The ground changed little in the following years with the next major improvement being the building of banking on the Lancaster Road side of the pitch with tons of cinders. It was during the late 1950s and early 1960s that the ground saw its next development. The team was doing well and with crowds rising the town end was concreted and a roofed standing area built. This was opened on September 27, 1958.

The club's first major floodlights were erected as well and opened officially on October 27, 1960, when an All Star XI lost 4-3 to a Morecambe side. In a period of great change the new £10,000 Auxiliary Club was opened just a few weeks later – December 7, 1960. Two years later, January 6, 1962, saw Christie Park draw its biggest ever crowd when officially 9,383 paid to watch Morecambe's FA Cup third round tie against Weymouth and at the end of that season the present main stand was built at a cost of £20,000. In all the club spent more than £35,000 in the space of a few months on ground improvements – a figure that would surely be a million or so pounds in today's prices. The new stand was officially opened on October 17, 1962 by club chairman Robert Altham, after a commemorative friendly with Leeds United which saw the Yorkshiremen win 7-1.

Six years later, came another major step in the shaping of the modern Christie Park, when the old 'Scratching Shed' was demolished and a new £8,000 covered terrace built at the Christie Avenue end of the ground – currently the Umbro stand.

It was nearly 20 years before the ground was altered again when new floodlights, costing £40,000, were erected in 1993 and officially opened on August 4, prior to a friendly with Burnley, by the great Sir Tom Finney. This was the start of a major facelift for the ground as the club endeavoured to be ready for Conference football if the chance arose. Grass bankings were replaced by concrete terracing and with a general tidy up, the Shrimps were ready to move up the Pyramid when the opportunity arose in 1995. The work didn't stop there however, and the club took the ambitious step of building a new £560,000 stand at the town end of the ground. The stand was first used by supporters on Saturday, March 21, in a Conference fixture with Cheltenham Town, but officially opened by Sir Bobby Charlton on Wednesday, September 2, prior to a friendly with a full strength Southampton side brought by boss, Dave Jones. Not long after the ground was passed as fit for the Football League and the club now has a venue it can be justifiably proud of.

CHURCH ROAD: Home of Hayes where Morecambe won on their first visit in the Conference on March 8, 1997. The Shrimps won 3-2 in front of a crowd of 558.

CHURCHMAN, DESMOND: 1956-58. Outside-left 39 (10 cup) apps; 4 (1 cup) goals. Joined in August, 1956, after playing for Bretherton, Bolton Wanderers and Bentham Utd. Moved to BAC Preston.

CLARK, JONATHON: 1988-89. Midfield 10 apps; 1 goal. Wales Schoolboy, youth and Under 21 international who began his career with Manchester Utd, making one appearance as a substitute before moving to Derby County for £50,000 in September 1978. Moved to PNE on a free transfer in August 1981 and made 106+3 apps, scoring 10 goals. Ended his career by playing for Bury and Carlisle Utd. Joined the Shrimps in February 1989 before being sold to Southport for £1,000 in the August.

CLARKE, ALAN: 1960-61. Outside-right 30 (6 cup) apps; 10 goals. Joined in August 1961 but moved to Horwich RMI. Rejoined in September.

CLARKE, CHARLES (CHARLIE): 1924-28 and 1931-33. Goalkeeper 92 (29 cup) apps. Bentham-born keeper with a tragic story. In his second spell at Christie Park he received serious internal injuries while playing against Dick Kerr's on January 7, 1933 and died of the injuries on June 30, 1933.

CLARKE, CHRISTOPHER (CHRIS): 1993-94. Goalkeeper 10 (4 cup) apps. Played on loan from Bolton Wanderers between August and October 1993. Later played for Rochdale (30 apps), Chorley, Barrow and Marine.

CLAYTON, HARRY: 1926-29. Right-half 91 (25 cup) apps; 8 (2 cup) goals. Former Stoke City player who joined in August 1926 from Nelson. Moved on to Manchester Central, Nelson and Bacup Borough.

CLAYTON, JIMMY: 1978-81. Midfield/Forward. 75 (22+2 cup) apps; 9 goals. Joined in August 1978, aged 23. Moved on to Lancaster City, Chorley and Hyde Utd.

CLAYTON, RONNIE: 1969-71. Half-back 22 (6 cup) apps; 3 (1 cup) goals. A footballing legend who won 35 England caps, Ronnie had a relatively unsuccessful period as Morecambe boss. Ronnie made 577 appearances for Blackburn Rovers and captained the side for 18 years in an illustrious career. It was seen as a great coup when he took over the manager's reins from Ken Waterhouse (first time round) in 1969. Things did not turn out to plan however and Ronnie soon found life tough in non-league circles.

After three great seasons under Waterhouse, Morecambe struggled in 1969/70 and many of the Shrimps' supporters blamed the new manager for the decline in the club's fortunes. After coming third the season before, Morecambe finished 15th. Ronnie *(pictured right)* was appointed as a player-manager, but the Shrimps' faithful never managed to see the best of him as a rib injury kept him out of the side for much of the season. Ronnie made 22 league and cup appearances in the season and scored two league and one cup goal. A bad season he may have had but a man of Clayton's stature certainly did not deserve to leave the club the way he did. He was sacked after just one game of the 1970/71 season, despite scoring Morecambe's goal in a 3-1 home defeat by Stafford Rangers. Ronnie went on to play for Great Harwood with a number of former Blackburn team mates before retiring.

CLEMENTS, DENNIS: 1956-58. Inside-left 67 (24 cup) apps; 30 (15 cup) goals. Former PNE Junior and Lancaster City player who joined in August 1956. Moved on to Netherfield and Lancaster City.

CLIFF, EDDIE: 1975-76. Defender/Midfield 12 (4 cup) apps; 1 goal. Former Burnley, Notts County, Lincoln City and player who joined from American side Chicago Sting in 1975. After a short spell at Christie Park moved back into the Football League, making 44+6 appearances for Tranmere and 25+1 for Rochdale.

CLIFTONVILLE: Irish League side who visited Christie Park for a friendly which ended 2-2 at the beginning of the 1979-80 season.

CLITHEROE: The Blues were formed in 1877 with little success until recent times. There were many matches in the Lancashire Combination League between 1925-26 and 1967-68. The first meeting was at Shawbridge in the FA Cup extra preliminary round on September 5, 1925, drawing 2-2. The gate was given as 3,000.

CLOSE, RICHARD: 1992-94. Defender 26 (13+1 cup) apps. Joined in October, 1991, and progressed to the first team after making some impressive performances in the reserves. Returned to home club Netherfield after a loan spell at Ilkeston in November 1993. Twin brother Jamie also played for Morecambe reserves.

CLUB CALL CUP: One of those unnecessary cups originally called the GMAC Cup. Was renamed the Premier Inter-League Cup for its final season in 1990-91.
Reached the semi-final in 1987-88 losing 2-1 at home to Weymouth on Sunday, April 24, 1988. Att: 974.

CLYDEBANK: The Bankies visited Christie Park for a pre-season friendly on August 1, 1993. John Coleman scored a penalty for Morecambe in a 1-1 draw.

COATES, JOHN: 1971-75 and 1977-78. Goalkeeper 100 (41 cup) apps. Southport-born John was the club's goalkeeper during their FA Trophy winning season. He signed for the Shrimps towards the end of the 1971-72 season, after impressing Morecambe officials while playing for Kirkby Town. Born in Southport in 1944, John started off his career at Burscough, before moving to his home town club where he made five Football League appearances in the 1964-65 season. He moved to Chester in 1966, but made just one league appearance for them, before a move to Tranmere Rovers – where he failed to make a first team start. He moved out of the league and returned to Burscough before his move to Kirkby Town and then Morecambe. A firm favourite with the Morecambe fans the Lancashire Evening Post described him as: *"A spectacular goalkeeper and generally acknowledged as one of the best in the NPL."* He left the club after a 2-1 home defeat by South Liverpool on April 30, 1975, and joined Skelmersdale United and Southport before making a brief return to Christie Park in 1977, making just four league and one cup app. His last game was a 1-0 home defeat by Matlock Town on September 3, 1977.

COLCHESTER UTD: Morecambe visited Layer Road to meet the U's in an FA Trophy 3rd Rd tie on February 22, 1992. Colchester won 3-1. Att: 3,206.
Colchester Utd: Barrett, Donald, Roberts (Masters), Kinsella, English, Cook, Collins (Dart), Stewart (2), McDonough, McGavin (1), Smith.
Morecambe: Allison, Tomlinson, Armstrong, Parillon, Lodge, Brown, Lavelle (McInerney), Coleman (Holden), McMahon, Cain (1).

COLEMAN, GORDON: 1984-85. Forward 8 (1 cup) apps. A PNE favourite who scored 25 goals in 248+21 apps at Deepdale. A spell with Bury followed before a brief period at Christie Park, signing in August, 1984, and being released a month later.

COLEMAN, JOHN: 1990-96. Centre-forward 199+13 (74+6 cup) apps; 141 (60 cup) goals. The best goalscorer at Christie Park in modern times. Coleman, now manager of Accrington Stanley, chalked up an impressive 201 goals in 273 games and bagged a number of records along the way. These included hitting the fastest ever FA Cup hat-trick in a victory over Gainsborough Trinity in 1993, with three goals in four minutes. It was a record that makes him the club's second highest goalscorer behind Steve Done.
Signed for a bargain price of £1,000, by Bryan Griffiths (from Witton Albion) in August, 1990. He made his debut v Mossley on August 18, scoring his first league goal two days later against Horwich, holds the club record for scoring in 13 consecutive games in the 1994/95 season. The sequence started on September 6 with a goal at Knowsley and followed by goals at Bishop Auckland, Boston, Witton, Spennymoor, Hyde Utd, Barrow, Horwich, Frickley and Chorley in the league and Brigg Town, Chorley and Congleton in the FA Cup. The run was ended with a blank in a FA Cup clash with Witton Albion, although he did make it 11 league games on the trot with a goal at Matlock, the following Saturday. Coleman holds the club record for the most goals in a Northern Premier League season, with 32 in 1990/91 and 1992/93, scoring 46 goals in total in the 1992/93

campaign. He was the only Morecambe player to score 100 NPL goals in his career and was the league's top scorer for 3 of the 5 seasons he was at Christie Park. The only setback Coleman *(pictured below)* had at Morecambe came in 1993 when he broke his leg in a pre-season game against Lancaster City. He was only able to make 12 league appearances that season but in true Coleman fashion scored 13 goals. His last game for Morecambe was on Saturday, March 9, 1996, against Bath City. He joined Lancaster City and went on to manage Ashton United and Accrington Stanley, taking the latter into the Conference as Unibond League champions. President's Cup winner in 1991-92. Lancashire Cup winner in 1993-94.

The light at the end of the tunnel

COLKIN, LEE. 2001-03. Defender 52+2 (16+1 cup) apps. A former Northampton player who made 74+25 apps for the Cobblers between 1992-98.
After a loan spell at Leyton Orient he joined Hednesford. He moved in May, 2001, and was released in May, 2003. He later played for Burton Albion and Tamworth.

COLLINS, JIMMY: 1989-91. Midfield/Forward 49+7 (17+4 cup) apps; 1 goal. Former Derby County, St Helens Town and Fleetwood player who signed in August, 1989. Joined Accrington Stanley and later played for Garswood Utd.

COLLINS, LEE: 2002-04. Midfield 16+2 (3 cup) apps; 1 (1 cup) goals. Former Albion Rovers, Swindon and Blackpool player who joined in August 2003 after a successful loan spell at the end of the 2002-03 season. Released in December 2003 and moved to Stranraer in January 2004.

COLNE DYNAMOES: A club who came to the fore in the late 1980s with a big spending chairman who relieved Morecambe of their manager Joe Wojciechowicz and half of the first team squad.They won the NPL and the Lancashire Cup but when promotion to the Conference was refused the club disbanded.

COLNE TOWN: An earlier club for Colne who had two seasons in the Lancashire Combination in 1925-26 and 1926-27. The first meeting was on October 17, 1925, at Rosebery Park. Of the four games played Morecambe won 3 and lost 1.

COLWYN BAY: Morecambe have met them in away games at Ellesmere Port, Northwich Victoria, Rhyl and their own Llanelian Road ground. The first meeting was at Rhyl in the FA Cup, 1st Qualifying Rd, on September 16, 1989. The 'home' team won 4-1. Att: 352. The last meeting was the Shrimps' last match in the NPL at Colwyn Bay on May 2, 1995. A crowd of 606 watched a 0-0 draw.

COMMON ROAD: Home of Evesham Utd who Morecambe met in the FA Trophy 4th Rd on February 3, 2001. Att: 738. The game ended 0-0 with Morecambe winning the replay.

COMSTIVE, PAUL: 1994-96. Defender/Midfield. 28+10 (10+1 cup) apps; 4 goals. Paul joined from Southport in March, 1985, and helped Morecambe win promotion to the Conference. A vastly experienced midfielder who had spells at Blackburn Rovers (3+3 apps); Rochdale (9 apps, 2 goals); Wigan Athletic (35 apps, 2 goals); Wrexham (95+4 apps, 8 goals); Burnley (81+1 apps, 17 goals), Bolton Wanderers (42+7 apps, 3 goals) and Chester City (55+2 apps, 6 goals). Moved to Chorley in March, 1996, and went on to play for and manage Hesketh Bank.

CONFERENCE: Morecambe joined the league in 1995/96 and played their opening game on August 19, 1995, beating Telford Utd 2-0. Att: 1,533. Paul Burns scored the opening goal in the Conference with a penalty in the 82nd minute.
Biggest win: 7-0 v Altrincham at home on February 17, 1996.
Record defeat: 7-0 v Leek Town away on August 25, 1998.

Highest gate: 4,353 v Yeovil Town at Huish Park on January 18, 2003.
Highest home gate: 3,914 v Halifax Town on October 28, 1997.
Lowest gate: 402 v Gateshead at the International Stadium on October 16, 1996.
Lowest home gate: 645 v Halifax Town on March 12, 1996.

Morecambe's full record in the Conference is:

	P	W	D	L	F	A	Pts	Pos
1995/96	42	17	8	17	78	72	59	9th
1996/97	42	19	9	14	69	56	66	4th
1997/98	42	21	10	11	77	64	73	5th
1998/99	42	15	8	19	60	76	53	14th
1999/00	42	18	16	8	70	48	70	3rd
2000/01	42	11	12	19	64	66	45	19th
2001/02	42	17	11	14	63	67	62	6th
2002/03	42	23	9	10	86	42	78	2nd
2003/04	42	20	7	15	66	66	67	7th

CONGLETON TOWN: Morecambe first met the Bears at Christie Park on December 18, 1961, in the Cheshire League/Combination Inter-League Cup. Congleton surprisingly won 2-1 in a season where Morecambe lost only six league and cup games. Att: 1,900.

CONNERTON, STUART: 1987-88 and 1989-90. Defender 13+2 (8+1 cup) apps; 2 (1 cup) goals. Played for Morecambe Reserves when they won the Lancashire League Division 2 title in 1983/84. Moved to Netherfield but returned to play for the Reserves. Joined Netherfield again but returned in December 1989. Later played in the North Lancashire League for Phoenix Celtic and Marsh Utd.

CONSETT: Just one meeting with the Steelmen which came in the FA Cup 1st Qualifying Rd at Christie Park on September 19, 1981. A crowd of 200 saw Morecambe lose 3-2. Just two days later, Morecambe went on to lose 9-0, at home to Bangor City.

CONWAY, CHRIS: 1982-83. Midfield 10 apps. Chris joined in March, 1983, aged 19. Moved to Glossop and Mossley.

COOKE: 1920-22. Full-back 17 (3 cup) apps. He joined in March, 1921, after playing for Carlisle.

COOMBES: 1932-33. Right-half 15 (5 cup) apps. Former Fleetwood player who joined in August, 1923.

COOPER, JAMES (JIM): 1920-21. Centre-half 11 (1 cup) apps; 1 goal. Played in Morecambe's first game in August 1920. One of the club's first professionals the former Sunderland and Newcastle Utd player was club captain and referred to as the *"team manager"*.

CORNTHWAITE, J: 1933-34. Left-half 22 (2 cup) apps. Joined in November 1933 and moved back to Galgate with brother H Cornthwaite who made 4 (1 cup) apps.

CORR, PETER JOSEPH (PADDY): 1953-54. Outside-right 23 (2 cup) apps; 2 goals. An Eire international, 4 caps, who played in his country's famous 2-0 victory over England in 1949 at Goodison Park. After playing for Dundalk, Preston North End, Everton, Bangor City and Wigan he moved to Morecambe in December 1953. Born in Dundalk on June 26, 1923, Paddy died in Preston on May 27, 2001.

COULTHARD, LAURIE: 1976-77. Defender 13 (6 cup) apps. Joined in June, 1976, but moved to Kuwait in December, 1976. Played for Carlisle Utd from 1977-80.

COYLE, NICK: Coyle was an academy player who was capped 5 times and captained the England Schoolboys Under 18s side in the 1999-2000 season. Later played for Blackpool Mechanics.

CRABBLE ATHLETIC GROUND: Home of Dover Athletic and, for a temporary basis, Margate in 2003-04. Morecambe's first visit was on March 30, 1996, beating Dover 3-2 after being 2-0 down at half-time. Att: 1,090.

CRAIG, J: 1932-33. Centre-forward 15 (4 cup) apps; 6 (2 cup) goals. Former Warton player who joined in December 1932.

CREWE ALEXANDRA: The Railwaymen have been to Christie Park just once. A pre-season friendly on July 20, 2000, ended in a 0-0 draw.

CROFT, BILL: 1938-40. Outside-right 25 (3 cup) apps, 8 goals. Also 17 (3 cup) apps and 20 (3 cup) goals during 1939-40 and 1940-41 in the North Lancashire League. Leading goalscorer in 1939-40 with 22 goals.

CROFT PARK: Home of Blyth Spartans where Morecambe lost 1-0 in the FA Cup 1st Rd on November 3, 1962. Att: 4,490.

CROMPTON, DENIS: 1967-69. Half-back 34 (17 cup) apps; 3 goals. Denis joined in December 1967 from Altrincham. He formerly played for Wigan Athletic, Burnley, Doncaster Rovers and Bolton Wanderers. Moved on to Netherfield and Rossendale.

CROMPTON'S RECS: Works team in Ashton-in-Makerfield who faced Morecambe in the Lancashire Combination League. The first meeting was away on February 15, 1958 which Morecambe won 2-0.

CROWDS: The biggest crowd to watch Morecambe was the 19,000 who saw the club beat Dartford in the 1974, FA Trophy final at Wembley on April 17, 1974. The only other five figure crowds for the first team were in 1925, when the Shrimps battled it out with Chorley for the Lancashire Junior Cup final. Incredibly it took three games for the result to be resolved and all three crowds topped 10,000. The first game was at Preston on February 20, 1926, and saw 13,324 witness a 2-2 draw. The replay on March 6, was held at Burnden Park, Bolton and was watched by 12,981. The silverware was finally sealed after a third game, again at Preston. A crowd of 10,009 saw the Shrimps win 3-1. A total of 36,314 people watched the three games. Morecambe's Youth team once attracted an amazing crowd of 11,000 at Old Trafford when they met the mighty Manchester United in an FA Youth Cup tie on October 12, 1959. Unfortunately Morecambe lost 14-0. The biggest crowd at Christie Park was 9,383 for the FA Cup third round tie with Weymouth on January 6, 1962. Despite the huge crowd the Shrimps went down 1-0 and missed the chance of a fourth round meeting with Preston North End. The best gates in the NPL came when the Shrimps met Wigan Athletic. Nearly 6,500 saw the game against Wigan on August 14, 1968. Morecambe's best crowd at Christie Park while in the Northern Premier League came against Wigan when 2,689 watched on September 10, 1968. The lowest crowd to watch Morecambe is 24 for a NPL game against Kirkby Town on April 17, 1972. Those that were there witnessed a 1-0 Morecambe win. Another low crowd was announced at the annual meeting for the 1940/41 season when a North Lancashire League fixture drew gate receipts of 3d.

CUBBAGE, DON: 1960-67 and 1968-71. Right-back 290 (86 cup) apps; 7 (2 cup) goals. The former Blackpool junior made his name as a player in the successful Shrimps side which took the Lancashire Combination by storm in the late 1960s. A fierce tackler, he was a virtual ever present for the Shrimps in the 60s after signing from Altrincham. He went on to make 376 appearances in a Morecambe shirt and scored nine goals. After spells at Penrith and Trimpell as a player, Don was appointed manager in November, 1979. The highlight of Don's reign was undoubtedly the FA Cup tie against Rotherham at Christie Park, the first time the Shrimps had ever been drawn at home to a Football League club in the competition. After holding the full timers to a draw at Christie Park, the Shrimps narrowly lost the replay. The 1980-81 season proved a disaster however, as Don was faced with a cash crisis. The Shrimps finished in 21st place and had to seek re-election for the first time ever. The 1981-1982 season started off just as badly with a record 9-0 home defeat in an FA Cup tie against Bangor City. It was all too much and Don resigned on Tuesday, September 23, 1981.

CULLINGFORD, ROBERT (BOB): 1975-76 and 1979-81. Defender 32+2 (3+1 cup) apps. A former England Schoolboy international who won two Under 18 caps in 1972. He joined Morecambe from Lancaster City in May, 1975, was released in May, 1976, but returned in August, 1979.

CURTIS, JOHN: 1981-84. Defender 78+2 (24 cup) apps. Joined in January, 1982, the former Blackpool, Blackburn Rovers and Wigan Athletic defender was released in January, 1984.

CURTIS, WAYNE: 1997-2004. Forward 69+38 (10+12 cup) apps; 39 (5 cup) goals. Former Holker Old Boys Junior who made his debut for the Reserves in February, 1998. He scored for the first team on his home and away debuts and has proved to be a regular goalscorer ever since.

He helped Morecambe win the Spalding Cup in 1997-98, scoring in the second leg of the He was loaned to Barrow in November, 2003, but returned to the first team and scored regularly again. Lancashire Cup winner in 1998-99 and 2003-04. Spalding Cup winner in 1997-98.

CURZON ASHTON: Morecambe first visited the Blues in the President's Cup 1st Rd on October 2, 1993, winning 3-0. Att: 162.

D

DAGENHAM & REDBRIDGE: Morecambe first met the Daggers in the Conference on September 16, 1995 at Dagenham, drawing 2-2. Att: 834.

DAINTY, ALBERT: 1953-56. Centre-forward 53 (6 cup) apps; 25 (3 cup) goals. Albert was born in Lancaster, December 4, 1923. Died Lancaster, March 23, 1979. Albert was a popular player on both sides of the River Lune. Albert played for several local junior teams before signing for PNE just as war was breaking out. He made a guest appearance for Manchester United and two for Millwall in 1942/43. He played twice for North End in the 1944/45 season before making his full debut after the war had finished. Unfortunately, he made just one first team appearance for Preston in the 1946/47 season, before joining Stockport County, where he scored 16 goals in 36 appearances. The next season he was Stockport's top scorer with 12 goals. A move to Southport saw him score 11 goals in 49 games. He then joined Lancaster City where he played from 1951 to 1954. He became a Shrimps' player in March 1954, where his 7 goals in 10 games helped save the club from relegation. In two years at Morecambe he made 53 league and 6 cup appearances, scoring a total of 28 goals, before being appointed manager for the 1955/56 season. He was the Shrimps' second ever manager, but unfortunately did not have a successful time, and was replaced by Ken Horton.

DAIRY CREST FLOODLIT LEAGUE: Morecambe's manager Les Rigby started this competition in 1983-84, the only season the club entered, with little success.

DALTON, JOHN: 1965-68. Forward 20+1 (12 cup) apps; 12 (4 cup) goals. Former PNE A and Chorley player who joined in August, 1965.

DALZIEL, IAN: 1994-95. Defender 20+1 (5+2 cup) apps; 1 cup goal. Signed by Jim Harvey in July, 1994, but saw appearances restricted by injury. He returned to the club as assistant manager in September, 2000, resigning in November, 2001, for business reasons. Ian's clubs included Derby County, Hereford Utd and Carlisle Utd.

DANSON, DICKIE. 1957-58. Inside-right one appearance in March 1958. Former PNE Junior who moved into the local league with Galgate 1966-67, Trimpell 1968-69, Lansil, Galgate and Storeys. He returned to play for Morecambe reserves in 1971-72 and moved to Lancaster City in 1974. He was manager at Giant Axe from 1982-90 before being sacked in November, 1990. Dickie was appointed manager of Morecambe reserves in September, 1991. Was caretaker manager before Leighton James was appointed in December, 1993 and became assistant manager to Jim Harvey. He also had a spell as a club director and academy coach.

DARK LANE: Home of Rossendale Utd. Morecambe's first visit was on November 20, 1920, winning 4-1 – their second ever win.

DARLEY, JACK: 1946-49. Left-back 53 (12 cup) apps; 1 goal. Joined in May, 1947, but unfortunately broke his leg playing at Wigan Athletic in the 1948-49 season.

DARLEY, STUART: 1987-90. Midfield/Forward 25+3 (12+2 cup) apps; 1 (1 cup) goals. Joined in April, 1987, from Horwich RMI. He later played for a host of clubs including Gt. Harwood Town, Bamber Bridge, Lancaster City, Netherfield and Gretna.

DARLING, MALCOLM: 1977-78 and 1978-80. Forward 72+3 (21+1 cup) apps; 20 (7 cup) goals. A vastly experienced player, who first joined in 1977, but moved to Sheffield Wednesday. Made one appearance for the Owls and two for Hartlepool before returning to Christie Park in October, 1977. Moved to Bury in March, 1978, but was back again in April and even had a spell as caretaker manager in November, 1979. Released in April, 1980, and moved on to Workington and Darwen where he had as spell as player manager. His league career included 114+13 apps and 30 goals at Blackburn Rovers, 16 apps and 5 goals for Norwich City, 82+4 apps, 16 goals for Rochdale, a short spell at Bolton Wanderers and 100+4 games for Chesterfield where he scored 33 goals.

DARLINGTON ROAD GROUND: Former home of Ferryhill Athletic where Morecambe lost 2-0 in the FA Trophy 1st Qualifying Rd, in September 23, 1989. The ground was sold for redevelopment in 1995.

DARTFORD: Only meeting came at Wembley in the FA Trophy Final in 1974 which the Shrimps won 2-1.

DARWEN: The first meeting between the clubs, was in the Lancashire Combination at Woodhill Lane on September 11, 1920, Morecambe losing 6-1. Att: 1,500.

DAVIES, ANTHONY: 1932-33. Outside-right 1 app in January 1933. Was Morecambe's trainer but played to make up the 11.

DAVIES, MARK: 1982-83. Midfield 14+6 (5+1 cup) apps, 2 goals. Joined from Lancaster City in July, 1982, but moved back to Giant Axe in February, 1983.

DAWSON, PAUL: 1980-81. Defender 27 (4 cup) apps. Former Blackburn Rovers apprentice who joined from Fleetwood in October, 1980.

DE HAVILLAND: Just one meeting with the works team in an FA Cup, Preliminary Rd, game at Christie Park on September 20, 1947, which Morecambe won 3-1. Att: 3,000.

DEAN STREET: Home of Shildon where Morecambe first played on October 20, 1984, in the 1st Qualifying Rd, of the FA Trophy. Morecambe won 5-3. Att: 97.

DEBUTS: Wayne Curtis and Mike Bignall both scored on both their home and away debuts. Curtis scored at Dover Athletic on April 25, 1998, and at home to Stalybridge three days later. Bignall bagged on his home debut against Dover on March 22, 1997, and then scored twice at Kidderminster Harriers on March, 29. Morecambe's best ever debut boy though was Fred Bedford who scored hat-tricks in both his home and away debuts. He chalked up his first trio against Horwich RMI on August 25, 1928, and at Bacup Borough on August, 30. He also scored a hat-trick in his third game at Barnoldswick Town on September, 1.

DEEPDALE: Famous home of Preston North End. Although Morecambe have never played the North End first team at Deepdale the club has regularly played finals of the Lancashire Cup there. The first final was on February 20, 1926, when 13,324 watched a 2-2 draw with Chorley.

DEFEATS: The original Morecambe town team, before the club formed in 1920 lost 16-0 at Scotforth on Saturday, October 1, 1898, but the full Morecambe's record defeat is 14-1 and came at Chorley in the Lancashire Combination league on a Good Friday, April 19, 1946. The excuse? Morecambe had eight players making their debuts. The club's record home defeat is 10-1 by the RAF in a North Lancashire League Challenge Cup, 2nd Rd, tie on October 12, 1940. The heaviest defeat in the NPL was 9-0 against Bangor City on Monday, September 21, 1981.

DEMPSEY, FRED: 1928-31 Outside-right 18 (2 cup) apps, 5 (1 cup) goals. Local player who had a trial with Everton but released by Morecambe in 1930. Joined Canforth Rangers and later Edmondsons.

DENABY UTD: First met in the FA Trophy 2nd Rd at Christie Park on February 12, 1972, winning 4-0. Att: 875.

DENEHY, CHARLES: 1959-60. Outside-left 21 (3 cup) apps, 4 (3 cup) goals. Ex-Blackpool Reserve team player who joined in August 1958. Moved on to Netherfield and Fleetwood.

DEVA STADIUM. The new home of Chester City, Morecambe's first visit was on January 27, 2001, in the Conference in a 1-0 defeat.

DEVANEY, PHIL: 1988-89. Forward 8+2 (8+1 cup) app. Former Burnley apprentice who joined in July, 1988. He moved on to Marine in February, 1989. Phil later played for Warrington Town, Goole Town, Burnley Bank Hall, North Ferriby Utd and Emley.

DEVINE, PETER: 1982-83. Midfield/Forward 5 (1 cup) apps, 1 goal. A former league player with Bristol City who joined in August 1982. Moved on to Blackburn (8 apps, 4 goals) and Burnley (46+10 apps, 4 goals). Later played for Chorley, Clitheroe and Lancaster City where he became famous for a celebrated penalty miss in the NPL, Division One Cup final. After playing, he became Blackburn's Football in the Community Officer.

DEWHURST, JACK: 1921-22. Centre-half 8 apps. Played for Darwen in their first season on the Football League before spending six years as a striker at Blackburn Rovers (1899-1905), making 169 appearances, scoring 43 goals. Joined in February 1922, aged 45.

DIAMOND, BARRY: 1987-88. Forward 5 (8+1 cup) apps, 3 (3 cup) goals. Much travelled lower league striker who joined in January 1988 before moving to Colne Dynamoes in March and helping them to win the FA Vase competition that year. In the league played for Rochdale, Stockport County, Halifax Town and Wrexham. After leaving Morecambe played for Mossley, Hyde Utd, Altrincham, Chorley, Stalybridge Celtic, Curzon Ashton, Rossendale Utd, Horwich RMI, Droylsden, Gt Harwood, Leigh RMI and Castleton Gabriels.

DICK KERR'S: Morecambe played against the Preston works team from 1920-21 until 1935-36 when they withdrew from the league.

DICKINSON: 1925-28. Half-back 14 apps. Former Lancaster Town player who joined in February, 1926. Broke his leg playing for the Shrimps in March, 1928.

DIGGLE, HARRIET ELEANOR: Photographs from the 1920s show Mrs Diggle as the club's Dame President. She continued in her Vice-President's role until she died on May 3, 1935, aged 65.

DIXON, STEVE. 1987-88. Defender 1 cup app. Must be the only player to play his only game for the club in a cup final! He was in the team that lost to Colne Dynamoes in the Lancashire Cup final in April 1988. He then moved to Bishop Auckland.

DOBSON, ROY: 1978-81. Goalkeeper 21 (2 cup) apps. Joined in December, 1978 after playing for Chelsea in Australia. Moved to Lytham in October, 1981 and went on to play for Lancaster City and Fleetwood where he was a member of their FA Vase final team.

DONCASTER ROVERS: First meeting was in a pre-season friendly at Christie Park on July 22, 1997 when Morecambe beat the struggling Division 3 side 4-0.

DONE, STEVE: 1968-78. Midfield/Forward 392+4 (132+3 cup) apps; 44 (12 cup) goals. The man to hold the record for the most apps in a Morecambe shirt joined the Shrimps as a 19-year-old in the summer of 1968 and went on to play a total of 524 league and cup games for the club. Born in Blackburn, Steve was a junior at Burnley and had two seasons as a reserve team regular and even played against Morecambe for Burnley in a

5-0 pre-season win for the Clarets on August 8, 1968. An intelligent man, Steve wanted to concentrate on a career in teaching and joined Morecambe as a part-timer, ironically making his debut in a 2-1 friendly defeat against his old club Burnley. Steve made his debut at home to Boston United on August 24, 1968, and scored Morecambe's goal in a 1-1 draw. From there he became a virtual ever present for the next 10 years and made 392 league starts, scoring 44 times. He played a further 132 cup games, scoring another 12 goals. He was an influential member of the Shrimps' FA Trophy winning side of 1974 and also played a part in the club's Lancashire Junior Cup win over Great Harwood in the 1968-69 season. His last game for the club came on April 28, 1978 – a 1-1 draw with Gainsborough Trinity. Steve still has links with the area through his son Ryan, a golf professional with Heysham Golf Club. He scouts for Manchester United and can be seen at some of the club's junior games. FA Trophy winner in 1968-69. Lancashire Cup winner in 1968-69.

DOVECOTE: Home of Shepshed Charterhouse (later Shepshed Albion and now Shepshed Dynamo). Travelled there in the NPL from 1988 to 1992. The first visit, on October 8, 1988, ended in a 2-2 draw. Att: 210.

DOVER ATHLETIC: First meeting with the Whites was in the Conference at Christie Park on November 18, 1995. Morecambe won 3-1. Att: 1,047.

DOWE, JULIAN: 2000-01. Forward 7 (4 cup) apps, 1 cup goal. Joined in September 2000 and was a member of the team that knocked Cambridge Utd out of the FA Cup on a memorable day at Christie Park. Released in February 2001 and later played for Bacup Borough, Colne and Hyde Utd. Before landing at Morecambe he had a string of clubs including Marbella and Real Mallorca in Spain.

DRAWS: Highest draws have been 5-5. On Boxing Day, 1936, Morecambe drew 5-5 with Barrow Reserves at Christie Park. Att: 2,096. The opening game of the 1946-47 season on August, 31, at Fleetwood, also ended 5-5. Att: 4,536. The benefit match for Borrowdale, Cubbage, Fawcett, Mitchell and Scott on March 15, 1966 against an All Stars XI was also drawn 5-5 with goals from Borrowdale, Fawcett, Howarth, Scott and Varcoe.

DRILL FIELD: Former home of Northwich Victoria, which claimed to be the oldest football ground in the world. The first meeting between the sides was in the North West Floodlit League on November 13, 1967 which ended in a 2-1 defeat. Att: 1,914.

DROYLSDEN: The Shrimps' met the Bloods many times in the Lancashire Combination and the NPL. The first meeting was at Christie Park on March 6, 1937, losing 1-0. Att: 894.

DRUMMOND, STEWART: 1992-2004. Midfield 254+17 (58+14 cup) apps; 37 (5 cup) goals. Player who came up through the ranks at Christie Park to skipper the side and become an England semi-pro regular. Played for the junior and reserve sides from 1991 to

1995 before making his first team debut in January 1995. Drummond *(pictured right)* signed professional forms in June 1995 and became a regular in the 1997-98 season. He established himself among Morecambe's great players winning a number of player of the year awards, winning 12 England caps and being selected for the FA XI between 1999 and 2002. Player of the year 1998-99 and 1999-2000. Left the club in May 2004 to join Chester City after they had won promotion to the Football League. Conference team of the year 1999-2000 and 2003-04. Lancashire Cup winner in 2003-04. Spalding Cup winner 1997-98.

DRY DOCK UTD: Played against the team who played at Caton Road and then Far Moor in the North Lancashire League during the 1939-40 and 1940-41 seasons. Lost the first meeting in November 4, 1939 4-3 away.

DRYBURGH, THOMAS: 1958-59. Outside-left 31 (11 cup) apps; 8 (6 cup) goals. A former ice hockey player who only took up football after wartime service with the Royal Navy. Played professionally with Aldershot and Rochdale before making the switch to Leicester City in August 1950 for a fee of £6,500. Scored 29 goals in 95 games before moving to Hull City and Kings Lynn. Joined in September 1958 and later moved to Rossendale.

DULLAGHAN, GARY: 1989-96. Defender 177+14 (72+5 cup) apps; 11 (7 cup) goals. Another Liverpool-based player who seemed to thrive under the guidance of Bryan Griffiths this no-nonsense central defender played a big part in Morecambe's promotion to the Conference. Joined in January 1990 along with Robbie Armstrong after spells with South Liverpool, Lucas Sports, Witton Albion, Oswestry Town and Rhyl. Moved to Lancaster City in March 1996 and later played for Witton Albion, Ashton Utd and Chorley. President's Cup winner in 1991-92. Lancashire Cup winner in 1993-94.

DUNDEE: The Dark Blues visited Christie Park for a pre-season friendly on July 26, 1994, drawing 2-2. Dundee returned on July 24, 1997 and won 1-0 with O'Driscoll scoring.

DUNDERDALE, S: 1933-34. Outside-right 2 apps in January 1934.

DUNN, JOE: 1961-64. Right-Half 62 (19 cup) apps; 5 goals. A true Morecambe great Joe was a hero both as a player and a manger for the club. Joe was a Glaswegian born on

September 25, 1925 and first made his name playing for junior sides Ashfield and Springburn United before moving up the ranks to play for Clyde from 1949 to 1951, making 29 appearances as a defender. So impressive was Joe that Preston North End splashed out £1,500 for his services in July 1951 and they were not to be disappointed as he made 224 league and 14 FA Cup appearances for the Deepdale club, scoring 2 league goals.

Joe was released by Preston North End at the end of the 1960/61 season and joined the Shrimps as player manager, replacing another former PNE favourite Ken Horton. Nobody can deny that Joe took over a good squad but he certainly made it an even better one as he led Morecambe to some of their greatest days. In the 1961/62 season the club won the Lancashire Combination League and the Lancashire Junior Club as well as reaching the third round of the FA Cup for the only time in the club's history. His debut came in a 5-3 home win over New Brighton on August 19, 1961 and his influence was there for all to see. A Visitor report of a later game said of Joe: *"He was an inspiration to the side, his rugged Scots accent so clear during the game when he gave instructions which acted as a spur to the Morecambe team."*

Success followed in the 1962/63 campaign with another league and cup double but 1963/64 proved an anti-climax and Joe was sacked on March 30, 1964. The Shrimps finished in 10th spot that season. Joe later went on to manage Fleetwood and is still remembered with great affection by many at Christie Park.

DURHAM CITY: The original Durham City played at Holiday Park in the Football League in 1921-28. Disbanded in 1938 they reformed in 1949. Morecambe faced Durham City in the FA Cup 2nd, Qualifying Rd, on September 28, 1991, winning 4-1. Att: 213.

DURHAM FA: In 1986-87 Morecambe represented the Lancashire FA in the Northern Counties Cup. After beating the East Riding FA Morecambe met Durham, represented by Bishop Auckland. The first game ended in a 1-1 draw at Christie Park on February 8, 1987.

E

EARLESTOWN: Morecambe first met the Lilywhites in the Lancashire Junior Cup 1st Rd at Christie Park on September 29, 1945, losing 2-1 after extra time.

EARLY YEARS: Although the present club was formed in 1920 the town had a team before the turn of the century. The club was in existence from 1897 to 1912 and was known as Morecambe Association Football Club in contrast to Morecambe Football Club which was the town's rugby team until its demise in 1906. The early Morecambe played in blue or blue and white and played on various grounds around Woodhill Lane and a pitch on West End Road which was called New Road Ground. The formation of the club at this time is rather vague but during the first season in 1897/98 only friendlies were played with the first result traced being a 0-0 draw with Moorlands Athletic on

November 4, 1897. In 1898/99, the club joined the Lancaster & District League (which became the North Lancashire League in 1905) and the side started disastrously, losing 16-0 away to Scotforth in their third match. But results did improve and by 1899/1900 they finished second. But the following seasons were mixed and they finished bottom in the 1905/06 season. The season after, saw renewed hope. The rugby team disbanded and football became the premier sport in the town and the club finished second. A shortage of fixtures in the local league resulted in the club also joining the Ulverston & District League in 1907/08 and 1908/09 and they managed to end both years as champions. One notable date in the early years was on January 30, 1909, when the then president of the Football Association, Lord Kinnard, visited the area and kicked off for the club in a 2-1 defeat at Giant Axe against Lancaster reserves. In 1909/10, Morecambe entered the West Lancashire League, while also playing in the North Lancashire League, but although they continued to enjoy success in the latter the new league was a step too far. A couple of years later, the club fell out of existence due to the general apathy to football in the town and a lack of money to improve the team and rugby league returned as the town's main sport.

EAST GATESHEAD STADIUM: Now known as the International Stadium. Morecambe's first visit was on April 23, 1975, losing 4-1 to Gateshead Utd.

EAST RIDING FA: Represented the Lancashire FA against East Riding in the Quarter-Final of the Northern Counties Cup at East Ferriby, winning 2-0.

EASTERBY, JOE: 1950-60. Outside-right/Inside-right 225 (37 cup) apps; 32 (5 cup) goals. A regular throughout the 1950s Joe has been described as a brilliant ball player in the Tom Finney mould. Born in 1928, Joe was a right winger and inside right who after being demobbed from the army was spotted playing for Caton United in the North Lancashire League. He made such an impression that the legendary Wolves manager Stan Cullis invited him to Molyneux for a trial. He had two games for Wolves, and was invited to sign but turned down the offer to remain part time. After signing for Morecambe in

1950, he made his debut at Blackpool B in the Lancashire Combination on September 23, in a 3-1 defeat. The 1950s were not particularly good times for Morecambe but Joe did play in two cup finals which both ended in defeat. The first was a Lancashire Junior Cup defeat against Rochdale reserves in 1950/51 and a two-legged Combination Cup reverse against Horwich RMI in the 1956/57 season. Joe was awarded a benefit match on May 2, 1957, with a Morecambe XI beating Joe's XI 5-3. A groin injury restricted his appearances towards the end of the 1950s and that injury eventually forced him to retire in 1959. His last game was on September 9, 1959, a 2-1 defeat at Fleetwood.

EASTWOOD, EDMUND (EDDIE): 1923-29. Left-back 213 (63 cup) apps. A regular defender in the great side of the 1920s, winning a Combination League Championship medal in 1924-25. He joined in August, 1923, and moved to Clitheroe 1929-30. Lancashire Combination League winner in 1924-25. Lancashire Cup winner in 1925-26 and 1926-27. Combination Cup winner in 1926-27.

EASTWOOD HANLEY: Only one meeting with the now defunct club with a 2-1 away defeat on January 30, 1989, in the 2nd Rd of the Northern Premier League Cup. Att: 215.

EASTWOOD, PHIL: 1999-2002. Forward 45+28 (5+11 cup) apps; 21 (6 cup) goals. Former Burnley player who made 7+9 first team apps, scoring 1 goal before being released in 1999. Had loan spells in the Conference with Telford Utd and Kettering Town before joining Morecambe in the summer of 1999.
Moved to Southport in October 2001 and then to Stalybridge Celtic in July 2002, scoring 30 goals in the 2002-03 season.

EATOUGH, MARTIN: 1979-80, 1983-84 and 1989-90. Defender/Midfield 82 (19 cup) apps; 5 (2 cup) goals. Had three spells at Christie Park starting in August, 1978, when joining from home town team Great Harwood. Had a spell in America before moving to Barrow and Southport for four figure fees on both occasions. Returned to Morecambe in December, 1983, but moved on to Clitheroe, Accrington Stanley and Fleetwood. Had a spell as assistant manager at Christie Park after joining for a third time in July, 1989, but soon moved on again, joining Wren Rovers. Once described as 'one of the best players in non-league football' he continued to move on regularly with a spell as manager at Bamber Bridge and two successful periods at Lancaster City.

ECCLES, BILLY: 1950-51 and 1953-56. Half-back/Forward. 20 (4 cup) apps; 6 goals. A local player who joined in January 1951 before moving to Morecambe Lads Club. Returned in August 1953 and continued to play for the reserves until the 1957-58 season.

ECCLES UTD: Met in the Lancashire Combination from 1920-21 to 1924-25. First meeting was at Eccles and ended in a 3-1 defeat on October 30, 1920. Att: 6,000. In the last meeting at Rosebery Park on February 21, 1925, Morecambe won 11-1.

EDGAR STREET: Home of Hereford Utd. First visit was in the Conference on February 14, 1998 with Hereford winning 1-0. Att: 1,720.

EDGE, DAVID JOHN: 1983-84. Goalkeeper unused sub in one pre-season cup game in August 1983. Played locally for Greaves Utd, Nicholsons and Carnforth Rangers and became Morecambe's Reserve team manager when the club reformed a second team in the 1983-84 season. Had a brief spell as caretaker manager in February, 1985, after Sean Gallagher quit and went on to manage Netherfield before returning to Christie Park as physio in the summer of 1989. Son, Lewis Edge, made his first team debut for Blackpool at the age of 17 against Bristol City on May 8, 2004.

EDGELEY PARK: Home of Stockport County where Morecambe first visited to play their reserves in the Lancashire Combination on January 7, 1922. Almost 4,000 watched Stockport win 2-0.

EDMONDSON, ALBERT: 1930-31 and 1932-34. Centre-Forward 42 (7 cup) apps; 17 (1 cup) goals. A local player who went to West End School and represented Morecambe Schoolboys in 1925-26. Played for Lancaster Town, Thornton Athletic and Edmondsons before joining Morecambe in January, 1930. Played for Edmondsons in 1931-32 before returning to Christie Park in August, 1932.

EDMONDSON, 'WAXY': 1950-53. Right-half/Inside-right 13 (4 cup) apps; 1 goal. Joined in March, 1951. Later played for Carnforth Rangers.

EDMONDSONS: Met while in the North Lancashire League in the 1939-40 season. Both games were played at Christie Park with a 2-2 draw on October 28 and a 4-2 win on May 6. After war broke out Morecambe had 3 weeks without a game before playing Edmondsons in a friendly which was the club's first wartime game. Edmondsons won 4-3. They also beat Morecambe 6-2 on the Railway Meadow in the 1st Rd of the North Lancashire League Challenge Cup.

EDWARDS, ANDY: 1987-88. Forward 20+1 (9 cup) apps; 9 (2 cup) goals. Player who scored 27 goals in 88+25 apps for Wrexham before joining in September, 1987 after a spell in Australia. Loaned to Northwich Victoria in March, 1988, and later moved to Colne Dynamoes.

EDWARDS, COLIN: 1983-84. Defender 15 (5 cup) apps. Joined in December, 1983, from Southport. Made 350 apps for Marine between 1972-80.

ELAM, LEE: 2002-03. Midfield/Forward 37+3 (9 cup) apps; 14 (2 cup) goals. Ex-Bradford City schoolboy who joined from Southport in August, 2002. Scored a number of important goals before leaving to join Halifax Town in May, 2003. Signed by newly promoted Yeovil Town where he was loaned out to Chester. While with Morecambe won 3 England semi-pro caps in 2002-03. Moved to Hornchurch in May, 2004.

ELLESMERE PORT TOWN: Met for 2 seasons in the NPL in 1971-72 and 1972-73. First meeting was a 2-1 defeat away on September, 25, 1971. Att: 600.

EMLEY: Joined the NPL in 1989-90 and faced Morecambe in that season in Rd 4 of the Northern Premier League Cup at Christie Park on March, 13, drawing 0-0. Att: 380. Morecambe won the replay 2-1. The club are now known as Wakefield & Emley and play at the Belle Vue Stadium in Wakefield.

EMMISON: 1921-22. Inside-left 10 apps; 1 goal. Joined from Blackburn in November 1921.

ENGLISH, J: 1926-28. Half-back/Inside-left 11 (2 cup) apps; 10 goals. Joined in August, 1926, and moved to Dick Kerr's. Despite scoring 10 goals in 11 games a local reporter said rather harshly he *"was weak in front of goals.'"*

ESH WINNING: Team from County Durham who Morecambe beat 8-0 at Christie Park on September 13, 1986, for their best ever win in the FA Cup. Att: 288.

ETON PARK: Home of Burton Albion who Morecambe played in the NPL from 1979-80 to 1986-87 and in the Conference. First visit was on April 19, 1980, with a 1-0 defeat. Att: 770.

EVANS, RAY: 1961-64. Half-back/Inside-right 90 (24+1 cup) apps; 18 (5 cup) goals. One of the club's best players in the Combination championship winning seasons of 1961/62 and 1962/63 India-born Evans was signed by Joe Dunn after impressing in a trial match in 1961. After making 33 league and one FA Cup appearance for Preston North End he moved on to Bournemouth in the summer of 1959 and made a further 36 league appearances, scoring nine goals. After being somewhat surprisingly released Ray made his Morecambe debut on August 19, 1961 in a 5-3 victory over New Brighton. He made his mark with the local press.
In the 1961/62 FA Cup tie at South Shields the Guardian wrote: *"Evans played his usual artistic game"* while against Chester he was said to be: *"the mastermind in Morecambe's attack. He delighted everyone with some brilliant runs sometimes beating three men by his body swerves."*
His final game came on April 27, 1964 in a 2-2 draw at Horwich RMI. Combination League winner in 1961-62 and 1962-63. Lancashire Cup winner in 1961-62.

EVERTON: One memorable fact is that Howard Kendall's successful spell as Everton manager began at Christie Park. His first game in charge was a pre-season friendly on August 8, 1981, which Everton won 3-0. Att: 2,000.

EVESHAM UTD: Met the Robins in the FA Trophy 4th Rd on February 2, 2001, drawing 0-0. Morecambe won the replay 4-1 at Christie Park on February 6. Att: 634.

EWEN FIELDS: Home of Hyde Utd and now called the Tameside Stadium. First meeting was a 1-1 draw on November 30, 1968, in the NPL. Att: 1,300.

EWOOD PARK: Home of Blackburn Rovers with the first visit being on March 19, 1973, in a FA Trophy, 4th Rd, 2nd Replay. Wigan won 1-0 in front of 5,693.

EXETER CITY: First met the Grecians in the Conference on November 15, 2003, at St James Park. A crowd of 2,993 watched Exeter win 4-0.

EYRES, DAVID: 1985-87. Forward 0+3 apps. It is hard to believe that one of the North West's leading players in the 90s did not make the grade at Christie Park.
He was a regular member of the reserve team managed by Dave Edge in the mid 1980s and was selected to make his first team debut during the 1985/86 season but only made two starts. The season after, he was selected only once, and left to join Southport. He also failed to make the grade at Haig Avenue and it was only when he was at Rhyl that his obvious skill began to catch the attention of scouts. It still took three years before he was given a professional contract when Blackpool came in for him when aged 24. He went on to play for Burnley, Preston North End and Oldham Athletic.

EYRIE GROUND: Former home of the original Bedford Town where Morecambe won 1-0 in the FA Trophy, Quarter-Final, on March 9, 1974. Att: 2,515. Malcolm Richmond scored the winner.

FA Cup Action 1995 - Ian Cain at Witton Albion.

The light at the end of the tunnel

F

FAIRCLOUGH, TONY: 1957-61. Winger 113 (27 cup) apps; 32 (5 cup) goals. Former Preston North End Reserves and Accrington Stanley player who joined in September, 1957. Moved to Wigan Athletic for £50 in January, 1961, and later played for Lancaster City.

FARNBOROUGH TOWN: First meeting against the club from Hampshire was in the Conference away on January 6, 1996, with 729 watching the home side win 3-1.

FARNWORTH, JACKIE: 1920-29. Half-back 295 (73 cup) apps; 15 (4 cup) goals. Born in Preston in 1901, Jackie served with the Kings' Own Royal Borders in France in 1916 and joined the club in its first season in 1920. He was an almost ever present for nine seasons and an essential member of the team during the 20s winning a Lancashire Combination League winners medal in 1924/25. He also picked up cup winners medals in the Lancashire Junior Cup (1925/26 and 1926/27) and the Lancashire Combination Cup (1926/27). Moved on to Rossendale United in October 1929.

FARRAR ROAD: Home of Bangor City where Morecambe lost 2-1 on their first visit on April 15, 1939, in the Lancashire Combination. Att: 2,500.

FARRELL, ANDREW: 1999-2000. Defender 30+1 (5 cup) apps. A highly experienced defender who joined in July 1999 from Rochdale where he made 113+5 apps, scoring 6 goals. Began his career by making 98+7 apps for home town club Colchester. He moved to Burnley for £13,000 in August, 1987, and played 237+20 games, scoring 19 goals between 1987-94. A £20,000 move to Wigan followed in September, 1994, with 51+3 apps and one goal before being released and joining Rochdale. Moved to Leigh RMI in July, 2000, making 61+4 apps and having a short spell as assistant manager.

FARRELL, GERRY: 1978-80. Full-back 50 (15 cup) apps. Liverpool-born defender who was an apprentice at Wolves and had a short spell at Watford before joining Blackburn Rovers in 1971. Made 21+1 appearances until leaving in February 1973 and moving to South Africa. Joined Morecambe in 1978 and played for Toronto (Canada) in 1979. Moved to Workington Town and also played for Lancaster City where he had a spell as coach. Became a respected estate agent in Morecambe.

FARSLEY CELTIC: There has been only one meeting with the Villagers with Morecambe beating them 4-2 in the 3rd Qualifying Rd of the FA Cup at Christie Park on October 19, 1998. Att: 520.

FAULKNER, MIKE: 1969-71. Half-back/Inside-forward 7+1 apps; 2 goals. Former Oldham and Rochdale player who joined in March, 1970. Released in September, 1970. Later played for Denaby Utd and Gainsborough Trinity.

FAWCETT, ROY: 1960-67. Outside-right 227 (65 cup) apps; 99 (22 cup) goals. Another of the Shrimps' stars in the 1960s. Roy was born in Leeds on January 20, 1938, and was a professional at Blackpool for five years. Unfortunately for Roy, a right winger who was an understudy to the great Stanley Matthews, he made just three first team appearances in that time and joined Morecambe in the summer of 1960. His first appearance in a Morecambe shirt came in a 4-1 home win over Bacup Borough on August 20, 1960. He certainly made a good impression as the Visitor reported that Roy was: *"Star of the Morecambe cast."* The report added: *"Left winger Fawcett's speedy raids and bullshot shooting gained the plaudits of the hard-bitten Christie critics."*
Roy went on to become a regular for six seasons and won two championship medals as well as being a member of two Junior Cup and one Combination Cup winning sides. His last first team game was a 1-0 away defeat at Burscough on December 17, 1966.
Roy left Morecambe and joined Lancaster City in February 1967.

FENSOME, ANDY: 1998-2002. Defender 114+5 (26+1 cup) apps. Experienced defender *(pictured right)* who joined from Barrow in March, 1999. Started his career as an apprentice at Norwich City but made his mark at Cambridge Utd under John Beck where he made 122+4 appearances, as Cambridge won successive promotions from Division Four and Division Three and made the FA Cup Quarter-Finals. Moved to Preston North End with Beck in October 1993 for £7,500 and made 93 apps, scoring one goal. Made a further 80+2 apps for Rochdale after moving on a free transfer in July 1996. Was Morecambe's player of the season in 2000-01. Moved to Lancaster City in July 2002 but retired in June 2003 and moved into coaching with PNE. Lancashire Cup winner in 1998-99.

The light at the end of the tunnel

FERBER, TOMMY: Tommy was club coach during the reign of Johnny Johnson (1976-77) and was promoted to boss in June 1977 after Johnson was sacked. Unfortunately, Ferber's reign was short and not very sweet. In the space of a year he was sacked not once, but twice. After just three months in charge he was sacked when the club wanted to appoint ex-Southport player Alex Russell but Formby wanted more than £500 in compensation and the Shrimps refused. Ferber was reinstated and several directors resigned as the club suffered a number of disappointments and a lack of cash, but perhaps he should have known better as he was shown the door again in February, 1978.

FERENS PARK: Former home of Durham City where Morecambe won an FA Cup, 2nd Qualifying Rd, tie on September 29, 1991, 4-1 with goals from Coleman, Brown, McMahon and Holden. Att: 212.

FERN, TOM: 1961-63. Right-half/Inside-right 24 (4 cup) apps; 3 goals. Former Dumbarton player who joined in September 1961. Lancashire Cup winner in 1961-62.

FERRYHILL ATHLETIC: First met at Christie Park on October 22, 1983, in the 1st Qualifying Rd of the FA Trophy, winning 2-1. Att: 225.

FINCH, JIM: 1981-82 Midfield 10 (2 cup) apps. Signed by Les Rigby who also managed the Sunday League side Lisieux Hall that Jim played for.

FINNEY, TOM SIR: The great Preston North End winger played three times at Christie Park. His first appearance came on October 27, 1960, when he switched on the club's new floodlights. He then went on to play for an All Stars XI against Morecambe. He played centre-forward with Stan Mortenson scoring a hat-trick at outside left in a game Morecambe won 4-3. His next appearance came a couple of months later on December 7, 1960, in another All Star XI side. This time the game marked the opening of the club's new Auxiliary Club. Tom was outside-right with another former great, Liverpool's Billy Liddell, at outside left. Despite the great names Morecambe won again – this time 6-5. His final Christie Park showing came on August 30, 1962, in a Grand Charity Match. Finney played outside-right for an Augmented Press XI against Stan Stennett's Showbiz XI. The game was a 6-6 draw. In the Press side was Brian London who once played for Blackpool Mechanics against Morecambe Reserves in the Lancashire Combination.

FISHER, ELLIS: 1929-32. Right-back/Centre-half 23 apps. Born Lancaster 1902. Died 1982. Ex-PNE player who had two spells at Lancaster Town where he won three Lancashire Cup winners medals in 10 years. Played rugby before joining Morecambe in January 1930. Moved to Fleetwood for the 1932-33 season. Retired and became Lancaster's groundsman for 34 years from 1933-67 before retiring in October, 1967.

FLAPPER FOLD: Home of Atherton. First visit was on October 9, 1920, losing 4-0 in the Lancashire Combination.

FLEETWOOD: A Fleetwood Rangers side existed from the 1880s to the end of the century. A new club, Fleetwood Amateurs, was formed in 1902, dropping the Amateurs in 1908. Fleetwood played Morecambe in their first match on August 28, 1920 at Woodhill Lane. A gate of 3,000 saw Fleetwood win 4-1. Fleetwood were the first visitors to Christie Park on August 27, 1921, and won 4-0. Att: 3,000. The club closed in 1927-28.

FLEETWOOD WINDSOR VILLA: Formed in 1920. A West Lancashire League side that beat Morecambe 2-1 in the 2nd Rd of the Lancashire Junior Cup on November 22, 1930. The club joined the Lancashire Combination in 1931-32 and became known as Fleetwood. They enjoyed great success in the 1930s and became founder members of the NPL until once again the club folded at the end of the 1975-76 season.

FLEETWOOD TOWN: The new club were formed in April 1977 and worked their way back into the NPL with the highlight being a 3-1 FA Vase Final defeat by Halesowen Town at Wembley on April 27, 1985. Morecambe visited Highbury on December 8, 1979, winning a Lancashire Junior Cup, 1st Rd tie, 2-1. Att: 211. Again the club was wound up.

FLEETWOOD FREEPORT: Formed in 1998 as Fleetwood Wanderers but became Fleetwood Freeport before playing a game. First meeting was in Rd 2 of the ATS Lancashire Challenge Trophy at Highbury on January 13, 1999, winning 4-2. Now known as Fleetwood Town.

FLIXTON: Morecambe won their only meeting with the Valiants 6-2 on October 12, 1996 in the 3rd Qualifying Rd of the FA Cup at Christie Park.

FLOODLIGHTS: Morecambe's first floodlit match was at Ashton Utd in the Lancashire Combination League on March 22, 1954, winning 3-1. Morecambe's floodlights, costing £4,500, were switched on by club doctor Fred Hogarth on October 27, 1960 when Morecambe beat an All Stars XI 4-3. New £40,000 floodlights were switched on by Sir Tom Finney on August 4, 1993 before a 2-1 victory over Burnley in a pre-season friendly.

FA CUP: Morecambe's first game in the FA Cup was against Breightmet Utd at Woodhill Lane on September 25, 1920, drawing 1-1 with Parker scoring. The club did not enter the FA Cup in 1931-32 to save money and did not enter in 1945-46 due to difficulties straight after the war. The club reached the 1st Rd proper for the first time in 1936-37, losing 1-0 away to South

Liverpool. Morecambe have reached the 3rd Rd, three times. The first run of note was in 1961-62 when the club made Rd 3 after beating Clitheroe 4-2, Penrith 2-1, Burscough 8-1, Wigan Athletic 2-0, South Shields 2-1, and Chester 1-0 before losing at home to Southern League side Weymouth at Christie Park. In 2000-01 Morecambe lost 3-0 to Premiership side Ipswich Town at Christie Park after beating Bedlington Terriers 2-1, Forrest Green 3-0, and Cambridge Utd 2-1. Ipswich were again the opponents in 2002-03 with a 4-0 defeat at Portman Road after beating Grantham Town 3-1, Chesterfield 2-1 and Chester City 3-2. Biggest FA Cup win is 8-0 over Esh Winning in 1986-87. Biggest defeat is 5-0 v Wigan Athletic in 1934-35 and Bishop Auckland in 1974-75.

FA TROPHY: A FA Cup for the semi-professional non league clubs was finally introduced in the 1969/70 season with the final being at Wembley.
The inaugural season saw the Shrimps make the long journey to North Wales to play NPL rivals Bangor City. Hopes had been high of success in this competition but Morecambe crashed out, losing 4-2 at Farrar Road. Macclesfield were the first winners of the competition beating Telford 2-0 at Wembley in front of a crowd of 28,000. In the early years of the Trophy Morecambe built up a growing reputation. In the 1971/72 season Morecambe progressed through four qualifying rounds beating Boldon, Lower Gornal, Tamworth and Denaby before losing at Macclesfield 2-1 in the third round. The following season the Shrimps went a step closer to Wembley by reaching the quarter-finals for the first time before falling to arch rivals Wigan Athletic after two replays. The next season saw the Shrimps achieve their goal of getting to the final in the club's biggest day, Saturday, April 27, 1974 - *(pictured below, with the trophy)*.

The path to Wembley was a difficult one. After a comfortable 3-0 victory over Mexborough old foes Bangor City were beaten 2-1 at Christie Park. Ron Atkinson's Kettering Town were next and after a 0-0 draw at Christie Park the Poppies declared that victory was a foregone conclusion at Rockingham Road. Morecambe thought otherwise and put on a magnificent display winning the game 2-1 with Tony Webber scoring both goals. Another non-league 'giant' Bedford Town lay in wait for the Shrimps in the next round and a late Mal Richmond goal sent the 1,000 or so Morecambe fans home happy. That took the club into the semi-finals for the first time and a two-legged tie against South Shields. The job was more or less done with a 2-0 win at Croft Park and when Jimmy Sutton scored after 17 minutes of the 2nd leg to make it 3-0 on aggregate the crowd of 3,535 could start to think about the Twin Towers. In the following 30 years the club has never managed to rekindle the glory of that day, the closest being a semi-final appearance in the 2001/2002 season which ended with defeat at Stevenage. There have been a number of quarter final appearances as well. In 1977 the Shrimps went down 2-0 to Slough Town after beating Tooting & Mitcham 3-2. One of the biggest disappointments came in the 1993/94 season when the Shrimps were hot favourites to reach the semi-finals after being drawn against Guiseley who were then playing in the first division of the Unibond League. Morecambe went down 3-2 however after a sub standard performance and once again the dreams of a return to Wembley were dashed.

FA YOUTH CUP: First entered the competition from 1956-57 until 1960-61 before re-entering in the 1990s. Lost the first match in the competition 4-0 at Bloomfield Road against Blackpool on October 3, 1956. The most interesting tie was in Rd 1 on October 12, 1959, when a Morecambe team lost 14-0 to Manchester United before a crowd of 10,882.
Man Utd: Briggs, R Smith, Ackerley, Nicholson (2), Atherton, Donaldson, Moir (2), Nobby Stiles (4), Chisnall (3), Spratt (1), McMillam (2).
Morecambe: Broadman, Wylie, Holt, Langridge, Armistead, Wilkinson, Ainsworth, Croft, Palmer, T Webb.

FOREST GREEN ROVERS: First met the Gloucestershire club at Christie Park on November 7, 1998, winning 3-1. Att: 812.

FORFAR ATHLETIC: Met the Lions in a pre-season game at Christie Park on July 23, 1994, winning 1-0. Att: 214.

FORMBY: First met the Squirrels in the 1st Rd of the Lancashire Junior Cup at Christie Park on January 16, 1960, winning 6-0. Att: 1,500.

FOSTER, CLIFFORD LAKE: 1926-27. Outside-left 22 (9 cup) apps; 8 (1 cup) goals. Born Rotherham 1904. Died January 8, 1959. Joined in September, 1926, and moved to Manchester City in April, 1927, making three appearances as City won the Division Two championship. Later played for Oldham Athletic and Halifax Town.

FOSTER, MIKE: 1979-81. Defender 48 (16 cup) apps; 1 cup goal. Joined in July, 1989, from Barrow where he made 88 apps, scoring one goal. Morecambe's player of the year in 1979-80 but released in April, 1981, and joined Fleetwood Town. Worked at the Football League headquarters in Lytham.

FOWLER, GEORGE: 1935-38. Forward 30 (2 cup) apps; 11 (3 cup) goals. Signed in September, 1935. Moved to Kells Utd in 1938-39.

FRICKLEY ATHLETIC: First met the Blues, the South Yorkshire colliery team, in the NPL at Christie Park on January 29, 1977, winning 5-0. Att: 505.

FRIENDLIES: First club friendly was on October 9, 1920 at Woodhill Lane with a 1-0 win over the famous amateur club Northern Nomads. Att: 550.

FRYATT, JOE: 1934-35. Outside-right 28 (9 cup) apps; 6 (2 cup) goals. Former Northern League player who joined with his brother in September 1934. Moved to Heysham LMS in March 1935.

G

GAFFNEY, ROBBIE: 1990-92. Midfield 13+7 (1+5 cup) apps; 2 goals. Former Carlisle Utd, Runcorn and South Liverpool player who joined in March 1991. Released in January 1992 and later played for Knowsley Utd, Skelmersdale and Camaes Bay in Wales.

GAINSBOROUGH TRINITY: Founder members of the NPL who Morecambe first met at Christie Park on October 26, 1968. A crowd of 1,800 saw the Shrimps win 5-0.

GALGATE: Morecambe met Galgate in the North Lancashire League during 1939-40 but when Galgate withdrew from the league the games were declared void.
The first meeting was at Christie Park on December 2, 1939 with Morecambe winning 4-0. The return game saw Galgate win 1-0.

GALLAGHER, SEAN: 1952-53, 1955-56 and 1973-74. Forward 17 (2 cup); 2 goals. Born in Remelton, Co Donegal Sean has served the club in numerous roles. Joined in September 1952 as a 16-year-old but moved to Carnforth Rangers from 1953-55. Re-signed by Albert Dainty in August 1955 but moved to Netherfield in October 1955 in a swap with Bert Keen. Was there between 1955-58 before spending nine seasons at Lancaster City 1958-67. Sean had spells with Derry City, Darwen and Carnforth Rangers before becoming Morecambe reserve team manager in July 1972. He was asked to make 1 first team app in April 1974, a full 29 years after making his debut – a Morecambe record. Sean then spent six largely successful years as manager of Lancaster City between 1974-80 and was then in charge at Workington from March 1980 until October 1981 when he was replaced by Joe Wojciechowicz. Returned to Christie Park as temporary manager in January 1984 and was appointed officially in April before resigning in February 1985. Resumed playing for a number of local sides until retiring. Is still coaching at the club.

GALLAGHER, SIMON: 1977-81. Defender 87+1 (17 cup) apps; 1 cup goal. Joined in August 1977 from Lancaster City. Released in April, 1981, and moved to Mossley. Later played for Stalybridge Celtic.

GALLEY, KEITH: 1972-76, 1977-79, 1981-87 and 1988-91. Forward 275+39 (106+15 cup) apps; 86 (38 cup) goals. A great servant Keith *(pictured below)* had four spells at Christie Park over 17 seasons. During that time he became the club's top scorer in the NPL, scoring 86 league goals in 275 starts and 38 cup goals in 106 cup appearances. Born in Worksop on October 17, 1955, he played for local junior clubs before having a trial with Morecambe Reserves in the 1971/72 season.

After a trial with Manchester United Keith made a bigger impact in a second trial period at Christie Park. He scored a hat-trick in a 3-1 away win at Preston North End A on April 7, 1973 and went on to make his first team debut at the age of 17 in a 0-2 defeat at Bangor City on April 30, 1973.

When Russ Perkins left, Keith took over the centre forward role finishing the 1973/74 season as top scorer with 23 goals from 36 league and 21 cup games. He was named as a substitute in the FA Trophy final and came on to replace manager Dave Roberts. On January 5, 1974 he scored four times in a 4-2 victory at Bangor City, a record haul for a NPL game. Keith had trials with Arsenal in May 1973 and Leicester City in April 1974 but his ambition to play league football was finally achieved in December, 1976, when he moved to Southport for £2,500. He finished his first season as the Sandgrounders' top scorer with nine goals in 24 starts. The next season was not as fruitful however as he scored just twice in 26 league and 3 cup starts and was released. Keith joined Telford United but briefly returned to Morecambe at the end of the

1977/78 season before leaving for Netherfield early in the 1981/82 season In August 1980 he joined Macclesfield for £2,000 but was back at Netherfield for the 1981/82 season. A fee of £400 saw him rejoin the Shrimps in January, 1982, where he stayed longer. He was the club's joint leading goalscorer with 21 goals in the 1985/86 season and made sporadic appearances up until the 1990/91 season with another short spell at Netherfield in between. Keith's son James has turned out for Morecambe Reserves and also followed his father's footsteps at Kendal Town. FA Trophy winner 1973-74. Lancashire Cup winner 1985-86.

GAMBLE, FRANK: 1985-88. Forward 57+1 (23 cup) apps; 22 (7 cup) goals. Former Derby County, Barrow and Rochdale player who joined in March 1986. Had a spell on loan at Northwich Victoria in October 1987 before moving to Southport in December 1987 for a small fee.

GARDEN WALK STADIUM: Home of Lower Gornal Athletic (now known as Gornal Athletic). Just one meeting in the FA Trophy, 3rd Qualifying Rd, on December 4, 1971, which ended in a 2-1 win. Att: 150.

GARDNER, DAVID: 1998-2000. Forward 13+16 (3+5 cup) apps; 3 goals. Former Manchester Utd trainee who joined in October 1998 after spells with Macclesfield, Witton Albion and Stalybridge Celtic. Later played for Leigh, Salford City and Altrincham. Made the headlines as a sports agent and friend of David Beckham. Scored the winning penalty as Morecambe beat Darwen to win the Lancashire Cup by spot kicks in 1998-99.

GARNETT, SHAUN: 2003-04. Defender 10 (1+1 cup) games. Experienced former professional who joined for a short spell from Halifax Town in December 2003 after being on loan for a month.
Played in the league with Tranmere Rovers, Chester City, Preston North End, Wigan Athletic, Swansea City (£200,000), and Oldham Athletic (£150,000). Released in May 2004. Lancashire Cup winner in 2003-04.

GATESHEAD: Football League club South Shields, moved to Gateshead in 1930, and changed their name accordingly, playing at Redheugh Park. They lost their League status in 1960 and dropped down into non-league football.
First met Gateshead in a pre-season friendly at Christie Park on August 15, 1964, with Morecambe winning 2-0. Att: 1,000. Later met in the NPL in 1968-69 and 1969-70. This club closed down in August, 1973, and as in 1930, the South Shields club moved to Gateshead for the 1974-75 season, renaming themselves Gateshead Utd. First met at Christie Park in the NPL on March 31, 1975, winning 2-1. Att: 337. Again the team folded. The present club was formed almost immediately after the demise of Gateshead Utd. First met at Gateshead on October 3, 1977, losing 3-2.

GAY MEADOW: Home of Shrewsbury Utd with the first visit being in the LDV Vans Trophy on October 22, 2002. A crowd of 1,602 watched the home side win 3-0.

GEBBIE, BERT: 1964-66. Goalkeeper 56 (18 cup) apps. Scottish-born keeper who made 112 apps for Bradford City before signing in August 1964. Combination Cup winner in 1964-65.

GIANT AXE: Home of Lancaster City/Town. Morecambe's first win there was on October 2, 1920 with a 1-0 victory. Att: 3,500.

GIBSON, ALAN: 1977-79 and 1980-81. Forward 30+4 (4 cup) apps; 7 goals. Joined in March, 1978, from Wren Rovers. Moved to Blackpool Mechanics but returned in August 1980. Joined Lytham in the 1981-82 season.

GILL, GRAHAM: 1985-88. Forward 95+5 (4+2 cup) apps; 24 (6 cup) goals. Signed from Workington in August, 1985, for a then record fee of £1,000 after proving to be one of the best strikers in the North. Played 315 games for Workington between 1978-85 with spells at Lancaster City and Netherfield before that.
Was another player to move to Colne Dynamoes in 1988-89 and went on to help Barrow to the NPL title in 1988-89 despite scoring just 2 goals in 34 games. Had a second spell at Lancaster City 1991-93. Lancashire Cup winner in 1985-86 and 1986-87.

GILLIBRAND, JEFF: 1950-53. Inside-right 57 (8 cup) apps; 15 (2 cup) goals. Joined in December 1950 and moved to Chorley 1953-54.

GILLIBRAND, BILLY: 1936-38. Inside-right 66 (10 cup) apps; 17 (2 cup) goals. Ex-PNE player who helped Fleetwood win the Combination Cup in 1932-33 and Lancashire Cup in 1934-35 before signing in August 1936.

GLENNON, CHRIS: 1972-73. Forward 19 (11 cup) apps; 1 (2 cup) goals. Joined from Northwich Victoria in October, 1972, before being released and rejoining Northwich in April, 1973. A player who made three appearances for Manchester City between 1965-71.

GLOSSOP: Only one first team meeting which was a pre-season friendly at Christie Park on August 9, 1980. Glossop won 1-0. The club was reformed in 1992 and returned to its former name of Glossop North End.

GOALSCORERS (Top):

Keith Borrowdale	.289	Tommy Ross	.114
John Coleman	.201	John Norman	.112
Arnold Timmins	.133	Jim McCluskie	.99
Keith Galley	.124	Ray Charnley	.98
Roy Fawcett	.121	Ian Cain	.96
Ian Whitehead	.116	Steve Holden	.90

GOALSCORERS (pre-Conference year by year)

Season	Player	Lge	Cup	Total
1920/21	Gornall	14	0	14
1921/22	Aldred	7	0	7
1922/23	Manley	11	5	16
1923/24	Matthews	10	13	23
1924/25	Brown	21	8	29
1925/26	Wagstaff	21	7	28
1926/27	Gras	33	10	43
1927/28	Iddon	25	0	25
1928/29	Bedford	23	2	25
1929/30	Straughton	22	1	23
1930/31	Nairn	22	4	26
1931/32	Wiseman	9	0	9
1932/33	Edmondson	14	1	15
1933/34	Tracey	13	0	13
1934/35	Spencer	12	7	19
1935/36	McCormick	27	2	29
1936/37	Ross	39	11	50
1937/38	Ross	31	2	33
1938/39	Otley	11	0	11
1939/45	WAR			
1945/46	Holmes W	9	7	16
1946/47	Ashworth	19	2	21
1947/48	Ashworth	29	4	33
1948/49	Ashworth	24	3	27
1949/50	Wilson	22	1	23
1950/51	Smith WJ	11	5	16
1951/52	Smith WJ	19	1	20
1952/53	Johnston	10	1	11
1953/54	Johnston	9	7	16
1954/55	Dainty	18	3	21
1955/56	Hayes	22	3	25
1956/57	Charnley	31	12	43
1957/58	Clements	14	3	17
1958/59	Lawrenson	18	7	25
1959/60	Speakman	29	8	37
1960/61	Vizard	14	6	20
1961/62	Borrowdale	42	10	52
1962/63	Whitehead	45	4	49
1963/64	Borrowdale	27	4	31
1964/65	Borrowdale	27	13	40
1965/66	Fawcett	19	1	20
	Timmins	16	4	20
1966/67	Timmins	28	5	33
1967/68	Timmins	32	15	47

Northern Premier League

Season	Player	Lge	Cup	Total
1968/69	Wroth	15	3	18
	Lancaster	13	5	18
1969/70	Lancaster	9	1	10
1970/71	Lancaster	14	2	16
1971/72	Richmond	17	12	29
1972/73	Perkins	14	8	22
1973/74	Webber	17	6	23
	Galley	15	8	23
1974/75	Webber	16	6	22
1975/76	Webber	17	12	29
1976/77	Thomas	15	9	24
1977/78	Towers	10	3	13
1978/79	McLachlan	11	1	12
	Darling	9	3	12
1979/80	Parry	10	4	14
1980/81	Parry	14	1	15
1981/82	Walsh	10	0	10
1982/83	Brownbill	13	8	21
1983/84	Beesley	13	6	19
1984/85	Barnes	13	5	18
1985/86	Galley	10	11	21
	Thornton	8	13	21
1986/87	Gamble	14	7	21
1987/88	Lancaster	16	9	25
1988/89	Poskett	13	5	18
1989/90	Cain	11	5	16
1990/91	Coleman	32	6	38
1991/92	Holden	25	11	36
1992/93	Coleman	32	12	44
1993/94	McCluskie	20	10	30
1994/95	Coleman	31	15	46

John Coleman

GOOLE TOWN: Founder members of the NPL. First met the Vikings at Christie Park on January 11, 1969, losing 3-2. Att: 1,610. The club was reformed as Goole AFC in 1997.

GORDON, KENNY: 1985-86. Defender 35+1 (20+1 cup) apps; 2 (3 cup) goals. Son of Billy Gordon, Barrow's record goalscorer in the Football League. Played for Barrow himself between 1977 and 1985 before joining Morecambe in August, 1985. Returned to Barrow in June, 1986, and went on to make a total of 534 apps for the Cumbrians. His greatest moment came when he scored two goals as Barrow won the FA Trophy in 1989-90. Later emigrated to Australia. Lancashire Cup winner in 1985-86.

GORE, TOMMY: 1948-58. Right-back/Centre-half. 278 (48 cup) apps; 10 goals. Ex-PNE junior who was a loyal servant just after the war after joining in October, 1948. Later became a PNE director between 1969-82.

GORNALL, FRANK: 1920-23. Inside-forward 43 (4 cup) apps; 20 (1 cup) goals. Former PNE player who joined in December, 1920. Released in May, 1923.

GORST, HARRY: 1922-23 and 1924-28. Left-half 4 (1 cup) apps; 1 goal. Former rugby league player with Leigh who also played rugby union for the Vale of Lune and football locally with Poulton Athletic, Bare Ramblers and Morecambe AFC. An amateur player who joined in September, 1922, where he spent eight years with the club as trainer. Sacked in May, 1930, because of a lack of finances but was reappointed. Moved on to Barrow as trainer and then Lancaster Town 1932-35. After WWII became Morecambe's first first team trainer until 1947 when he was replaced by his brother Jack.

GORST, JOHN (JACK): Trained Morecambe Reserves after WWII before taking over from brother Harry as first team coach in 1947. Was also the club's full-time groundsman before retiring in 1964. Continued in the role part-time until 1968-69. Died on October 22, 1977, aged 79.

GORST, JOHN HENRY (JACKIE): 1946-52. Left-half/Inside-left 63 (11 cup) apps; 21 (1 cup) goals. Ex-Euston Road pupil who played for Morecambe Schoolboys and Edmondsons before joining in September, 1946. Died on March 8, 1995, aged 73.

GOUCK, ANDY: 2001-03. Midfield 28+14 (3+1 cup) apps; 4 goals. Former league player with Blackpool (121+27 apps; 12 goals) and Rochdale (58+8 apps; 8 goals). He was signed from Southport in May, 2001. Loaned to Accrington Stanley in December, 2002, and signed for them in January, 2003, helping them to win the NPL title to win a place in the Conference. Released by Stanley in May, 2004.

GRADWELL, ALFRED: 1920-23. Left-back 69 (13 cup) apps; 3 goals. Ex-Horwich RMI player who joined in August 1920. One of the club's early professional players. Joined Bradford City in August 1923.

GRADWELL, SYDNEY: 1931-32. Full-back 14 (1 cup) apps. Ex-Horwich player 1920-29. Joined in August, 1931. Brother of Alfred.

GRADWELL, WILLIAM: 1921-26. Outside-right 81 (27 cup) apps; 15 (1 cup) goals. Former Lancaster Town player who joined in April, 1922. Later moved to Horwich RMI.

GRANGE LANE: Home of North Ferriby Utd where Morecambe represented the Lancashire FA against the East Riding FA, winning 2-0 on November 29, 1988.

GRANT, PAUL: 1984-85. Forward 17 (7 cup) apps; 7 (1 cup) goals. Former Bedford Town and Hitchin Town striker who joined in April, 1984 .

GRANTHAM: The Gingerbreads faced Morecambe in the NPL from 1979-80 to 1984-85. First match was at London Road on April 16, 1980, with Grantham winning 3-1.

GRASS, GEORGE 'PINKY': 1925-27. Centre-forward/Inside-left 32 (9 cup) apps; 35 (10 cup) goals. One of the first Morecambe players to move into the professional game. The Morecambe-born forward played for the Shrimps between 1925 and 1927 with phenomenal success. In 32 league games he scored 35 goals. Add 10 cup goals in nine appearances and it was clear that he had a future at a higher level. George scored 43 league and cup goals in the 1926/27 season and scored the only goal of the game to beat Lancaster Town in the Lancashire Junior Cup final on April 13, 1927. His form brought him to the attention of Blackburn Rovers who signed him for £450 but unfortunately a broken leg prevented him from making any first team appearances. Moved to Lancaster and then Bury before ending his career at Giant Axe. George died on April 23, 1988. Lancashire Cup winner 1926-27.

GRAVESEND & NORTHFLEET: First met the Fleet in the Conference on November 30, 2002, at Christie Park, winning 2-0, Att: 1,062.

GRAY, ANDY: 1988-90. Goalkeeper 23 (6 cup) apps. Former Mossley, Curzon Ashton and Radcliffe Borough keeper who joined in November 1988. Moved to Clitheroe in 1990-91.

GREAT HARWOOD: Many meetings in the Lancashire Combination and latterly in the NPL until their demise at the end of the 1977-78 season.
First met at the Showground on September 18, 1920, losing 2-1. Att: 2,000.

GREAT HARWOOD TOWN: The Robins were formed in 1965 as Great Harwood Wellington. Moved from their Memorial Park Ground to take over the Showground and worked their way back up to the NPL. First met in the Dairy Crest Floodlit League at Christie Park on December 13, 1983, winning 2-1. Att: 135.

GREATOREX, BILLY: 1924-28. Right-back 132 (46 cup) apps; 1 goal. Another PNE regular who found his way to Christie Park in the 1920s. Born in Preston in 1899 William

Greatorex played wartime football in the army and in London until 1919 before being spotted by North End playing for a works team. Billy made his league debut as right back in a 1-1 draw with Burnley on December 27, 1919. He went on to make 17 first team appearances that season and added 6 more in the 1920/21 campaign. Billy was considered to be the fastest right back North End had ever had but his Deepdale career came to an unfortunate end when he broke his leg.

He moved on to Southport in the new Division 3 North making 58 appearances before transferring to Chesterfield where he played 13 games in the 1923/24 season.

He came to Christie Park for the 1924/25 season and played a big part in the club's championship winning side. He was a regular for four seasons and also helped the club to two Lancashire Cup (1925-26 and 1926-27) and one Combination Cup success (1926-27). Died in Preston, July 20, 1971.

GREEN, ANDY: 1992-93. Forward 6+3 (6+2 cup) apps; 3 (2 cup) goals. A prolific goalscorer with South Liverpool who had a spell playing in Belgium before signing from Macclesfield Town for £1,500 in September, 1992. Was released in April, 1993, and moved to Knowsley Utd. Later played for Altrincham (24 goals in 50 games), Barrow (15 goals in 66 apps) and Droylsden.

GREENGATE UTD: Met in a pre-season friendly at Christie Park on July 30, 1980, winning 2-0 with goals from Foster and Hughes.

GREENWOOD, ALBERT: 1930-31. Inside-right/Centre-forward 23 (4 cup) goals; 7 goals. Joined in August 1930.

GREGOIRE, MATTHEW: 2002-04. Goalkeeper two cup appearance. Morecambe Youth team player who graduated to the reserves. He gave up football to pursue a career in modelling after winning the Visitor newspaper's Face of 2004 competition.

GREGORY, PAUL: 1977-78. Defender 42 (10 cup) apps. Former Burscough, Wigan Athletic, Netherfield, South Liverpool and Lancaster City full-back who joined in August 1977. Moved to South Liverpool 1978-80.

GRESLEY ROVERS: First visited the Moatmen for a FA Trophy, 2nd Rd, tie on February 11, 1995, winning 3-2. Att: 1,113.

GRETNA: First played this now Scottish League club at Ryedale Park in an FA Cup 3rd Qualifying Rd tie on October 12, 1985, winning 2-0. Att: 179.

GRIFFITHS, BRYAN: A successful manager who earned a lot of plaudits for his work as boss between 1989 and 1993 and before his sacking on December 18, 1993. A player with Everton, where he made his first team debut at 18, and Southport Bryan moved into management after his playing career came to a premature end through injury. After 12 months out of the game he joined his local club Formby as boss. He then joined Burscough and South Liverpool where he won the ATS Lancashire Cup, The Northern

Premier League Cup and the Liverpool Senior Cup in the 1983/84 season. Southport spotted his potential and he steered them to the FA Trophy quarter final and the FA Cup 1st Rd where they met Port Vale at home.

A disagreement with the directors saw him resign and join Mossley where he won four trophies in 18 months. On Thursday, December 7, 1989, he was appointed as first team boss to replace Larry Milligan bringing Dave Jones with him as his assistant.

In his first season the Shrimps reached the final of the Lancashire ATS Challenge Cup but lost 2-0 to Northern Premier League champions Colne Dynamoes.

Over the next three seasons Bryan led Morecambe to three third place finishes and is credited with getting together the nucleus of the side that would see Morecambe win promotion to the Conference with star signings such as John Coleman, Jim McCluskie, Andy Grimshaw, Paul Tomlinson, Robbie Armstrong, Paul Burns and Gary Dullaghan. Although he couldn't take the side one step further he did enjoy cup success in the NPL President's Cup where they beat Stalybridge Celtic 3-2 on aggregate in the 1991/92 season. Highlights included a 1st Rd FA Cup tie against Hull City at Christie Park and FA Trophy runs that earned them ties with Wycombe Wanderers and Colchester United. Later managed Knowsley Utd, Witton Albion, Chorley and Netherfield. Was assistant manager at Rossendale Utd 2002-03.

GRIMSHAW, ANDY: 1992-98.
Midfield 182+8 (75+7 cup) apps; 30
(13 cup) goals *(pictured right)*.
One of the most popular players at the club in recent times. Rossendale-born Grimshaw spent six seasons at Christie Park between 1992-98 making 182 league and 76 cup appearances, scoring 43 goals. Joined the Shrimps from Witton Albion where he helped the Cheshire club win the NPL in the 1990/91 season and reach the FA Trophy final at Wembley against Colchester in 1992. Always a winner he came to the fore as a member of the all conquering Colne Dynamoes side which between 1986 and 1990 won the NPL Division One and Premier Division title. In his early days played 6 reserve teams games for Manchester United but wasn't offered a contract. After leaving Morecambe Grimshaw

played for Chorley, Rossendale and Bamber Bridge and enjoyed a spell as manager at Ramsbottom Utd but quit through work commitments at the end of 1993. Lancashire Cup winner in 1993-94 and 1995-96.

GRIMSHAW, BOB: 1982-85. Forward 95+5 (27+4 cup) apps; 16 (4 cup) goals. Former Darwen, Rossendale, Horwich RMI and Stalybridge Celtic player he later moved on to Chorley, Netherfield and another spell at Horwich RMI and Rossendale United. Also known as a very useful Lancashire League cricketer.

GRIMSHAW, CHRIS: 1988-89. Forward 10 (2+1 cup) apps; 2 cup goals. A forward who had success in the non league game – but not at Morecambe. Made only 10 appearances for the Shrimps in the 1988/89 season but went on to win the NPL Division One title with Colne Dynamoes and play in the 1996 FA Vase final with Fleetwood Town. Made 352 apps for Accrington Stanley.

GRUNDY, BRIAN: 1973-76. Forward 83+6 (20+3 cup) apps; 7 (6 cup) goals. Former Bury (10 goals in 94+6 apps), Netherfield and Bangor City striker who signed in April 1974. Released in May 1976 and moved to Lancaster City. Later played for Northwich Victoria, Winsford Utd and Mossley. Was player-manager at Glossop and managed Mossley.

GRUNDY HILL: Former home of Horwich RMI with its famous sloping pitch. Many visits in the Lancashire Combination and Northern Premier Leagues. First visit was on April 16, 1921, with Morecambe winning 3-1.

GUINNESS EXPORT: Morecambe played the Aughton/Ormskirk club in the Lancashire Combination from 1965/66 to 1967/68. The first meeting ended in a 2-2 draw at Middlewood Road on November 20, 1965. The game was marked by the sending off of Morecambe keeper Gebbie for fighting with a spectator behind the goals.

GUISELEY: Tough Yorkshire opponents who Morecambe first met at Christie Park in the FA Cup 1st Qualifying Rd on September 17, 1983. Morecambe won 1-0. Att: 305.

H

HAGEN, OWEN: 1931-33. Outside-right 22 (4 cup) apps; 1 (1 cup) goals. Former Workington player who joined in February 1932.

HAIG AVENUE: Home of Southport where Morecambe first visited in April 26, 1924, to play Southport Reserves in the Lancashire Combination. Southport won 2-0.

HALIFAX TOWN: Recent meetings in the Conference but first game was in a pre-season friendly at Christie Park on July 28, 1983, losing 2-0.

HALL, ARTHUR (IKE): 1933-36. Outside-Right/Inside-Right 62 (15 cup) apps; 10 (3 cup) goals. Joined from the Blackburn area in September 1933. Moved to Clitheroe 1936-37.

HALL, DAVID: 1998-99. Defender 24 (6+1 cup) apps. A former England Schoolboy international who had a short spell at Christie Park after signing in June 1998. The ex-Oldham Athletic trainee joined from Stalybridge Celtic but made just 24 league and one cup appearance with much of his spell blighted by a niggling back injury. Lancashire Cup winner in 1989-99.

HALL LANE: Home of Northern League side Willington where Morecambe visited in a FA Cup 4th Qualifying Rd tie on November 1, 1975, which ended 2-2.

HALSALL, ALAN: 1971-73. Goalkeeper 49 (21 cup) apps. Former Skelmersdale Utd, Blackpool, Oldham and Wigan keeper who joined from Netherfield in September 1971. Released April 1973.

HALSALL, NIGEL: 1981-84. Forward 85+2 (24+3 cup) apps; 8 (6 cup) goals. Ex-Southport, Runcorn and Chorley player who was signed in February 1982 for £400. Released in March 1984 and later played for Wigan, Chorley, Southport and Burscough.

HALSTEAD, DAVID: 1967-73. Defender 193 (66 cup) apps; 1 cup goal. A defender who was one of the first names on the teamsheet for five seasons after making his debut in a 4-1 away win at St Helens on October 7, 1967. David was a junior at Burnley before making the switch to Blackburn Rovers where he failed to make a first team appearance. He was signed as a left back by Ken Waterhouse in the summer of 1967 for Morecambe's last year in the Lancashire Combination. His debut was marred by the broken leg picked up by Ken Waterhouse that ended his playing career. David made great progress during his time at Christie Park and helped the club to win the Lancashire Senior Cup and Combination League and cup double in the 1967/68 season and the Lancashire Junior Cup in 1968/69 season. In the 1972/73 season he lost his place and his last game was a 3-0 away defeat at Ellesmere Port Town on August 26, 1972. He became the first Morecambe player to join Colne Dynamoes where he made 456 apps for first team and reserves. Combination League and Cup winner in 1967-68. Lancashire Cup winner in 1968-69 and Lancashire Senior Cup winner in 1967-68.

HAMER, J W: 1947-48. Outside-Right 28 (6 cup) apps; 4 goals. Joined in November 1947. Moved to Nelson in October 1948 for £10.

HAMILTON ACADEMICALS: The Accies visited Christie Park for a pre-season friendly on July 28, 1973, drawing 1-1.

HAMILTON, SYDNEY (MICKY): 1934-36. Outside-left 21 (4 cup) apps; 7 goals. Former Penrith player who joined in April, 1935. Moved to play for Carlisle Reserves in November, 1935, and later played 33 games for the first team, scoring 10 goals.

HAMPDEN ROAD: Former home of the now defunct Mexborough Town and visited during Morecambe's successful FA Trophy year. The clubs met in the 1st Rd with Morecambe winning 3-0 on January 12, 1974. Att: 274.

HAMPSON: 1921-22. Outside-left 13 apps; 3 goals. Joined in October, 1921.

HANDLEY, PAUL: 1981-82 and 1982-83. Forward 16+3 (3 cup) apps; 2 goals. The Morecambe-born former PNE junior played for Netherfield from 1974-80 before signing for Workington for a fee of £1,250 in October, 1980. Joined Morecambe for a short spell in May 1981 but moved to Lancaster City in January, 1982. Re-signed for the club in July, 1982. A successful local cricketer with Morecambe and Carnforth.

HANKINSON, TOM: 1957-59. Forward 39 (4 cup) apps; 17 goals. Former Fleetwood and Netherfield striker who joined in November, 1957. Returned to Fleetwood for the 1959-60 season.

HANSON, NEIL: 1988-89. Midfield 10 (7 cup) apps. Former PNE apprentice who had spells with Halifax Town, Chorley and Accrington Stanley before signing in June, 1988. Unfortunately, injuries forced him to retire in January, 1989.

HARDIKER, JOHN: 1998-2002. Defender *(pictured right)*. 68+4 (22+2 cup) apps; 4 cup goals. The most successful of the club's first batch of academy players. After making his debut at just 16 the young centre-half impressed a clutch of scouts before eventually signing for Stockport County in January, 2002 for £150,000, the club's biggest transfer sale. Born in Preston on July 7, 1982 he was a schoolboy player with Everton, Blackburn Rovers and Bury before joining the Shrimps' academy and signing professional forms in May 1999.

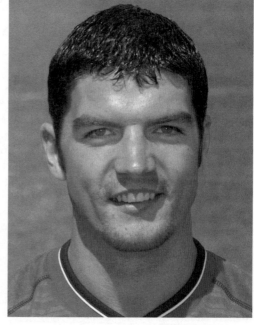

HARDY, NEILL: 1999-2000. Forward 17+14 (6 cup) apps; 9 (2 cup) goals. Former YTS with Bolton Wanderers who played for Northwich Victoria and Altrincham before signing in July 1999. Released in July 2000 and moved to Radcliffe Borough where Stockport signed him for £15,000 in June 2001. Made just four starts, scoring two goals, before returning to Radcliffe Borough and later Altrincham.

HARRISON PARK: Home of Leek Town. First game was a 1-1 draw in the NPL on March 23, 1991. Att: 564. On August 25, 1998, Morecambe suffered their heaviest Conference defeat at Harrison Park when they went down 7-0. Att: 501. Ironically Leek were relegated in the same season.

HARRISON, WAYNE: 1987-88. Midfield 9 (3 cup) apps; 2 cup goals. Experienced player who made 78+5 apps for Blackpool between 1979-82 before having spells in America and Finland. Had two terms as manager at Workington before joining Morecambe in September, 1987. Went on to manage Workington for a third time and also had spells in charge at Bamber Bridge and Accrington Stanley.

HARROGATE RAILWAY ATHLETIC: Only one meeting which came with a 3-2 win in the FA Cup 4th Qualifying Rd on October 27, 2001. Att: 940.

HARROGATE TOWN: Morecambe beat the Town 2-0 in an FA Cup 1st Qualifying Rd tie at Wetherby Road on September 7, 1985. Att: 266.

HART: 1932-33. Goalkeeper 18 (5 cup) apps. Joined in August 1932.

HARTLEPOOL UTD: The Pool visited Christie Park for a pre-season friendly on August 4, 2001 for a pre-season friendly, winning 3-1.

HARTLEY, DEREK: 1976-78 and 1984-85. Forward 27+6 (8 cup) apps; 5 (2 cup) goals. Joined in April, 1976, and played for the Reserves between 1976 and 1979 being a sub in two games. Had four seasons at Lansil and a spell at Lancaster City 1982-84 before rejoining Morecambe in August, 1984. Moved back to Lancaster City 1985-87 and later played for Twente Enschede in Holland, Colne Dynamoes, Netherfield, Lancaster City and Wren Rovers.

HARTLEY, TOMMY: 1935-36. Outside-right 18 (1 cup) apps; 1 goal. Joined in November, 1935. Moved to Horwich.

HARSTDOWN PARK: Home of Margate where Morecambe first visited on March 16, 2002, in an FA Trophy, 6th Rd, tie which was won 2-1. Att: 1,244.

HARVEY, JIM: 1993-2004. Midfield 27+14 (16+4 cup) apps; 1 (1 cup) goal *(pictured right)*. The manager who took Morecambe into the Conference, Harvey originally joined the club as assistant manager to Leighton James on January 6, 1994. Became the boss on June 7, 1994, and oversaw huge changes at the club. His own career began a Glenavon where he helped the side to the runners-up spot in the Irish League and was voted Ulster's Young Player of the Year 1976-77. A move to Arsenal followed in August, 1977, where he made 2+1 first team apps. Joined Hereford Utd on a free transfer in June, 1980, and went on to make 276+2 apps for the Bulls, scoring 39 goals along the way. Bristol City then paid £25,000 for him in March, 1987, but the move didn't work out and he went to Tranmere Rovers where he became a Prenton Park favourite as the club moved up the leagues. Signed in October, 1987, and made 174+10 apps, scoring 19 goals. Moved to Crewe on a free transfer in July, 1992, and later played for Southport before becoming Reserve team coach and head of the school of excellence at Chester City. Won one Northern Ireland U21 cap against the Republic of Ireland on March 8, 1978. In January, 2000, joined the Northern Ireland international set-up as assistant to Sammy McIlroy, resigning in March, 2003. Celebrated 10 years as Morecambe manager on June 7, 2004.

HASLAM, PHILLIP: 1979-82. Midfield 66+4 (12 cup) apps; 7 (3 cup) goals. Morecambe-born player who joined in August 1979 and had 3 good seasons with the club. Moved to Trimpell and later played for Lancaster City and Netherfield before playing locally for a number of years.

HASTINGS, JIMMY: 1949-51. Inside-left 18 (1 cup) apps; 6 goals. A Lancaster policeman who joined in January, 1950. Had to retire in 1952 through ill-health.

HAWORTH, TOM: 1963-64. Centre-half 11 (3 cup) apps. Ex-Blackburn Rovers player who made his debut for Morecambe reserves in August, 1962. Moved to Chorley and later became a coach at Blackburn Rovers. Also had a brief spell as manager of Chorley in 1983-84.

HAWORTH, TOMMY: 1923-26. Right-half 91 (35 cup) apps; 5 goals. Another regular in the early days after joining in August, 1923. Moved to Great Harwood and later retired to become a teacher.

HAWTHORNS: The home of Brigg Town where Morecambe won an FA Cup 1st Qualifying Rd tie 4-0 on September 10, 1994.

HAYES: First met the Missioners in the Conference at Christie Park on December 7, 1996, losing 4-2. Att: 1,012.

HAYES, NORMAN: 1955-56. Forward 35 (4 cup) apps; 22 (3 cup) goals. Former Bolton Wanderers, Burnley and Lancaster City striker who joined in August, 1955. Moved on to Fleetwood, Lancaster City, Darwen and Bacup Borough. After playing became a referee and was an official in the NPL between 1968 and 1975.

HEALY, BRIAN: 1996-99. Midfield 71+2 (25 cup) apps; 13 (5 cup) goals. A player who had done the rounds in his native north east playing for West Auckland Town, Billingham Town, Bishop Auckland, Gateshead and Spennymoor Utd before joining in March, 1997, for £3,000.
Became a firm fans favourite and was selected for the England semi-pro squad and Middlesex Wanderers where he toured Brunei and Burma in 1998. Moved to Torquay Utd

for £25,000 on December 16, 1998. Made
55 +4 appearances but unfortunately
missed the 2000-01 season with injury.
Joined Darlington but only made 1+1
appearances, scoring one goal. Spalding
Cup winner in 1997-98. *(Pictured right).*

HEATON, ALAN: 1978-80. Forward
19+2 apps; 6 goals. Former Longridge Utd
player who joined in February, 1979.
Moved to Darwen in December 1979. Later
played for Leyland Motors before going
back to Longridge where he is still
involved.

HEATON, MICK: 1978-79. Forward 12
(3 cup) apps. Sheffield-born player who
tragically died in a car crash on April 11,
1995. Played 168+2 games for Blackburn
Rovers between 1971-77 after a £7,000
move from Sheffield Utd in October 1971.
A serious knee injury effectively ended his career in December, 1975, but he did make a
comeback with Great Harwood and Morecambe, signing in Augus,t 1978.
Made a name for himself after his playing career as Howard Kendall's trusted right-hand
man. First linked up with Kendall as Reserve and first team coach at Blackburn Rovers
between 1978-81, Everton (first team coach) 1981-87, Manchester City (assistant
manager) 1989-91. Also had a short spell managing Workington – December, 1988, to
October, 1989.

HEDNESFORD TOWN: Morecambe first met in a FA Trophy, 3rd Qualifying Rd, on
November 22, 1986, at their old Cross Keys Ground, winning 3-1.

HELLIWELL, DAVE: 1977-78 and 1978-79. Midfield/Forward 22+2 (3+1 cup) apps;
1 (1 cup) goals. Began his career by making 15 apps for Blackburn Rovers before
moving to Lincoln City. Made 184+13 apps for Workington between 1970-76, scoring
20 goals. Made 20+11 appearances for Rochdale before joining Morecambe in August
1977. Released November, 1977. Rejoined in March, 1979. Born in Blackburn on
March 28, 1948. Died in March, 2003.

HELME, TEDDY: 1934-35 and 1936-37 at Inside-Left/Outside-Left and 1945-46 at
Full-Back. 29 (6 cup) apps; 7 goals. Former Edmondsons player who began his career
with Morecambe in January, 1935. Moved back to Edmondsons 1935-36 and 1937-39.
Also played for Morecambe 1939-40 in the North Lancashire League. Also had two
spells at Lancaster City.

HENDON: Morecambe met the Dons in a pre-season friendly at Christie Park on July 31, 1988, which finished 0-0. Att: 200.

HEREFORD UTD: The first match was in the Conference at Christie Park on November 1, 1997, losing 5-1. Att: 1,860.

HIGGINS, BOB: 1981-82. Defender 15+1 (6 cup) apps; 2 goals. An England Schoolboy U18 international who was a professional with Burnley, Hartlepool Utd and Rochdale. Joined in August, 1981, and moved to Burnley Utd in February, 1982.

HIGHBURY STADIUM: Not Arsenal's famous ground but the third home of Fleetwood! First visit was on August 31, 1946 which ended 5-5. Att: 4,536.

HIGHAM, PETER: 1960-61. Centre-forward 20 (4 cup) apps; 15 (2 cup) goals. A vastly experienced striker who signed from Rhyl for £125 in November 1960.
Not his biggest transfer by any means for the prolific goalscorer who joined Nottingham Forest for £6,000 from PNE in August, 1955, and helped them to win promotion from Division 2. Also played for Bolton Wanderers, Doncaster Rovers and Wigan Athletic. Left Morecambe for Wigan Athletic and then moved to Stalybridge Celtic where he scored 130 goals in three seasons.

HILL, KEITH: 2002-03. Defender 19+1 (4 cup) apps. A player who was part of the team that took Blackburn Rovers into the Premiership in 1991-92. He made 89+7 apps, scoring four goals for the Ewood Park side before moving to Plymouth Argyle for £175,000 in September, 1992. Made 117+6 apps, scoring two goals as Plymouth won promotion to Division Two. Moved to Rochdale on a free in August 1996 before ending his League career with Cheltenham and a loan spell with Wrexham. Joined Morecambe in August, 2002, and released in May, 2003, when he retired. Made a comeback with Chorley.

HILLIER, JOHN: 1988-89. Defender 25+1 (5 cup) apps. Former Penrith and Netherfield player who joined in the close season of 1988 but moved to Penrith in October, 1988. Rejoined in November, 1988 but released in May, 1989.

HILLSHEAD PARK: Home of Whitley Bay where Morecambe visited for 4 seasons in the NPL. First trip was on September 24, 1991, a 1-1 draw. Att: 401.

HILTON PARK: New home of Leigh RMI after Horwich RMI moved there in 1994 from Grundy Hill. First visit was in the 2nd Rd of the FA Trophy on November 21, 1998, losing 4-1. Att: 455.

HILTON, RAY: 1975-78. Defender 18+1 (1+1 cup) apps. Former Dolphinholme junior who had a trial with Bolton Wanderers in February 1976. Moved to Workington and Lancaster City 1983-84.

HINDLEY GREEN ATHLETIC: Morecambe met Hindley for three seasons in the

Lancashire Combination League between 1925-26 and 1927-28. First meeting was at Christie Park on November 28, 1925, with a 3-3 draw. Att: 974.

HINDSFORD: Met in the Lancashire Junior Cup, 1st Rd, at the Hindsford Ground on January 19, 1935. The game ended 2-2.

HOBSON, RAY: 1964-65. Inside-right 32 (7 cup) apps; 21 (2 cup) goals. Former Clitheroe and Chorley player who joined in August 1964. Returned to Clitheroe in 1965-66.

HODGSON, BERT: 1938-40 and 1945-46. Forward 19 (2 cup) apps; 11 (4 cup) goals. Ex-Heysham LMS player.

HODGSON, ERIC: 1946-51 and 1952-53. Outside-right 25 (1 cup) apps; 2 goals. Local player who joined in September, 1946, and returned in January, 1953. Played for Williamsons from 1953-62.

HODGSON, STEVEN: 1995-98. Defender 17+6 (5+4 cup) apps; 1 goal. Played for Morecambe reserves before signing a contract in June 1995. He was loaned to Gretna in September 1996 and August 1998. Moved to Gretna 1998-99 and later played for Netherfield (Kendal Town). Steven was a member of the Spalding Cup winning side in 1997-98.

HOGARTH, MICK: The Kendal born Hogarth was a former England youth international and respected as manager of the British Telecom national team. Unfortunately, his career faltered a little and he was released by Blackpool as a junior. He signed for Morecambe in 1958 and made 24 appearances for the Shrimps before moving on to Leyland Motors, Netherfield and Lancaster City. He was originally Morecambe's reserve team boss before replacing Tommy Ferber in February, 1978. He resigned in October, 1979. One of his most notable achievements was persuading former England stars Keith Newton and Mick Heaton, who went on to become Howard Kendall's successful assistant manager at Everton, to sign for the Shrimps.

HOGHTON ROAD: Second home of St Helens Town. First visit was in the Lancashire Combination League on February 25, 1956, winning 2-0. Att: 200.

HOLDCROFT, HARRY: 1947-48. Goalkeeper 36 (10 cup) apps. Former PNE goalkeeper who made 266 apps for the Deepdale club between 1932-45, playing in the FA Cup winning side of 1937-38. Won two England caps in 1936-37 v Wales and Northern Ireland and represented the Football League v Scottish League in 1936-37. Signed for Morecambe in September, 1947, and moved to Chorley in August, 1948.

HOLDEN, D: 1938-39. Outside-Left 13 (2 cup) apps; 1 goal. Ex-Silverdale Youth who joined in August 1938. Moved to Carnforth Rangers 1938-40. Played for England v Scotland in a junior international at Giant Axe on April 22, 1939.

HOLDEN, STEVE: 1989-90 and 1991-94. Centre-forward *(pictured below - left)* 118+12 (52+10 cup) apps; 67 (23 cup) goals. Joined for the first time in August, 1989, from Fleetwood Town but moved to Southport in December, 1989, for £2,000 and scored 40 goals for the Sandgrounders in the 1990-91 season. Returned to Morecambe in June, 1991, and was the club's leading goalscorer in the 1992-93 season with 25 league and 10 cup goals. Moved to Barrow in the close season of 1994 and later played for Lancaster City and Northwich Victoria. Managed Thornton ICI in the West Lancs League 2002-03. President's Cup winner in 1991-92.

HOLDING, STUART: 1965-71. Forward 121+5 (52+5 cup) apps; 36 (14 cup) goals. A regular in the Lancashire Combination League championship winning sides of 1966/67 and 1967/68 Stuart was brought to the club as a nippy winger to replace Roy Fawcett. A player who had trials with England amateurs, Stuart signed from Rossendale United and made his debut on November 20, 1965, in a 2-2 draw at Guinness Export. In his home debut, a 7-0 win over St Helens Town, the Visitor reported: *"St Helens were unfortunate to meet latest signing Stuart Holding in dazzling form on the right wing. His wingman waltz had his opposing full-back almost dizzy."* He became an integral member of the side but suffered a broken leg in an FA Cup 4th Qualifying Round tie at Mossley on November 2, 1968. He came back on September 30, 1969, at Netherfield in a 2-1 Lancashire Senior Cup defeat. His final game for the Shrimps was at Goole Town on April 3, 1971, a 1-0 defeat.

Combination League and Cup winner in 1966-67 and 1967-68 and Lancashire Senior Cup winner in 1967-68.

HOLKER STREET: Home of Barrow. Venue of first ever away match on August 30, 1920, which ended in a 4-0 defeat.

HOLLINGS, CLARRY: 1951-54. Half-back 2 apps. Morecambe-born player who has been an amazing servant for the club as player, Reserve team coach and groundsman in a partnership with the club that has lasted more than 50 years. Played his first team games in May, 1952, and April, 1953. Received an FA Long Service Medal for his efforts.

HOLLY PARK: Former home of South Liverpool when they reformed in 1934. First visit was on September 7, 1935, losing 1-0. Att: 3,000.

HOLMES, MARK: 1982-83 and 1983-85. Defender 42+1 (6 cup) apps. Joined in September, 1982, and released in February, 1983. Moved to Middleton 1983-84 but returned to Morecambe in February, 1984. Rejoined Lancaster City 1984-87 and retired.

HOLMES, BILL: 1945-48. Centre-forward 26 (11 cup) apps; 21 (7 cup) goals. Joined in September 1945 and moved to Lancaster City in September, 1948. Later played for Wolves Reserves, Doncaster Rovers, Blackburn Rovers (21 apps; 16 goals), Bradford City and Southport. Played for the Rest v England Amateurs on December 13, 1949 and gained 4 England Amateur caps. Bill was in the GB Olympic Squad that played in Helsinki in 1952. Combination Cup winner in 1945-46.

HOLT HOUSE. Home of the late Colne Dynamoes although still used by the new Colne FC. First visit was on New Year's Day, 1990 in the NPL, losing 3-1. Att: 1,187.

HOLT, TONY: 1959-61. Inside-Right 12 (7 cup) apps; 3 (5 cup) goals. Joined in September 1959 and moved to Netherfield for £20 in October 1961. Later played for Lancaster City and Nelson.

HOPE STREET: Home of Prescot (later Prescot Cables/Town). Now known as Valerie Park with the club's first visit being on November 5, 1927, winning 3-1 in Rd 2 of the Lancashire Junior Cup.

HORDEN COLLIERY WELFARE: Visited Welfare Park for a 1st Rd, FA Trophy, tie on January 12, 1980, winning 2-1. Att; 381.

HORNBY, BILL: 1929-31. Goalkeeper 34 (4 cup) apps. Former Lancaster Town player who joined in September, 1929. Moved back to Lancaster in 1931-33. Later played for Morecambe Victoria, Storeys and Williamsons.

HORROCKS, STEVE: 1991-93. Midfield 16+10 (8+5 cup) apps; 1 goal. Signed in August, 1991, and moved to Lancaster City 1993-97. President's Cup winner in 1991-92.

HORSFALL STADIUM: New home of the reformed Bradford Park Avenue where Morecambe visited on February 8, 1997, in a FA Trophy 2nd Rd tie, winning 1-0. Att: 915.

HORTON, KEN: 1956-61. Inside-right 86 (42 cup) apps; 24 goals.
Although a popular player manager Ken was unfortunate not to collect any silverware in his spell at the helm. Preston-born Ken joined PNE as an amateur in 1937 and became a professional in January, 1942, making 31 appearances and scoring two goals in war time football. A half-back or inside forward Ken made a further 166 appearances scoring 36 goals between 1946 and 1952.
Ken then spent three years at Hull City making 76 appearances and scoring 13 goals before a season at Barrow where he made 22 starts and scored four times.
He joined the Shrimps in 1956 and became player manager making 86 league and 42 cup appearances scoring 40 goals. He was sacked in 1961.

HORWICH RMI. Many meetings in the old Lancashire Combination. The first meeting was at Grundy Hill on April 16, 1921, winning 3-1.

HOSKER, JOHN (HUSTLER): 1924-26. Inside-right 49 (16 cup) apps; 26 (7 cup) goals. Former PNE and Accrington Stanley player who signed in December 1924. Described as *"a dashing energetic, all-action inside forward."*
Combination League winner in 1924-25. Lancashire Cup winner in 1925-26.

HOTHERSALL, JOHN: 1928-29 and 1932-33. Outside-right/Inside-right 21 (6 cup) apps; 3 (2 cup) goals. Signed from Chorley in September, 1920, and returned there in 1929-30. Had spells with Lytham and Lancaster Town before returning to Morecambe in March, 1933.

HOUGH, BOBBY: 1966-68. Forward 19+1 (16+4 cup) apps; 4 (8 cup) goals. Ex-PNE amateur and Netherfield player who joined for a small fee in August 1966.

HOUGHTON, THOMAS: 1923-24. Inside-right 19 (10 cup) apps; 2 (4 cup) goals. Joined in August 1923 and moved to Lancaster Town 1924-25.

HOUSTON, GRAHAM: 1988-89. Forward 22 (7 cup) apps; 1 (3 cup) goals.
A player who made 90+39 apps for PNE, scoring 11 goals between 1978 and 86. Later played for Wigan, 16+1 apps and 4 goals between 1986-87. Also played for Carlisle Utd before joining Morecambe in November 1988. Released in September 1989 and later played for Chorley, Colne Dynamoes, Leyland Daf, Skelmersdale Utd and Bamber Bridge. Joined the police and played for Lancashire Constabulary.

HOWARD, GEORGE: 1954-56. Left-Half 54 (6 cup) apps. Joined in August 1954 from Chorley.

HOWARTH, GORDON: 1961-62. Outside-left 31 (14 cup) apps; 13 (9 cup) goals. Will always be remembered at Christie Park for the goal that earned the Shrimps a famous FA Cup victory over league club Chester City in the 1961/62 season.

Born in Prescot on October 7, 1939, Gordon was an amateur with Prescot Cables before joining Bury where he failed to make a first team appearance. A move to Netherfield followed before being signed for a fee by Morecambe at the start of the 1961/62 season. He started off well with a goal on his league debut in a 5-3 home win over New Brighton. The cup winning goal gave Morecambe their first ever win against league opponents. The Guardian reporter at the game described it in details stating: *"Morecambe were soon on the attack and Borrowdale was going through when he was nudged from behind and lost possession. Hardie, the Chester keeper had run out to clear but miskicked and the ball flew to Howarth who at the second attempt put the ball into the corner of the net from a narrow angle."* Gordon had a great season helping the Shrimps win the Lancashire Combination League and Lancashire Junior Cup but lost his place for the following season and spent the year in the reserves, making his last appearance on May 7, 1963, in a 1-0 defeat at Chorley. His son Kevin is a well known local cricketer who was Carnforth's professional for a couple of seasons. Combination League winner in 1961-62. Lancashire Cup winner in 1961-62.

HOWELL, DEAN: 2003-04. Midfield/Forward 24+6 (5 cup) apps; 3 (2 cup) goals. Former Notts County and Crewe youngster who signed from Southport, where he made 54+7 apps, scoring four goals, in the summer of 2003.

HUCKNALL TOWN: One meeting with the Nottinghamshire club in the FA Trophy 2nd Rd at Christie Park on November 27, 1999, winning 6-1. Att: 736.

HUDDERSFIELD TOWN: The Terriers played Bury in a pre-season friendly at Christie Park in the winter of 1962-63.

HUGHES, TONY: 1995-2000. Defender 77+4 (32+3 cup) apps; 1 (1 cup) goals *(pictured right)*.
A player with huge potential who was one of the first players to ever attend the FA School of Excellence at Lilleshall. Made his debut for Crewe as a teenager and made 18+5 appearances, scoring one goal, before seeing his career hit by injury. Signed for Morecambe in August, 1995, and was released in September, 1999, after suffering another string of injuries. Moved to Winsford Utd 1999-2000, Rhyl and Droylsden. Made 8+2 appearances for England Under 16s and won 4 caps for the Under 18s playing alongside the likes of Ryan Giggs and Nick Barmby. Lancashire Cup winner in 1995-96.

HUISH PARK: New home of Yeovil Town. First visit was in the Conference, winning 3-2 on March 7, 1998. Att: 2,140.

HULL CITY: The Shrimps met Hull City in the FA Cup, first round, at Christie Park in the 1991/92 season. After beating Great Harwood, Durham City, Penrith and Colwyn Bay Morecambe faced the Football League side for the only time in their history. Despite dominating for long periods they went down 1-0 although they were robbed of a superb equaliser when a Tommy Miller free kick hit the back of the net and bounced back into play but the referee waved play on. A crowd of 2,853 watched the game which was only allowed to take place after the club spent £10,000 on ground improvements.

HUNTER, GARRY: 2003-04. Midfield/Forward 8+7 (3 cup) apps. Morecambe-born player who came through the ranks to make his debut in the 2003-04 season after playing for the Reserves. Picked for the English Colleges tour of America in March 2003. Lancashire Cup winner in 2003-04.

HURST: Former name of Ashton Utd until 1947.

HUSTLE-RITE: Three matches during 1939-40 with this Morecambe wood-working firm. The first match was at Christie Park in the North Lancashire League on November 25, 1939 which was abandoned after 77 minutes with Morecambe winning 3-2.

HYDE UNITED: Founder member of the NPL in 1968-69, Morecambe have met them many times in this league. First met in a pre-season friendly at Christie Park on August 14, 1965, with Morecambe winning 2-1. Att: 1,000.

I

IDDON, HARRY: 1949-50. Outside-right 11 (2 cup) apps; 2 goals. A Preston-born player who guested for a number of clubs during the war, including Aldershot, Chester, Chesterfield, Leicester City, Manchester City, Notts County, Reading, Wolves, York City and PNE. Joined Barrow in October, 1946, before a £500 move to Southport in June 1947. Joined Morecambe in October, 1949, and later moved to Stalybridge Celtic and Clitheroe.

IDDON, RICHARD: 1927-28 and 1929-30. Inside-right/Centre-forward 43 (7 cup) apps; 43 (9 cup) goals. A prolific goalscorer who played for Tarleton FC, Leyland, PNE and Chorley before joining Manchester Utd in May, 1925, and making 2 apps before being released. Had another short spell at Chorley before joining Morecambe in December, 1927. Moved to New Brighton in May, 1928, before rejoining Morecambe in August, 1929. He seemed to enjoy moving about as he joined Lancaster Town in December, 1929, and helped them win the Combination League in 1929-30 with 37 goals in 29 apps. A third spell at

Christie Park began in March, 1930, but again he went back to Lancaster and scored a hat-trick as Town won the Lancashire Cup. Later played for Horwich RMI and Altrincham.

ILLINGWORTH, J: 1932-34. Goalkeeper 45 (5 cup) apps. Young player from Galgate who joined in March, 1933. Moved to Lancaster Town 1934-35 and later played for Galgate 1935-38.

INTERNATIONALS: Graham Walsh became the first player to receive an international call-up while playing for Morecambe when in the 1981-1982 season he was chosen to play for England under 18 schoolboys. He was followed by star striker John Coleman who, along with Marine's Brian Ross, became the first NPL players to be selected for the national semi-professional squad for more than 10 years. Although in the squad for the game against Wales at Cheltenham Town FC, Coleman made his international debut as a substitute against Finland at Woking on Wednesday, April 14, 1993. Unfortunately England lost 3-1 though Coleman was marked by Liverpool's Sammi Hyypia! Mike Bignall became the second Shrimps to win an international semi-pro call-up when he was chosen to play against the Highland League in 1997. He was followed by Brian Healy who was selected by England for the game against Holland in 1998 Healy certainly made his mark by setting up both goals in a 2-1 win. The 1999/2000 season saw Morecambe have two players picked for the England semi-professional squad for the first time ever. Stewart Drummond *(pictured below)* was selected by manager John Owens for all three games during the season, against Italy in Verona, Holland at Northwich Victoria and Wales at Llanelli. Justin Jackson was also chosen for the final game of the season in Wales and both played a part in a 1-1 draw.

Drummond became a regular and was then joined by Lee Elam, David Perkins, Garry Thompson, Robbie Talbot, Adriano Rigoglioso and Danny Carlton. Goalkeeper Craig Mawson was also selected for one squad but unfortunately, missed out as the club, along with all other Conference sides, pulled their players out of the game because of a row with the FA over the timing of the fixture.

INTERNATIONAL MATCHES: Group matches in the European Police Championships involving Italy, Norway and Sweden were played at Christie Park in 1988-89.

Morecambe also hosted the FA Amateur XI v UAU in February 1970.

On March 15, 2001, the England Women's U18s side met Holland U18s and in 2002-03 an English Colleges XI met Tobago.

IPSWICH TOWN: Premiership side Ispwich visited Christie Park on January 6, 2001, for an FA Cup 3rd Rd tie which the Tractor Boys won 3-0. Att: 5, 923. In the same round of the FA Cup Morecambe visited Portman Road on January 4, 2003, losing 4-0.

IRONWORKS GROUND: Home of Tow Low Town where Morecambe played in the FA Cup 1st Qualifying Rd on September 18, 1982, winning 5-3.

Claims to be the highest ground in non-league football or as Kerry Miller writes in 'The History of Non-League Football Grounds', *"The football follower will not see a game nearer the moon than at Tow Law."*

IRVING, GERRY: 1964-69. Defender 172+1 (69+1 cup) apps; 3 goals.

A player and coach who enjoyed great times at Christie Park. Gerry was born in Maryport on September 19, 1937. Played for Workington under Bill Shankly and Queen of the South before joining the Shrimps. He was a regular member of Ken Waterhouse's all conquering team of the late 1960s and was a firm crowd favourite. After retiring as a player at the end of the 1968/69 season he was club coach between 1970 and 1974. Combination League and Cup winner in 1966-67 and 1967-68. Lancashire Senior Cup winner in 1967-68 and Junior Cup winner 1968-69.

Was also the coach of the team that won the FA Trophy for Morecambe in 1974.

ITALIANS FROM MILNTHORPE: The Shrimps did their bit for international relations when they met Italian prisoners of war from the Bela Prison River Camp in Milnthorpe in the 1945/46 season. Morecambe played two friendlies against the Italians winning 3-2 at Milnthorpe on January 12, 1946, and drawing 1-1 a week later at Christie Park.

ITC MIDDLETON: Infantry Training Centre at the camp at Middleton for military and wartime conscripts. Morecambe lost an away match on November 9, 1940, in the North Lancashire League. There was no return match as Morecambe failed to play their last five games.

J

JACKSON, BRIAN. 1987-88. Midfield/Forward 10 apps. Joined in April 1988 from Southport in exchange for Darren Brown. Former Southport, Blackpool, Oswestry Town and Witton Albion player who moved to Colne Dynamoes in 1988-89. Later played for Marine.

JACKSON, JUSTIN: 1995-97, 1998-99 (loan) and 1999-2000. Forward 69+5 (15+1 cup) apps; 50 (7 cup) goals *(pictured right)*. In three spells at the club Jacko was a goalscoring revelation scoring 57 goals in 84 league and cup appearances. Born in Nottingham on December 10, 1974, Justin joined Bolton Wanderers as a trainee in 1992 but was released in 1994. Went to Ayr United where he was their top scorer with four goals in 22 league and cup games in the 1994/95 season. Ayr were relegated and Justin was released and had spells at Penrith and Ilkeston Town before being brought to Christie Park by George Norrie. He seemed to thrive under the leadership of Jim Harvey and scored 14 goals in the 1996/97 season, bagging the winner in the Lancashire Cup final against Bamber Bridge. His goalscoring exploits were spotted by Woking manager Geoff Chapple who paid £30,000 for his services on January 18, 1997. He failed to live up to his reputation however scoring only 3 goals in 23 appearances for the

Cards although he did collect an FA Trophy winner's medal along the way.
Notts County saw enough potential in Jackson to sign him for £30,000 in 1997 but again he failed to shine, making just seven first team appearances, scoring one goal.
While at Meadow Lane he returned to Morecambe on loan where he scored some vital goals in a disappointing season. In January, 1999, he had two loan games at Rotherham scoring once before joining Halifax Town where he scored four goals in 16 games.

Jackson returned to Morecambe on August 19, 1999 for a then record £18,000 which proved to be a bargain as he finished the season as the Conference's top scorer with 29 goals. His form was so good that Rushden & Diamonds forked out a non league record fee of £175,000 to take him to Nene Park. He helped them win promotion to the Football League before being sold to Doncaster Rovers where he endured a nightmare spell. Released by Doncaster in 2004 he had a short spell at Accrington Stanley and a trial period at Chester. Lancashire Cup winner in 1995-96. Won one England semi-pro cap against Wales in the 1999/2000 season.

JACKSON, LEE: 1977-79. Forward 20+1 (5+1 cup) apps; 7 goals. Forward who was once bought by WBA for £10,000 from Oldham Athletic before short spells at Bolton Wanderers and Wigan Athletic. Signed for Morecambe in September 1977 and moved to Vancouver Whitecaps in Canada. Returned in January 1980 and played for Morecambe reserves.

JACKSON: 1928-29. Centre-half 13 apps. Joined in November 1928.

JAMES, LEIGHTON: 1993-94. Forward 1 app. A Wales football legend who became Morecambe manager in January, 1994, only to be sacked at the end of the season despite winning the Lancashire Cup final with a victory over Southport at Burnden Park and taking Morecambe into the quarter finals of the FA Trophy where they suffered a shock defeat at Guiseley. As well as managing the Shrimps he made one full appearance v Horwich RMI on April 4, 1994, at the age of 41 years and 79 days.
Born in Llwchwyr, Glamorgan, on February 16, 1953, he made 180 appearances for Burnley between 1970 and 1975, scoring 44 goals and helping the Turf Moor outfit to promotion to the old Division One along the way. Moved to Derby County, 67+1 apps, 15 goals, in November 1975 for £140,000 and then QPR, 27+1 apps, 4 goals, for £180,000 in 1977. A fee of £165,000 took him back to Burnley where he made a further 76 apps, scoring 9 goals and then helped Swansea City to promotion to Division One after a £130,000 move in 1979. After four years at the Vetch Field where he scored 28 goals in 88 starts his career continued with a move to Sunderland (1983/84); Bury (1984/85) and Newport County (1985/86) before a third and final spell at Burnley where he scored 10 goals in 42 apps in the 1986/87 season.
Won 54 full Wales caps and 7 Under 23 caps. After leaving Morecambe he managed Netherfield, Ilkeston Town, Accrington Stanley and Llanelli.

JJB STADIUM: The Shrimps made a bit of history on Sunday, August 1, 1999, when they became the first team to play at Wigan Athletic's new £30m, 25,000 all seater stadium. Jim Harvey's side drew 0-0 in an entertaining encounter watched by a crowd of 3,500.

JAMES THOMPSON CUP: An end of season charity cup played with Lancaster Town and Barrow in the 1923/24 and 1924/25 seasons. It was a competition Morecambe failed to win however. In the first season they lost in the semi-final 2-0 to Lancaster at Giant Axe. Revenge was sweet a year later when the Shrimps beat Lancaster in the semi-final

1-0 at Rosebery Park, watched by a crowd of 2, 659. Barrow proved too strong in the final, beating Morecambe 3-0 on April 15

JOHNSON, GERRY: 1953-55. Left-back 25 (5 cup) apps; 1 cup goal. Ex-Accrington Stanley player who joined in February 1954.

JOHNSON, JOHNNY: 1971-72 and 1975-77. Defender/Midfield 37 (18 cup) apps; 1 goal. Johnny's spell as player manager for the Shrimps began successfully when he helped save the club from seeking re-election after taking over from Alan Spavin in March, 1976. Unfortunately the 1977/78 season was a bit of a disappointment for the defender and he was sacked in April, 1977, after making 37 league and 18 cup appearances and scoring 1 goal. Another Liverpool-born player Johnny joined the club after being player manager at Netherfield. He started off his career with Bolton Wanderers before being a Central League player with Southport before moving into the non league with Nantwich, Chorley and Fleetwood.

JOHNSTONE, F: 1920-22. Right-back 47 (1 cup) apps. Joined in October, 1920, from the Manchester district.

JOHNSTONE, GLENN: 1994-97. Goalkeeper 19+1 (5+1 cup) apps. Former Lancaster City favourite (1985-93) who moved to PNE for £5,000 in January, 1993. Played 10 first team games but was forced to end his professional career after picking up a back injury in pre-season training. Returned to Lancaster City in March, 1994, and signed for Morecambe in December, 1994, in a swap move involving Mark Thornley. Moved to Gretna in October, 1996, and had another spell with Lancaster City before switching to Fleetwood Freeport in 1999-2000.

JOHNSTON, VINCE (BILL): 1952-54. Centre-forward 32 (7 cup) apps; 19 (8 cup) goals. Former Wigan Athletic and Accrington Stanley striker who joined in March, 1953. Joined Darwen in 1954.

JONES, ARTHUR: 1948-51. Inside-right 47 (10 cup) apps; 5 (2 cup) goals. An 18-year-old miner from Leeds who joined in August, 1948, with his brother Leslie.

JONES, DAVID: 1989-90. Midfield 1 (1 cup) apps in April, 1990 *(pictured right)*.
The current Wolves manager, was at Morecambe as the assistant to Bryan Griffiths and has maintained close links with the Shrimps ever since. As a player he began his career with Everton, making 79+7 apps, scoring one goal between 1971-79. A £250,000 moved to Coventry City followed in June, 1979, but a knee injury saw him make only 8+3 appearances

for the club. After a successful trial he signed for PNE in August, 1983, and made 50 appearances, scoring one goal at Deepdale before dropping into non-league. Had spells as assistant manager with Southport and Mossley before joining the Shrimps in December, 1989. His coaching skills were recognised by Stockport County and he joined them in July, 1990, as youth team coach. Worked his way up through the ranks until eventually becoming first team boss in March, 1995, and impressing bigger clubs. Became manager of Southampton in June, 1997, and then Wolves in January, 2001, taking them up to the Premiership in 2002-03. Kindly brought a full Southampton first team to Christie Park to officially open the new stand and has sent strong Wolves teams for pre-season friendlies.

JONES, GRAHAM: 1985-90. Defender 146+11 (76+2 cup) apps; 3 (3 cup) goals. Regarded as one of the club's best defenders in recent times Graham made his Morecambe debut in August, 1985, after joining from Gainsborough.
A Football League player with Bradford where he made four first team apps before he moved into the non-league game. Graham made 40 league and 23 cup appearances in the 1985/86 season and even chipped in with a goal.
He stayed at the club until 1990 and was a consistent, quality defender. His last game was at Marine in May, 1990. He went on to play for Netherfield and Bradford Park Avenue. Lancashire Cup winner in 1985-86 and 1986-87.

JONES, LESLIE: 1948-49. Winger 28 (4 cup) apps; 9 goals. Brother of Arthur.

JONES, MARK: 1979-81. Defender 50+5 (6 cup) apps; 1 (1 cup) goal. Former Southport player who joined in January, 1980. Released in April, 1981, and moved to Lancaster City. Later played for Lytham, Darwen and Wren Rovers. Twin brother of Nick Jones.

JONES, NICK: 1979-81. Forward 43+6 (8 cup) apps; 4 (3 cup) goals. Joined in October, 1979, and released at the same time as twin brother Mark in April, 1981. Followed his brother to Lancaster City, Fleetwood Town, Darwen and Wren Rovers.

JUPAN OF LVIV: Ukrainian youngsters who played at Christie Park in a testimonial for Robbie Armstrong, Ian Cain, Gary Dillingham and Paul Tomlinson on November 21, 1995. Morecambe won 6-1.

K

KAPLER, KONRAD: 1950-51. Outside-left 37 (10 cup) apps; 2 goals. Polish-born player who was in his country's army in WWII. Played during the war with Third Lanark and Forrest Mechanics in the Highland League. Made seven appearances for Celtic in the 1947-48 season and played for Rochdale and Altrincham before joining Morecambe in August 1950. Born in Tychy (Poland) on February 25, 1925. Died in 1991.

KEEGAN, JIMMY: 1927-28. Outside-left 26 (5 cup) apps; 13 goals. Former Barrow, Gillingham, Peterborough & Fleeton Utd and Poole player who scored four goals on his debut at Darwen on August 30, 1927. Match reports recorded his name as Keedon for his first three games. Moved to Prescot Cables 1930-31. Born in Barrow on October 23, 1896. Died in 1973.

KEELING, BARRIE: 1998-2001. Forward 17+28 (7+4 cup) apps; 1 (3 cup) goals. Ex-Manchester City junior who signed in September 1998. Released in November 2000 and signed for Bamber Bridge before moving to Marine Castle Utd in Singapore. Returned to the country and played for Radcliffe Borough and later Stalybridge Celtic. His father Alan helped coach the junior players and became assistant manager to Jim Harvey for a short time.

KEEN, HERBERT: 1955-56. Outside-left 26 (3 cup) app; 6 goals. Joined Morecambe in October 1955 from Netherfield in exchange for Sean Gallagher. Brother of Jackie Keen. Born in Barrow on September 9, 1926. Died in 1993.

KEEN, JACKIE: 1960-64. Left-half 126 (33 cup) apps; 14 (2 cup) goals. A popular player with the Shrimps who joined in August 1960 after being a great servant at Barrow. Made 273 appearances for the Holker Street club, scoring 19 goals. Brother of Herbert. Combination League and Lancashire Cup winner in 1961-62 and 1962-63.

KELLEHER, STEPHEN: 1969-71. Goalkeeper 26 (8 cup) apps. Former Bury Reserve team player who joined in August 1969. Released in May 1971 and later played for Darwen.

KELLS UNITED: Visited the Cumberland village in the FA Cup, 4th Qualifying Rd, on November 14, 1936, winning 4-1.

KELLY, JIMMY: Midfield. Born in Liverpool on February 14, 1973, he began his career as a trainee with Wrexham where he made 11+10 (6+2 cup) appearances before a move to Wolves on February 21, 1992. Made just 4+3 (1 cup) appearances before being released in the close season of 1996. Had loan spells at Walsall and Wrexham before joining Hednesford Town. Made 41+6 appearances and scored 1 goal before a £15,000 move to Doncaster Rovers where he chalked up 58+6 appearances, scoring 4 goals.

Joined Chester City for the 2002-03 season and made 29+3 appearances with one goal before joining Scarborough in the 2003-04 season. Moved to Morecambe on a free transfer in May 2004.

KENNEDY, ALAN: 1990-91. Defender 9+1 apps *(pictured right)*. A hero of Liverpool's European Cup successes Kennedy, who also played for Newcastle, Wrexham and Hartlepool, was signed by Bryan Griffiths.
He made his debut in March, 1991, at Bishop Auckland and went on to make nine appearances until the end of the season. He was released at the end of the season and joined Barrow before playing and managing Netherfield. Younger brother of Keith.

KENNEDY, JOHN. 1997-99. Defender 33 (7+1 cup) apps. Former Netherfield, Barrow and Accrington Stanley player who joined in March 1998. Was a member of the Spalding Cup winning team of 1997-98. Moved to Lancaster City in March 1999 and later played for Springfields in the West Lancs League. Spalding Cup winner 1997-98.

KENNEDY, KEITH. 1984-88. Defender 63+1 (31 cup) apps; 1 (2 cup) goals. Elder brother of Alan, Keith was also a left back, brought to the club along with a number of Barrow players by Joe Wojciechowicz. Keith, a former professional with Newcastle and Bury, joined in the 1984/85 season and made 11 appearances that campaign with one goal to his credit that came against Macclesfield. He was to appear in 41 of the club's league games and 23 cup matches the following season and made the number three shirt his own. Unfortunately, Barrie Stimpson joined the season afterwards, and Keith's appearances were limited and after 10 league and 7 cup apps he left Christie Park. Keith later played for Netherfield and Colne Dynamoes.

KENYON, DAVID. 1930-32. Left-back 24 (4 cup) apps. Joined in January, 1931.

KERSHAW, BARRY. 1973-76. Forward 99 (34+1 cup) apps; 9 (4 cup) goals. A member of the FA Trophy winning team Barry signed from Great Harwood in May, 1973, after previously playing for Bacup Borough and Netherfield. Released in March, 1976, and moved to Rossendale Utd. Later played for Horwich RMI, Macclesfield Town and Glossop. Was said to have *"an explosive left foot shot with considerable ability in the air."* FA Trophy winner in 1973-74.

KETLEY, FRANK: 1955-56. Left-half 16 (3 cup) apps. Former Mansfield Town and Runcorn player who joined in December, 1955.

KETTERING TOWN: Many meetings with the Poppies in the Conference but the first battle was during the successful FA Trophy campaign of 1973/74. Ron Atkinson was the player-manager of the Kettering side who travelled to Christie Park for a 0-0 draw in the 3rd Rd on February 23, 1974. Att: 1,788. Against the odds Morecambe travelled to Rockingham Road and won 2-1.

KEYS PARK: Hednesford Town's new ground where Morecambe recorded their first away win in the Conference on November 25, 1995. A crowd of 1,271 saw the Shrimps win 2-1.

KIDDERMINSTER HARRIERS: Lost 4-2 at the Aggborough Stadium in the club's first away match in the Conference on August 26, 1995. Att: 1,702.

KING, PETER: 1993-95. Midfield 49 (19+1 cup) apps; 2 (2 cup) goals.
Former Liverpool apprentice who made 55+9 apps for Crewe between 1983-85, scoring 5 goals. Played for a host of non-league clubs including Stafford Rangers, Barrow and Marine before joining in September, 1993. Proved to be a steadying influence in midfield for the Shrimps and went on to use his experience with Fleetwood Town, Lancaster City and Burscough where he was assistant manager from 1995-2002. Lancashire Cup winner in 1993-94.

KINGS LYNN: Met the Linnets in the NPL from 1980-81 to 1982-83. The first match was at the Walks Stadium on Sunday, March 29, 1981, with 326 watching a 0-0 draw.

KINGS OWN BORDER REGIMENT: Met the army side in a friendly on October 16, 1990, winning 12-1.

KINGS OWN HEYSHAM: Lost 9-5 in the North Lancashire League on February 1, 1941 but the Heysham side later pulled out of the league and the result was declared void.

KINGS OWN (LANCASTER): Lost away in a North Lancashire League Parkinson Cup game in 1941. The teams should have met again in December but Morecambe could not raise a team!

KINGSFIELD STADIUM: Home of Woking with the club's first visit ending in a 3-0 defeat on November 4, 1995. Att: 2,679.

KINGSMEADOW STADIUM: Home of Kingstonian with the first trip ending in a 0-0 draw on March 6, 1999. Att: 888.

KINGSTONIAN: First meeting with the Ks was in the Conference on August 22, 1998, a 0-0 draw at Christie Park. Att: 1,024.

KINGSWAY: Former home of Bishop Auckland with the first visit being in Rd 1 of the FA Cup on November 23, 1974, losing 5-0. Att: 1,250.

KIRKBRIGHT, JOHN: 1921-22. Left-back 14 (3 cup) apps. Joined in August, 1921, from Accrington Stanley. Later played for Bacup Borough and Rossendale Utd.

KIRKBY TOWN: First met the Eagles at Simonswood Lane in the Lancashire Combination, winning 4-0 on October 20, 1967. Later met in the NPL.

KNOWLEDEN, BRYN. 1938-40. Full-Back 44 (3 cup) apps. Bryn joined in August, 1938, but later swapped codes and became a very successful rugby league player. Started his career with Barrow 1946-47 before moving to Warrington where he was a member of their championship winning side of 1947-48. Scored a try at Wembley as Warrington beat Widnes 19-0 to lift the Challenge Cup Trophy in 1949-50. Scored 13 tries for Great Britain in 15 apps and played one Test match against New Zealand in Auckland.

KNOWLES, KENNETH: 1945-51. Outside-right 17 (6 cup) apps; 10 (3 cup) goals. After serving in the navy during WWII joined Morecambe in April, 1946. Later moved to Lancaster City and also played for Morecambe Grammar School Old Boys. Well known as a local solicitor with Whiteside & Knowles.

KNOWLES, MICHAEL: 1993-2000 and 2000-03. Defender/Midfielder 137+38 (43+15 cup) apps; 6 (5 cup) goals. Morecambe-born player who played for the Youth side and the Reserves before signing forms in May, 1993. Had trials with Liverpool in August, 1995,

playing for their Reserves and also Blackburn Rovers before becoming a popular regular for several seasons and helping the club to win promotion from the Unibond League. John, *(pictured left)* would have played many more games had he not been the victim of a string of bad injuries including a broken leg and then a fractured hip which he picked up while playing against Southport. Left to coach in America in May 2000 but returned in October 2000. Had a loan spell with Bamber Bridge before signing for Accrington Stanley in October 2002. Released by Accrington in December 2003. Played in the Spalding Cup win of 1997-98. Lancashire Cup winner in 1993-94 and 1995-96.

KNOWSLEY UNITED: Met in the NPL but the teams first clashed at Alt Park in a pre-season friendly on August 17, 1991, drawing 1-1.

L

LAIDLER, JOHN: 1948-50. Outside-left 48 (9 cup) apps; 10 (1 cup) goals. Born in Windermere on January 5, 1919. Made his name scoring 230 goals in four seasons as a junior. Before joining Morecambe in August, 1948 he played for Windermere, Barrow, Netherfield and Carlisle Utd.

LAKELAND SOFT DRINKS CUP: A two-legged pre-season cup held from 1990 to 1994 between Morecambe and Lancaster City. The inaugural tournament saw Lancaster win a penalty shootout 3-2 after two 1-1 draws. Lancaster also won the 1990/91 tournament with a 3-2 aggregate success.
The Shrimps then won the cup for three successive years. In 1991/92 they won 3-2 on aggregate and followed that up with a 5-1 aggregate victory in the 1992/93 season and a 5-3 aggregate triumph in 1993/94. The final year of the competition belonged to Lancaster with another win on penalties after two 1-1 draws.

LAMB GROUND: Home of Tamworth where the club first visited on January 22, 1972, in the FA Trophy, 1st Rd, which ended in a 4-1 win. Att: 999.

LAMBERT, EDWARD: 1932-33. Left-half 12 (4 cup) apps. Former Lancaster Town and Carnforth Rangers player who joined in January, 1933.

LANCASHIRE COMBINATION: Morecambe played in the Lancashire Combination from 1920 to 1939 and 1945 to 1968 with the reserves playing in Division Two from 1950 to 1953 and 1957 to 1968 before returning to the division One Combination from 1975 to 1978. Morecambe won the Combination title in the 1924/25 season with the main players being Sloane, Greatorex, Eastwood, Haworth, Carlisle, Farnworth, Macauley, Rawlings, O'Doherty, Hosker, Brown, Lomax.
The golden years were in the 1960s, however, with four titles. The first success came in the 1961/62 season with the regular players being: Udall, Cubbage, Richardson, Dunn, Ferns, Scott, Keen, Fawcett, Evans, Borrowdale, Whitehead, Armstrong.
The Shrimps were then crowned champions two years in succession.
The 1966-67 season regulars were: Millard, Varcoe, Cubbage, Scott, Mitchell, Irving, Martin, Waterhouse, Holding, Borrowdale, Timmins and Lea.
The following year saw few changes with the regular line-up being: Millard, Varcoe, Baldwin, Halstead, Irving, Martin, Crompton, Porter, Holding, Borrowdale, Timmins, Lea.

LANCASHIRE COMBINATION CUP: The Shrimps won the cup in the seasons 1926/27, 1945/46, 1964/65, 196/67 and were losing finalists in 1923/24, 1924/25, 1956/57. The reserves reached the final and lost in 1962/63.

1926/27 Morecambe 1, Lancaster Town 1, April 27. Att: 5.450.
Lancaster Town 1, Morecambe 2 (replay), May 4. Att: 5,000.

1945/46 Morecambe 4, Bacup Borough 2, May 4. Att: 5,113.
1964/65 Morecambe 1, Chorley 3 (1st leg), April 26. Att: 2,000.
1966/67 Morecambe 1, Fleetwood 0 aet, May 4. Att: 3,129.
1967/68 Horwich 1, Morecambe 2, May 15.
The losing finals were:
1923/24 Southport Res 2, Morecambe 0, May 2.
1924/25 Morecambe 0, Chorley 1, April 27.
1956/57 Horwich 2, Morecambe 1 (1st leg), Goalscorer: Horton. April 26.
  Morecambe 0, Horwich RMI 0 (second leg). April 30. Att: 2,400.
1962/63 Morecambe Res 1, Chorley Res 1, May 1. Att: 2,000.
  Chorley Res 1, Morecambe 0 aet (replay). May 7.

LANCASHIRE CUP: The Shrimps first entered the Lancashire Junior Cup as it is fully known in the 1920-21 season, losing 2-1 in the first round to Leyland Town in a game played at Woodhill Lane in front of a crowd of more than 1,400.

The first of the club's 16 finals came in the 1925-26 season when the Shrimps beat Chorley 3-1 in a second replay at Deepdale. Ross was the goal hero with a hat-trick in a game watched by 10,629. The first tie, at Deepdale finished 2-2 with the first replay at Burnden Park ending 1-1. The following season saw Morecambe retain the trophy, beating Lancaster 1-0 at Deepdale thanks to a goal from George Grass.

After back to back successes, it was 20 years before the Shrimps again reached the final when in the 1950-51 season they lost 1-0 to Rochdale Reserves at Burnden Park.

The next victories came in the early 60s. The 1960/61 competition saw Morecambe beat Wigan Athletic 3-1 at Deepdale with goals from Borrowdale, Fawcett and Keen and the following year Joe Dunn's team overcame Horwich 2-1 with Fawcett (again) and Armstrong on the scoresheet. Morecambe's first season in the NPL (1967-68) ended in success with Charlie Lea the scorer in a 1-0 triumph over Great Harwood.

The 1970s proved a barren period for the club and Morecambe had to wait until the 1985-86 season before they reached the final again. Once again, Chorley were the opposition and goals from Galley, Szabo and Gordon gave the Shrimps a 3-2 victory after extra-time at Deepdale. The following season ended in victory again over Chorley with two Dave Lancaster goals earning the silverware at Springfield Park, Wigan. It became a hat-trick of finals, but not victories when Morecambe lost 2-0 to Marine at Burnden Park and it was defeat again in 1989-90 when Colne Dynamoes took the cup with a 2-0 victory. The 90s saw Morecambe beat old rivals Southport 4-3 in extra time after a thriller at Burnden Park in 1993-94. The following year ended in a 2-1 defeat by Bamber Bridge though a year after revenge was sweet with Justin Jackson scoring the only goal of the game to beat Brig 1-0.

Southport gained their revenge in 1997/98 with a 2-0 win before the Shrimps ended the Millennium on top with a penalty shoot-out win against Darwen to take the 1998/99 crown. The latest victory came in a two-legged final in 2003/04 with a 3-1 aggregate win over Accrington Stanley.

The first leg saw a Danny Carlton goal give the Shrimps a 1-0 win. Att: 1,214.
Morecambe: Mawson, McKearney (Carlton (1)), Bentley, Swan (Garnett), Perkins, Walmsley, Drummond, Osborne, Curtis, Hunter, Sugden (Thompson).

The squad that took Morecambe to the FA Trophy final in 1974.

Players celebrate lifting the Lancashire Cup after beating Darwen on penalties in 1999.

The FA Cup takes its place in the Morecambe dressing room prior to the third round tie against Ipswich Town on January 6, 2001.

Sir Steve Redgrave and Matthew Pinsent do the draw that will pit Morecambe against their Premiership rivals.

MORECAMBE V IPSWICH TOWN

The light at the end of the tunnel

Action from the FA Cup tie against Ipswich Town.

Morecambe fans young and old get in the spirit

The light at the end of the tunnel

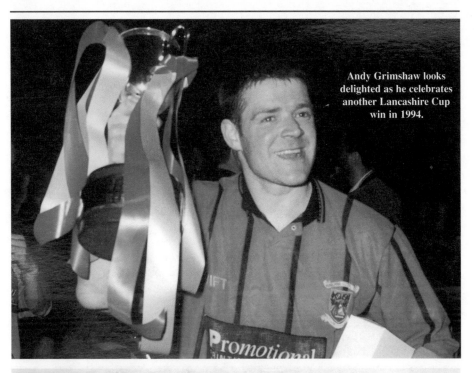

Andy Grimshaw looks delighted as he celebrates another Lancashire Cup win in 1994.

Stewart Drummond and Garry Thompson receive their England semi-professional caps.

The Conference runners-up trophy

Skipper Stewart Drummond receives the Conference runners-up trophy from Wolves manager Dave Jones.

Garry Thompson and Jim Bentley lead the celebrations after the Lancashire Cup victory over Accrington Stanley in 2004.

Morecambe FC 2003-04
D. Howell, J. Bentley, S. Drummond, M. Stringfellow, I. Swan, A. Rigoglioso, W. Curtis.
N. Rogan, C. Lane, G. Thompson, C. Mawson, K. Walmsley, D. Carlton, D. Gordon.
G. Hunter, P. Osbourne, J. Harvey, A. Mutch, L. Dodgson, D. Perkins.

Players model the latest Morecambe strip in July 2004. From left: Adam Sollitt, Danny Carlton, Michael Stringfellow, Michael Twiss and Jim Bentley

Jim Harvey, who celebrated 10 years as Morecambe manager in June 2004.

The light at the end of the tunnel

The 2nd leg at Christie Park was won 2-1. Att: 1,546.
Morecambe: Mawson, Walmsley, Perkins (sent off), Bentley, Murphy, Osborne
(Thompson), Hunter, Drummond, McFlynn (Rogan), Carlton (1) (Sugden), Curtis (1).
*Winners: 1925/26; 1926/27; 1961/62; 1962/63; 1968/69; 1985/86; 1986/87; 1993/94;
1995/96; 1998/99; 2003/04.*
Runners-up: 1950/51; 1987/88; 1989/90; 1994/95; 1997/98.

LANCASHIRE FA FLOODLIT CUP: One of those unwanted cups that Morecambe
entered between 1966/67 and 1974/75. There was little interest in the competition
although the club reached the final in the first season of entering, losing 2-1 to Wigan
Athletic over two legs.

LANCASHIRE POLICE: Visited Hutton to play in pre-season friendlies.
The first was a 3-2 defeat on August 15, 1989.

LANCASHIRE SENIOR CUP: Morecambe became the first non-league club to enter
the Senior Cup in 1963-64. They entered the competition each season between 1966-67
and 1973-74 when the competition was disbanded in its old form.
Morecambe won the competition in 1967-68 beating Blackburn Rovers first team 2-1 at
home, Netherfield (away) 1-0, Bury first team (home) 2-1, Netherfield (away) 1-0,
Oldham Athletic first team (away) 1-0 and Burnley Reserves 2-1 in the final on May 13,
1968. Att: 4,230. The club also reached the final in 1973-74, losing to Manchester City
Reserves 3-0.

LANCASTER, DAVE: 1986-88. Centre-Forward 75 (37 cup) apps; 28 (17 cup) goals.
One of the more recent players to leave Morecambe and end up in the Football League.
Dave was signed by Joe Wojciechowicz in the summer of 1986 from Leyland Motors
after coming to the fore as a goalscorer in the North West Counties League. His first goal
came in a 3-1 pre-season victory over Lancaster City and in the season that followed
scored 20 goals from 37 league and 21 cup apps.
The 1987/88 season was even better with 16 goals in 38 games, including a hat-trick in a
4-1 home win over Mossley. Unfortunately he was another to join the exodus to Colne
Dynamoes under Joe Wojciechowicz where he continued to impress as a striker and
moved into the Football League with Blackpool, Chesterfield, Rochdale and Bury.

LANCASTER, DEREK: 1968-73 and 1980-82. Forward 194 (54+1 cup) apps; 54 (17
cup) goals. Derek became another firm favourite with the Christie Park faithful by
scoring 71 goals in just under 250 appearances.
Born in Preston, Derek looked to have a big career ahead of him when he joined Chelsea
as an apprentice in 1965 but he failed to make the grade in his two years there. He was
released and joined PNE but failed to make a first team app despite being leading scorer
for the reserves with eight goals in 24 games. After being released from Preston, Derek
was snapped up by then manager Ken Waterhouse and it proved to be a shrewd move.
Not picked for the first game of the 1968-69 season Derek showed his worth with a hat-
trick for the Reserves in a 4-0 win at Crewe Alexandra. That was enough to persuade

Waterhouse of his worth and Derek made his debut on August 16, 1968, in a 1-1 draw at South Liverpool. He was then a regular in the starting line-up for the next five seasons finishing as joint leading scorer in the 1968-69 season with 18 goals. He followed that up by being top of the scoring charts in 1969-70 with 10 goals and 1970-71 with 15. Derek's first spell at the club ended on April 10, 1973, in a 1-1 draw at Skelmersdale United. The story did not end there however, as a full eight years later Derek rejoined the club in a shock move. On March 25, 1981, he scored in a friendly game for an Old Morecambe XI against an Old Lancaster XI and impressed manager Don Cubbage so much that he was re-signed and made his second debut in a 3-2 home defeat by Workington. Unfortunately, Derek's return was when the club was at one if its lowest ebbs and he was a member of the side that lost 9-0 to Bangor City. Cubbage resigned and Derek played just one more game under his successor Les Rigby.

LANCASTER CITY (LANCASTER TOWN 1905-1937): The club's local rivals were already members of the Lancashire Combination when Morecambe joined the league for the 1920/21 season. In fact the Shrimps enjoyed a good start against the Blues, winning the first league encounter 1-0 at Giant Axe in front of a crowd of 3,500.

Lancaster went on to win the league in the 1921/22 season though they did lose 3-0 to Morecambe at Christie Park on the final day of the season. The games always drew big crowds in the 1920s with the best perhaps being in the 1926/27 season when five meetings between the sides were watched by a total of 31,233 fans. A then record Christie Park crowd of 5,776 watched the first of those five games in a 1-1 draw on March 5, 1927. Just 21 days later City recorded a 2-0 victory in front of the then Giant Axe record of 6,507, although sources at the time believed the crowd to be nearer 8,000. After the league fixtures were completed the sides would meet again in the Lancashire Junior Cup final and the Lancashire Combination Cup final.

Deepdale was the venue for the Junior Cup clash on April, 13. Scores of local workers took advantage of the half-day holiday some factories allowed and the A6 was heavily congested with fans making their way to the ground. An official crowd of 8,500 saw George Grass score the only goal of the game to give Morecambe victory but again it was suggested that the crowd was more like 12,000.

The Combination Cup final saw 5,450 watch a 1-1 draw at Christie Park with the replay drawing 5,000 to Giant Axe as Morecambe won 2-1.

The most memorable meetings in recent years came in the FA Cup. The two sides were drawn against each other for the final qualifying round in the 1996/97 season and a titanic battle ensued. The first game was at Giant Axe and 2,500 watched a 1-1 draw. A replay at Christie Park on the Wednesday watched by 2,725 also ended all square after extra time and a toss of the coin decided the venue of the second replay. Christie Park won to be the venue again and 2,475 watched the Shrimps finally win through. The game ended up being an historic one as it was the last time the FA allowed a second replay to take place in an FA Cup game.

Games between the two sides became regular Boxing Day fixtures, drawing big crowds throughout the 40s, 50s and 60s. This changed when Morecambe joined the NPL in the 1968/69 season. The derby fixture was back on the agenda when City joined the NPL in the 1970/71 season.

LANCASTER LADS CLUB: Met in the North Lancashire League during 1940-41, winning 6-2 at Aldcliffe Road on September 28 and winning 3-1 at Christie Park on March, 15.

LANCASTER & MORECAMBE SUNDAY LEAGUE SELECT XI: Met in an end of season friendly on May 12, 1989.

LANE, CHRIS: 2003-04. Defender 15+1 (2 cup) apps; 1 goal. Former Football League player with Hereford Utd who joined Southport for £10,000 in January, 2001, making 89+1 apps for the Sandgrounders scoring seven goals. Joined Morecambe in May, 2003, and released in January, 2004. Signed for Leigh before moving to Chester where he was released in May, 2004. Chris rejoined Leigh in June, 2004.

LANSIL: Met in the North Lancashire League in 1939-40, winning 2-1 away on October, 7. Won 6-2 at home on April, 27.

LARGE, DAVID: 1984-87. Defender 50+1 (17+4 cup) apps; 2 cup goals. After 299 apps for Barrow between 1975-84 he joined in March, 1985. Described as *"a thoughtful constructive half-back"* he joined Vickers Sports Club in the 1987-88 season.

LATHAM, ALBERT: 1936-38. Centre-half 66 (14 cup) apps; 2 goals. A well-travelled player who joined in September, 1936, from Clitheroe. Moved to Lancaster City in September, 1938. Previous clubs included Wolves, Accrington Stanley, Rochdale, York City, Barnoldswick Town and Fleetwood.

LAVELLE, BEN: 1989-91, 1991-92, 1993-95 and 1995-97. Defender 129+22 (50+14 cup) apps; 1 (4 cup) goals. The likeable left sided player *(pictured right)* must hold the record for having the most spells at the club as he signed for the Shrimps on no less than seven occasions. He first joined in June, 1989, when signed by Larry Milligan from Southport. The Visitor described him as a *"versatile player who is at home equally at left back or as a left winger."* The writer proved to be a prophet of the highest order as over the next eight years Ben was a consistent performer for a number of managers. His debut came at Fleetwood on August 28, 1989, in a 2-1 win in a game which new record signing Ian Cain made the headlines. Ben moved to Blackpool Wren Rovers at the start of the 1991-92 season. From there,

he became something of a footballing nomad. He was brought back to Morecambe for the FA Trophy win against Welling United then loaned back to Wren Rovers and even played against Morecambe in a shock Shrimps Lancashire Cup defeat. He then re-signed in time to play at Colchester United in the FA Trophy before returning to Fleetwood for the 1992-93 season. Christie Park became his home again for the 1993-94 season and he proved a valuable member of the promotion winning squad. He was released again in October 1995 and joined Ashton United but by January he was back again and made 17 Conference appearances. His last appearance came as a substitute in a 2-1 win over Woking, on May 3, 1997. A truly popular player, Ben was a teacher at Our Lady's High School in Lancaster and was in the medals in the 1999/2000 season as a member of the Kirkham & Wesham team that won the Seat Cars West Lancashire League. Lancashire Cup winner in 1993-94 and 1995-96.

LAWN, THE: Home of Forest Green Rovers with the first visit coming on April 22, 1999, drawing 2-2. Att: 408.

LAWRENSON, TOMMY: 1957-60. Winger 107 (30 cup) apps; 40 (14 cup) goals. Father of former PNE, Brighton and Liverpool defender Mark, Tom signed for North End in 1949 but after just one league match he joined Southport. He made 37 league appearances for the Sandgrounders between 1955 and 1957. Tommy then joined the Shrimps and had some success. In the 1957-1958 season he was second top scorer with 12 league goals from 37 appearances. The next season he topped the scoring charts with 18 goals in 40 league games and in 1959-1960 helped the Shrimps to take fourth spot in the Lancashire Combination with 10 strikes in 30 league games.
Born in Preston on May 24, 1929, Tommy died in 1996.

LAWSON, ERIC: 1972-74 and 1974-75. Defender 33+3 (7+2 cup) apps (1 as goalkeeper); 2 goals. Moved to Lancaster City in September 1974 but returned in February 1975.

LAYER ROAD: Home of Colchester Utd where Morecambe lost 3-1 in the FA Trophy, 3rd Rd, on February 22, 1992. Att: 3,206. Ian Cain scored.

LDV VANS TROPHY: Since the 2000/01 season, the top clubs in the Conference have been included in the LDV Vans Trophy with the Football League's Division 2 and 3 clubs.
Morecambe have qualified 3 times to date. The first time was on November 28, 2000, with a 3-2 defeat in Rd 1 at Lincoln City. Att: 1,194.
On October 22, 2002, Shrewsbury beat the Shrimps 3-0 in another Rd 1 tie. Att: 1,602.
Morecambe bowed out of the competition in the 1st Rd for the third year running with a 4-1 defeat at Wrexham on October 14, 2003. Att: 1,079.

LEA, CHARLIE: 1966-73. Winger 201+10 (85+2 cup) apps; 51 (23 cup) goals. If you ask any long-term supporter, to name the most skilful Morecambe player he has seen, the answer is likely to be Charlie.

Still a regular around Morecambe his skills as a winger are unlikely to be matched as on his day, he was quite brilliant. Born in Preston, he played for North End A and B sides in the Lancashire League from 1960 to 1966 before going on to make seven appearances for the reserves before being released. He was snapped up by player-manager Ken Waterhouse and he made his Morecambe debut in a 2-0 win over Burscough on August 20, 1966. He scored two goals the following Tuesday in a 5-1 win over Marine and his status as a Morecambe legend was already assured. He was a regular in the side for the next six seasons and an integral member of the Lancashire Combination League winning sides in 1966-67 and 1967-68. He lost his place when trophy-winning manager Dave Roberts came to the club and his last game for Morecambe came on January 13, 1973, when he came on as a substitute in a 2-1 home defeat by Macclesfield Town. He left the club to join Lancaster City.

Combination League and Cup winner 1967-68 and 1967-68. Lancashire Senior Cup winner in1967-68 and Lancashire Cup winner in1968-69.

LEACH, JOHN: 1951-52. Outside-left 33 (4 cup) apps; 4 (2 cup) goals. Joined in September 1951 after making 74 apps for Barrow between 1947-49.

LEARMOUTH, JIMMY: 1948-49. Left-half 23 (5 cup) apps; 2 (1 cup) goals. Captain in the King's Own Regiment in Lancaster. Joined in November 1948. Moved to Lancaster City 1950-51.

LEAVER, DAVID: 1983-85 and 1996-97. Forward 27+3 (17+1 cup) apps; 2 (6 cup goals). Joined Morecambe for the first time in August 1983 and helped the reserves win the Lancashire League Division Two championship in 1983-84. Signed for PNE on non-contract forms before moving on to Leyland Motors and Bamber Bridge where he was an integral part of their major rise up the leagues as they won the NPL Division One title in 1994-95 and then the Premier Division title in 1995-96. Rejoined Morecambe in July 1996, but moved to Accrington Stanley for a four-figure fee in September, 1997. Later had another two spells at Bamber Bridge and one at Chorley.

LEE, DAVID: 2000-01. Forward 12 (7 cup) apps; 1 cup goal *(pictured right)*. Perhaps the most expensive player to have ever played for the club after being involved in transfers totalling almost £1m during a successful professional career.

Joined in January, 2001, from Halifax Town after being released as player-coach at Carlisle Utd. Moved to Wigan Athletic in April 2001 to take up a position as youth team coach. Had a celebrated career which started off with 203+5 appearances and scoring 35 goals for Bury. Joined Southampton for £350,000 in August 1991 and made a switch to Bolton Wanderers for £300,000 in December 1992. Made 124+31 apps for the Trotters scoring 17 goals as his side won the Division 1 title in 1996-97 and also reached the League Cup final at Wembley 1994-95. Joined Wigan for £250,000 in July 1997 where he made 61+22 appearances, scoring 11 goals. Played 9 games for Blackpool on loan in 1999.

LEEDS UTD: Visited Christie Park on August 7, 1962, to open the new main stand, winning 7-1. A crowd of 5,000 watched the late John Charles (recently signed back for £53,000 from Juventus) kick-off.

LEEK TOWN: Met the Blues in the NPL and in the Conference. First meeting was at Christie Park in the NPL on November 24, 1990, winning 3-1. Att: 440. The club's worst Conference defeat came at Harrison Park when Leek recorded a 7-0 win.

LEIGH RMI: The Railwaymen men, who started off life as Horwich RMI, first met Morecambe under the new name on January 16, 1996, at Christie Park, winning 2-0 in the 2nd Rd of the Lancashire Cup. Att: 266.

LEVETT, JACKIE: 1932-33, 1935-36 and 1945-47. Outside-left 67 (25 cup) apps; 17 (3 cup) goals. Former Edmondsons player who joined for the first time in September, 1932. Returned to Edmondsons before signing for the Shrimps once again in November, 1935.
Signed amateur forms with Manchester City in April, 1936, but in August, 1936, joined Lancaster City until 1939. After the war, he returned to Christie Park and played in the 1945-46 season. Combination Cup winner in 1945-46.

LEYLAND: Met in the Lancashire Combination League from 1920-21 to 1924-25. The first meeting was also Morecambe's first Lancashire Cup tie on October 16, 1920, at Woodhill Lane, losing 2-1. Att: 1,000.

LEYLAND MOTORS: First team or reserves met the Tigers in the Lancashire Combination between 1933-34 and 1967-68 and 1975-76 to 1977-78.
First meeting was in the West Lancashire League Junior Cup, Rd 1, on October 15, 1921, at Leyland. The home side won 3-1. Att; 200.

LEAGUE RECORDS

Lancashire Combination

	P	W	D	L	F	A	Pts	Pos
1920/21	34	10	5	19	58	83	25	13th
1921/22	34	10	6	18	36	56	26	14th
1922/23	34	9	8	17	41	60	26	16th
1923/24	38	15	5	18	60	63	35	15th

1924/25	36	24	7	5	88	31	55	1st
1925/26	38	21	10	7	103	58	52	2nd
1926/27	38	23	4	11	105	58	50	3rd
1927/28	38	17	6	15	92	72	40	8th
1929/29	38	20	2	16	89	73	42	10th
1929/30	38	12	7	19	74	111	31	15th
1930/31	38	12	8	18	76	97	32	16th
1931/32	36	6	6	24	41	93	18	18th
1932/33	38	11	10	17	68	84	32	14th
1933/34	38	9	9	20	65	101	27	18th
1934/35	38	17	5	16	63	60	39	8th
1935/36	38	19	9	12	78	65	47	6th
1936/37	40	17	10	13	95	75	44	10th
1937/38	42	21	10	11	90	70	52	6th
1938/39	42	14	10	18	67	76	38	14th
1939/40	3	2	0	1	5	4	4	---

North Lancashire League Division One

1939/40	18	9	9	4	57	41	23	2nd
1940/41	13	4	2	7	30	44	10	8th

Lancashire Combination League Division One

1945/46	22	6	6	10	54	68	18	9th
1946/47	42	23	5	14	133	85	51	4th
1947/48	42	24	6	12	98	59	54	4th
1948/49	42	22	6	14	80	60	50	3rd
1949/50	42	17	11	14	62	55	45	9th
1950/51	42	12	12	18	56	73	36	15th
1951/52	42	21	7	14	74	72	49	5th
1952/53	42	16	9	17	60	61	41	11th
1953/54	40	14	6	20	58	83	34	19th
1954/55	42	18	8	16	68	65	44	9th
1955/56	38	12	5	21	58	76	29	16th
1956/57	38	20	7	11	81	53	47	3rd
1957/58	42	18	12	12	66	50	48	7th
1958/59	42	22	9	11	77	44	53	5th
1959/60	42	28	2	12	103	54	58	4th
1960/61	42	23	5	14	96	76	51	6th
1961/62	42	32	6	4	143	51	70	1st
1962/63	42	31	6	5	153	40	68	1st
1963/64	42	19	8	15	93	71	46	10th
1964/65	42	30	2	10	132	50	62	3rd
1965/66	42	19	12	11	105	65	50	7th
1966/67	41	30	9	2	90	24	69	1st
1967/68	42	28	9	5	112	41	65	1st

LIGHTFOOT, CHRIS: 2001-02. Defender 15 (5 cup) apps; 2 (2 cup) goals. Experienced Football League campaigner who had a short spell at the club blighted by injuries. Made 263+14 appearances for Chester between 1987-95, scoring 32 goals. Joined Wigan for £87,500 in July, 1995, making 11+3 appearances; scoring one goal. In March, 1996, he joined Crewe for £50,000 and made 63+23 appearances, adding another five goals to his tally. Joined Morecambe in July, 2001, and released in May, 2002. Moved to Runcorn FC Halton and became manager in November, 2003.

LINCOLN CITY: Met the Imps, then managed by former England boss Graham Taylor, at Sincil Bank in the FA Cup 1st Rd on November 20, 1976, losing 1-0. Att: 6,111.

LIVERPOOL RESERVES: First met in a pre-season friendly at Christie Park on August 3, 1968, drawing 1-1. Later met in the Lancashire Senior Cup, 2nd Rd, on October 31, 1972, at Christie Park, losing 2-1.

LIVINGSTON: Met the Scottish Premier League side in a pre-season friendly at Christie Park on Sunday, July 28, 2002, losing 2-1.

LLANELIAN ROAD: Home of Colwyn Bay with the first visit in the FA Cup 4th Qualifying Rd on October 20, 1991, winning 2-0. Att: 781.

LOCK, FRED: 1921-23. Outside-left 16 (4 cup) apps; 3 goals. Joined in March, 1922, and moved to Altrincham in February, 1923.

LODGE, PAUL: 1991-94. Midfield 83 (39 cup) apps; 4 (2 cup) goals. An England Under 15 international who made 20+4 appearances for Everton before moving to PNE on a free transfer in February, 1983. Made 36+2 appearances before moving to Bolton Wanderers in July, 1984 and having loan spells at Port Vale and Stockport County. Played non-league for Barrow, Southport, Macclesfield Town and Witton Albion before signing for Morecambe for £3,000 in October 1991. Moved to Southport for £3,000 in November, 1993. Later played for Bangor City, Lancaster City, Burscough and Stalybridge Celtic. Was manager of St Helens Town 2003-04 before resigning in January, 2004. President's Cup winner in 1991-92.

LOMAX, C: 1923-25. Outside-right 23 (9 cup) apps; 6 (2 cup) goals. Former Lancaster Town player who joined in April, 1924. Moved to Barnoldswick Town 1925-26 and later Chorley. Combination League winner in 1924-25.

LONDON ROAD: Former home of Grantham where Morecambe visited in the NPL from 1979-85. The club was renamed Grantham Town and have played at the South Kesteven Sports Stadium since 1990. First meeting was at Grantham on April 16, 1980, losing 3-1.

LONRIGG, SIMON: 1989-90. Defender 0+1 app. Morecambe's youngest every player when he came on as a sub at Bishop Auckland on September 13, 1989 having just turned 16. Moved to Fleetwood Town 1992-93 and represented the RAF at football.

LONSDALE PARK: Former home of Workington from 1921 to 1937 in their North Eastern League days. The Shrimps played a friendly there on December 10, 1921, losing 5-4. Aldred, Bateson, Emmison and Hampson scored.

LORD, ALBERT ERNEST: 1970-72. Goalkeeper 29 (4 cup) apps. Joined Morecambe in October, 1970, from Clitheroe. Previous clubs had included Bolton Wanderers, Southport, Runcorn, Halifax Town and Horwich RMI.
Released in May, 1972. Joined Little Lever and later played for Nelson.

LOVETT, TOMMY: 1955-56 Outside-left and 1957-60 Left-back 57 (16 cup) apps. Former PNE junior.

LOWER GORNAL ATHLETIC: Now Gornal Athletic. Met the West Midlands club in the FA Trophy, 3rd Qualifying Rd, on December 4, 1971, winning 2-1. Att: 150. Sutton and Richmond scored.

LYDON, TONY: 1961-63. Outside-left 19 (1 cup) apps; 15 goals. Former Blackburn Rovers junior and Wigan Athletic player who signed for £20 in February, 1962. Moved to Horwich RMI for the same figure in July, 1963.

LYONS, ANDY: 1985-88, 1989-90 and 2000-01. Defender/Midfield/Forward 61+12 (26+3 cup) apps; 6 (6 cup) goals. Blackpool-born player who had three spells at the club. His first two were interspersed between spells at Fleetwood Town and Wren Rovers. His career took off when Crewe signed him from Fleetwood for £15,000 (some say it was £25,000) in October, 1992. Made 7+4 appearances, scoring two goals for Dario Gradi's side before a £7,500 move to Wigan Athletic followed in November, 1993. Scored 27 goals for the Latics in 78+6 apps and finished the 1993-94 and 1994-95 seasons as top goalscorer. This prompted Partick Thistle to pay £35,000 for him in March, 1996, and he went on to play 64+7 games and score 13 goals. Two seasons at Ayr United followed with 47+10 apps and eight goals with the highlight being the club's appearance in the Scottish Cup semi-final against Rangers in 1999-2000. Returned to Morecambe in July, 2000, and had a brief spell at Lancaster City in August, 2001, before retiring.

LYONS, DARREN: 1998-2000. Forward 51+3 (15+2 cup) apps; 9 (9 cup) goals. A non-league veteran winger whose pace proved to be a major asset. Played for a string of teams such as Rhyl, Droylsden, Macclesfield Town, Mossley, Ashton Utd and Accrington before being signed by Bury in March, 1992. Went on to make 23+13 appearances in the league scoring seven goals before being signed by Southport for £3,000 in 1993-94. A £2,000 move to Macclesfield Town in February, 1994, proved to be a successful one as he starred in Sammy McIlroy's side that won the Conference in 1994-95 and the FA Trophy in 1995-96. Moved on to Winsford, Halifax Town and Altrincham before joining Morecambe in September 1998. Moved to Southport but released after one substitute appearance. Managed East Manchester in the Manchester Air Miles Premier League between 2002-03. Lancashire Cup winner in 1998-99.

LYTHAM: Formed in 1880 and played at their Ballam Road ground until it was taken for housing in the 1980s. The Lytham club merged with St Annes Athletic in 1959-60 to become Lytham St Annes. First meeting was at home in the FA Cup 1st Qualifying Rd on October 7, 1922, winning 1-0. Att: 600.

M

MACAULEY, JIMMY: 1923-26. Inside-left 47 (21 cup) apps; 16 (3 cup) goals. One of the first internationals to play for the Shrimps. Jimmy won six caps for Northern Ireland while with Huddersfield Town and scored against England at Derby on February 11, 1911 in a 2-1 defeat. He also scored two goals in representative matches for the Irish League against the Football League and Scottish Leagues.
Jimmy was born in Belfast and began playing for Cliftonville, helping them to lift the Irish League title in the 1909/10 season. He was given a trial by Glasgow Rangers but failed to make an app and joined Huddersfield Town in October, 1910, where he made 95 appearances, scoring 32 goals. He then moved to PNE in November, 1913, and made his debut in a 1-0 home defeat by Liverpool. Jimmy eventually made 59 appearances for North End, scoring 24 goals before the advent of war. After the hostilities Jimmy played 19 games for second division side, Leicester City, scoring twice.
He then dropped down to the Lancashire Combination and had three years at Lancaster before joining Morecambe on and making his debut on August 25, 1923, in a 1-0 win over Fleetwood. He helped the Shrimps win the Lancashire Combination in the 1924/25 season with eight goals from 21 league and six cup appearances.
Injury saw him make only three appearances the season after and his last game before retiring was on March 20, 1926, a 3-0 home win over Barnoldswick Town.
Combination League winner in 1924-25.

MACCLESFIELD TOWN: Met the Silkmen in the NPL from 1968-69 to 1986-87 and then in the Conference from 1995-96 to 1996-97. First met at Moss Rose on September 28, 1968, drawing 2-2. Att: 2,675.

MACCLESFIELD FLOODLIT KNOCK-OUT CUP: Another early attempt to get the Combination and Cheshire clubs together before the formation of the NPL in 1968-69. This competition was held at Macclesfield Town's ground in 1965-66. Morecambe beat Runcorn 1-0 in Rd 1 on October 18 with Tulloch scoring. Att: 1,208. Lost 3-2 after extra time to Altrincham in Rd 2 on November, 22. Holden and Timmins scored in a game watched by 1,612.

McCLUSKIE, JIM: 1993-97. Forward 95+39 (43+16 cup) apps; 66 (33 cup) goals. Big Jim was a huge favourite with the crowd for his never-say-die attitude and aggression. Started off his life at Morecambe by earning the reputation 'Super Sub' as he was on the bench for 41 games in the 1996-97 season. Jim began his career at Rochdale where he made 14+5 appearances before being released in 1986. Played in Jersey and then for Mossley before being signed by Hyde Utd in December, 1989, for £8,000. Witton Albion then paid £10,000 for his services as he spearheaded their campaign to win the NPL in 1990-91. Jim *(pictured right)* was also part of the team that took Witton to the FA Trophy final at Wembley in 1991-92 along with Andy Grimshaw. In the space of two months in 1992 played for Barrow, Witton Albion, Mossley and Accrington Stanley before settling down at Accrington Stanley until being signed by the Shrimps for £2,000 in August, 1993. His goals were vital as Morecambe won promotion to the Conference. Had a brief spell as Jim Harvey's assistant between October, 1995, and February, 1996, before being released in July, 1997. Moved to Accrington Stanley before a

switch to Chorley in June, 1998, to become assistant player-manager, having a spell as caretaker manager in 1999. Took over as manager of Rossendale Utd before resigning in November, 2002. Returned as assistant manager in September, 2003, and became manager for a second time in January, 2004, resigning for a second time in May, 2004. Lancashire Cup winner in 1993-94 and 1995-96.

McCORMICK, PATRICK: 1935-36. Centre-forward 37 (4 cup) apps; 27 (2 cup) goals. Ex-Cleator Moor, PNE (amateur), Dick Kerr's and Lancaster Town player who joined in July, 1935. Moved to Oldham Athletic in May, 1936, and scored 13 goals in 38 appearances between 1936-39. Born in Cleator Moor on January 7, 1914, and died in 1991.

McCRAE, DON: 1948-49 and 1951-52. Centre-forward/Inside-left 10 apps; 6 goals. Joined in August 1948 and rejoined in January 1952. Played three games for Morecambe reserves in 1956-57.

McDONALD, ELIAS: 1930-31. Outside-left 30 (5 cup) apps; 2 goals. Made 18 appearances for Southampton and 37 for Southend Utd before joining Southport in May, 1925 and Doncaster Rovers in June, 1926. Became a firm favourite at Barrow where he made 97 appearances and scored 13 goals. Spells at Chorley and Ulverston Town followed before joining Morecambe in September, 1930. Born in Manchester on April 11, 1898 he died in Ribchester on April 8, 1978.

McDONNELL, PETER: 1984-88. Goalkeeper 125 (62 cup) apps. A former Liverpool goalkeeper who collected a European Cup winner's medal as a non-playing substitute. Peter was another big name player persuaded to join the club, signing on towards the end of the 1984/85 season. He became an instant success, appearing in the last 11 games of that season – a period which saw the fortunes of the team rise dramatically. The next season he appeared in 40 of the 42 league games, missing two games because of a suspension picked up because of a sending off at Mossley. He suffered a bad injury during a game against Gainsborough Trinity in February, 1987, but still managed to make 34 league and 21 cup appearances by the end of the season. The next season proved to be his last but once again he was a near ever-present with 40 league appearances. At the end of the season he left to rejoin Barrow and was sorely missed by the supporters, many of who still regard him as the best Morecambe goalkeeper of recent times. Lancashire Cup winner in 1985-86 and 1986-87.

McFLYNN, TERRY: 2003-04. Midfield 16+3 (4+1 cup) apps; 3 (1 cup) goals. Former QPR trainee who made one first team app before signing for Woking and then Margate where he made 39+11 apps; scoring six goals. Joined Morecambe in November, 2003, for £14,000. Played regularly for Northern Ireland U21s and more recently the U23s. Lancashire Cup winner 2003-04.

McGOWAN, JAMIE: 1989-92. Defender 12+2 (8+2 cup) apps. Morecambe-born player who had trials with Liverpool, Hearts, Burnley and Rangers before moving to Dundee in July, 1992. Made 32+3 appearances for the Dens Park side and scored one goal. Joined Falkirk and made 122+9 appearances, scoring eight goals. During his time there the team reached the Scottish Cup final in 1996-97 where they lost 1-0 to Kilmarnock after beating Celtic 1-0 in the semi-final. Won the Scottish League Challenge Cup in 1997-98 with a 1-0 win over Queen of the South. Later played for Motherwell, St Mirren and Alloa. President's Cup winner in 1991-92.

McGRAW, JOCK: 1946-51. Centre-half/Centre-forward 118 (20 cup) apps; 20 (6 cup) goals. Joined Morecambe in June, 1947, and moved to Ingleborough 1951-52. May be the same J McGraw that made 88 appearances for Leeds between 1939 and 46.

McGREGOR, NEIL: 1980-82. Forward 51 (11 cup) apps; 8 goals. Former Burnley youngster who joined in August, 1980. Moved to Burnley Utd in February, 1982.

McGUIRE, PAUL: 1998-2002. Defender 44+23 (11+2 cup) apps; 1 goal. Played for Morecambe Youths and the reserves before signing a contract in May, 1999. Moved to Hyde Utd in the close season of 2002 and later joined Northwich Victoria in October, 2003.

McHUGH, ARTHUR: 1983-85. Forward 17+2 (2+5 cup) apps; 1 goal. Joined in April, 1984 and moved to Lancaster City, 1985-88, before emigrating to Australia.

McILHARGEY, STEVE: 1994-2004. Goalkeeper 141 (46 cup) apps. Glasgow-born

Scottish Schoolboy international who had a great season as Morecambe won promotion from the NPL to the Conference. Former Walsall and Rotherham keeper who became a crowd favourite with Blackpool where he made 100+1 appearances between 1989-94. Played in two Division 4 play-off finals at Wembley before being released in 1994. Joined Morecambe in August, 1994, until retiring. Still involved with the club as goalkeeping coach. Lancashire Cup winner 1995-96 and 1998-99. Spalding Cup winner 1997-98.

McINERNEY, IAN: 1991-92. Midfield/Forward 13+3 (8+4 cup) apps; 3 (6 cup) goals. A professional with Huddersfield Town (5+5 apps; 2 goals); Stockport County (37+5 apps; 8 goals) and Rochdale (4 apps; 1 goal) before moving to Gateshead. Joined Morecambe for a short spell in September 1991. Later played for Runcorn (reaching the FA Trophy final in 1993-94), Worcester City, Halifax Town, Northwich Victoria and Leigh RMI.

McKEARNEY, DAVE: 1996-2004. Defender/Midfield 288+11 (71+5 cup) apps; 14 (5 cup) goals. Another very popular player *(pictured right)* in recent times after signing from Chorley in July, 1996. A versatile player who gave 100% wherever he played. Made his name with Crewe Alexandra where he made 95+13 appearances, scoring 12 goals after signing in October, 1989. Moved to Wigan on a free transfer in August 1993 and made 45+4 appearances for the Latics, scoring 9 goals. Was a member of the Shrimps' Spalding Cup winning team and picked up two Lancashire Cup winners medals in 1998-99 and 2003-04. Was released in May, 2004, and joined Burscough.

McKENNA, JOHN: 1981-85. Goalkeeper 133 (36 cup) apps. One of the best goalkeepers at Christie Park in recent times, John was signed from Formby by Les Rigby for £250 in February, 1982. He made his debut in a 1-1 draw at Matlock Town on February 6, 1982, and was almost an ever present until his last game against Goole Town at Christie Park on March 23, 1985. He left Morecambe when he emigrated to South Africa for a short time where he played for Durban City.
While at Morecambe he was selected for the Northern Premier League XI and later in his career while at Dagenham won seven caps as England's semi-professional goalkeeper.

McKENNA, TOM: 1922-23. Right-back 25 (8 cup) apps. Former Burnley, Barrow, Grimsby Town, Belfast Utd and PNE player who joined from Kendal Town in September, 1922. Returned to Kendal and later played for Ulverston Town.
Born in Dublin on October 1, 1891, Tom died in 1930.

McLACHLAN, NEIL: 1977-81. Forward 96+9 (17+4 cup) apps; 31 (3 cup) goals. Former Carnforth Rangers and Milnthorpe Corinthians player who joined in August, 1977. Had trials with PNE and Wrexham and moved to Horwich RMI 1981-85. Later played for Chorley and Atherton LR as well as two further spells at Horwich.

McLACHLAN, PETER: 1975-77 and 1978-79. Goalkeeper 86 (30 cup) apps. Joined in May, 1975, and had trials with Sheffield Utd and Carlisle Utd before moving to Carlisle City. Returned to Morecambe in July, 1978, before moving back to Carlisle City. Morecambe's player of the year in 1975-76.

McLELLAN, ALASTAIR ALEXANDER: 1949-50. Inside-left/Outside-left 25 (2 cup) apps; 8 (1 cup) goals. Joined in August, 1949, from Tranmere Rovers. Glasgow-born player who had earlier played for Raith Rovers, Huddersfield Town, Albion Rovers and New Brighton. Moved to Prescot Cables and later South Liverpool. An RAF air-gunner in WWII he was badly wounded over Germany. Nicknamed 'Cowboy'.

McMAHON, JOHN: 1990-93. Midfield 57+1 (25 cup) apps; 2 (4 cup) goals. Younger brother of Steve McMahon who signed from Altrincham in September, 1990, for a 'sizable fee'. Experienced non-league player with spells at Southport, South Liverpool, Runcorn and Witton Albion. Moved to Macclesfield Town in December, 1992, and later played for Knowsley Utd and Hyde Utd. Became part of the coaching staff at Tranmere Rovers in 2002 and had a spell as caretaker boss in September, 2003, before the appointment of Brian Little.

McNALLY, JOHN: 1991-95. Forward 36+40 (14+15 cup) apps; 10 (6 cup) goals. A player known as 'super-sub' after being on the bench for 35 games in the 1992-93 season. Joined in March, 1992, from Vauxhall GM. Moved to Southport in September 1994 but made just one appearance before moving on to Accrington Stanley and League of Wales side Camaes Bay. President's Cup winner in 1991-92. Lancashire Cup winner in 1993-94.

MADDOCK, WAYNE: 1995-96. Forward 10+1 (4+1 cup) apps. Joined in August, 1995, three goals. Moved to Bamber Bridge in December, 1995, and helped them to win the NPL title in the 1995-96 season. Later played for Accrington Stanley, Fleetwood Freeport and Kendal Town where he was player-coach in 2001-02.

MAGSON: 1938-39. Outside-left 14 (1 cup) apps; two goals. A local player who joined in November 1938.

MAINE ROAD: Former home of Manchester City with the first visit being in the FA Cup, 1st Rd, against York City on December 8, 1966, losing 1-0. Att: 4,283. Lost 2-1 to

Manchester City reserves in the Lancashire Senior Cup, 2nd Rd, on October 22, 1968. Att: 2,043. Morecambe used Maine Road as the home venue for a replay against York City in the FA Cup 1st Rd on November 19, 1985 when Christie Park was considered unsuitable for a League club to visit. York won 2-0. Att: 1,305.

MAINE ROAD FC: One of the biggest setbacks in the early 90s was a shock 2-1 FA Cup defeat at Maine Road. On September 12, 1992, Morecambe were hot favourites to beat the North West Counties side but in front of a crowd of 180, most of them from Morecambe, they went down 2-1. Mike Dunphy and Dave Swindells scored for the home side with John Coleman grabbing Morecambe's goal.

MALLEY, PHILIP:1988-91. Midfield 72+1 (26 cup) apps; 3 (1 cup) goals. Former Sunderland apprentice who made 91+4 appearances for Burnley, scoring five goals before joining in November, 1988. Moved to Great Harwood in September, 1989, but rejoined in November, 1989. Left in December, 1990, and played for Burnley Bank Hall, Rossendale Utd and Great Harwood.

MANAGERS: The Morecambe managers in chronological order are:

Jimmy Milne 1947-1948	Mike Hogarth 1978-1980
Albert Dainty 1955-1956	Jim Thompson 1980
Ken Horton 1956-1961	Don Cubbage 1980-1981
Joe Dunn 1961-1964	Les Rigby 1981-1984
Geoff Twentyman 1964-1965	Sean Gallagher 1984-1985
Ken Waterhouse 1965-1969	Joe Wojciechowicz 1985-1988
Ronnie Clayton 1969-1970	Eric Whalley 1988
Gerry Irving/Ronnie Mitchell 1970	Billy Wright 1988-1989
Ken Waterhouse 1971-1972	Lawrence Milligan 1989
Dave Roberts 1972-1975	Bryan Griffiths 1989-1993
Alan Spavin 1975-1976	Leighton James 1994
Johnny Johnson 1976-1977	Jim Harvey 1994 -
Tommy Ferber 1977-1978	

MANCHESTER CENTRAL: A failed attempt to get a 3rd League club in Manchester. Met in the Combination from 1928-29 to 1930-31. First meeting was a 1-1 draw in Manchester on September 8. Lost 3-0 at home on March 29.

MANCHESTER CITY: Met a City XI during Morecambe's Carnival Week on September 16, 1925, with the score not known. Wales's legend Billy Meredith was reported to have been the referee. A City XI, including Sir Matt Busby, visited Christie Park for Dick Woodhouse's benefit on March 21, 1928, a 1-1 draw.
First game in the Lancashire Senior Cup was a home game with City Reserves on November 4, 1963, losing 4-1. Att: 2,200. Lost 3-0 to Manchester City Reserves in the final of the Lancashire Senior Cup at Christie Park on May 11, 1974. Att: 3,221.
City brought a strong side to Christie Park for Geoff Street's testimonial game on August 13, 1977, drawing 1-1. Att: 721.

MANCHESTER NORTH END: Began life as New Cross in 1919 before moving to New Cross and joining the Combination in 1922-23. Changed their name to North End in 1923-24. Moved to the Cheshire League until they disbanded after the 1938-39 season. First met New Cross at home on February 3, 1923, drawing 1-1. Att: 1,250. Lost the return game 4-1. The last meeting was in the Combination Cup 3rd Rd at home, winning 2-1 on November 28, 1923 with Farnworth and Houghton scoring.

MANCHESTER UNITED: Morecambe played United reserves on New Year's Day, 1929, in Eddie Eastwood's benefit match at Christie Park, losing 6-2. Eastwood and Burrows scored for Morecambe. Beat a United reserve side in the semi-final of the Lancashire Senior Cup on May 8, 1974, at Christie Park. Att: 3,014. A crowd of 3,950 saw a pre-season friendly end 0-0 at Christie Park on August 12, 1996. On November 6, 1997, United sent along a team for Andy Grimshaw and Ben Lavelle's testimonial with the visitors winning 6-0 thanks to a hat-trick from Ben Thornley.

MANLEY, JOHN: 1921-23. Centre-forward 32 (8 cup) apps; 17 (5 cup) goals. Joined in January, 1922, and released in May, 1923. Moved to Kendal Town and later played for Morecambe Park Villa.

MANN: 1949-50. Left-half 28 (2 cup) apps. Former Chorley player who joined in August, 1948.

MANOR GROUND: Former home of Oxford United where Morecambe lost 3-2 in a FA Cup, 1st Rd, tie on October 30, 1999. Att: 3,504.

MANOR PARK: Home of Nuneaton Borough. First visit was in the Conference on February 12, 2000, drawing 1-1. Att: 1,411.

MARCELLINI, ALBERTO: 1973-76. Midfield 14+2 (2 cup) apps; 1 (1 cup) goals. Ex-Skerton Athletic and Lancaster Celtic player who joined as a 16-year-old in August 1973. Played largely for the Reserves from 1973-76 and 1977-79.

MARGATE: First met the Gate in the Conference at Christie Park on November 24, 2001, winning 2-1. Att: 1,588.

MARINE: Team from Crosby that have always found it hard to win at Christie Park. Their last win at Morecambe came in the Lancashire Junior Cup in the 1960-61 season and it is one of the few grounds that veteran manager Roly Howard has never won at during his 30+ years in charge. First met the Mariners in the Combination at Rossett Park on April 10, 1936, losing 3-1.

MARSTON, C E: 1933-34. Outside-right 20 (2 cup) apps; 1 goal. Joined from Lancaster Town in August, 1933.

MARSTON ROAD: Home of Stafford Rangers with the first visit being a 1-1 draw on October 18, 1969 in the NPL. Att: 2,027.

MARTIN, JOHN: 1966-70. Midfield 82+3 (39+2 cup) apps; 16 (9 cup) goals. A popular ball player Johnny was almost an ever present in the 1966/67 Lancashire Combination League winning side. Signed by Ken Waterhouse as an 18-year-old from Barrow, Martin made a big impression after making his debut in a 3-2 friendly victory over Workington on August 6, 1966. His league debut was a memorable one. In a 2-0 win over Burscough on August 20, he was booked, missed a penalty, had a goal disallowed for offside and set up both goals. In his first season he scored 14 goals in 41 league and 23 cup appearances. The following season he made 26 league and 12 cup appearances and scored eight goals. Unfortunately, the next two seasons were not as fruitful. He made just four starts in the 1968/69 season and 15 the following year.
His final game was in a 3-0 defeat at South Liverpool on January 31, 1970. He went on to join Netherfield and then Barrow. Combination League and Cup winner in 1966-67 and 1967-68. Lancashire Senior Cup winner 1967-68.

MASON, TOMMY: 1949-50. Goalkeeper 30 (4 cup) apps. Former Lancaster City and Netherfield player who joined in September, 1949. Moved to Horwich RMI.

MASSON, JACK: 1935-39 and 1945-46. Half-back/Inside-forward/Outside-left. 81 (16 cup) apps; 21 (5 cup) goals. Joined from Penrith in August 1935 and moved to Netherfield in October, 1938. Returned for one game in the North Lancashire League in April, 1940, and rejoined for a longer spell in February, 1946. Moved to Lancaster City in 1946-47. Lived locally and played snooker for Trimpell for many years.

MATLOCK TOWN: First met the Gladiators at Christie Park on August 23, 1969 in the NPL, winning 3-0. Att: 1,600.

MATTHEWS, J: 1923-24. Centre-forward 29 (13 cup) goals. Ex-Lancaster Town player who joined in August, 1923.

MATTINSON, HARRY: 1960-62. Centre-half 26 (7 cup) apps. Veteran defender who began his career with Sunderland and Middlesbrough before a £4,500 move to PNE in March, 1949. Made 124 appearances for PNE helping them win the Division Two title in 1950-51. Moved to Queen of the South and joined the Shrimps in February, 1961. Played his last game in October 1961. Born in Ireby, Carlisle, on July 20, 1925 and died on June 8, 2001.

MAWDESLEY, W H: 1931-34. Full-back/Left-half/Forward 66 (10 cup) apps; 3 (1 cup) goals. Signed from Chorley in September, 1931. Returned to Chorley in January, 1934. Later played for Lytham and also featured for Morecambe reserves 1935-36.

MAWSON, CRAIG: 2001-04. Goalkeeper 122+1 (27 cup) apps. Keighley-born keeper who joined from Halifax Town in the close season of 2001. Started his career as a youngster at Burnley and signed professional forms but did not make a first team app. Had a loan spell at Lincoln City before moving to Halifax Town where he played nine games in 2000-01. Player of the year in 2002-03. Lancashire Cup winner in 2003-04.

MAY PARK: The ground used by the old Leyland club where Morecambe played in the Combination from 1920 to 1925. PNE used the ground for their A team games 1925-26 until 1928-29 in the Combination. First game there against PNE was on April 15, 1926, winning 2-1.

MAYERS, KENNY: 1997-99. Defender/Midfield 53+19 (21+2 cup) apps; 5 (2 cup) goals. A player who came to the fore while playing for Bamber Bridge during their rise up the leagues. Between 1991-96 he was part of the team that won promotion from the NPL Division 1 and won the NPL a year later in 1995-96. Joined Chorley for £12,000 in November, 1995, before moving to Southport in December, 1996.
Signed for Morecambe in June, 1997, and moved to Lancaster City in June, 1999. Later played for Stalybridge Celtic, Hyde Utd and Barrow. Played for the Great Britain Post Office team in the European Championships against Italy, Belgium and Greece in 1996-97. Spalding Cup winner in 1997-98. Lancashire Cup winner in 1998-99.

MAYOR, JACKIE: 1934-36, 1939-40 and 1945-48. Half-back 39 (17 cup) apps; 9 (3 cup) goals. Joined Morecambe originally in April, 1935, before signing amateur Central League forms for Manchester United in March, 1936. Played for the A team at Old Trafford and then played for Oldham Athletic reserves 1936-38 and Lancaster City 1938-39. Returned to Morecambe in August, 1939, and again as Morecambe captain 1945-46. Played for the reserves until 1951-52. Emigrated to Australia in October, 1957, but returned and died in Lancaster on June 14, 1965, aged 61.
Combination Cup winner in 1945-46.

MEADOWS, JOHN: 1938-39, 1954-55 and 1957-58. Goalkeeper 6 apps. Joined originally in February 1939 and was another to play in the England v Scotland junior international match at Giant Axe on April 22, 1939. Made four apps in 1938-39. He was a Spitfire pilot for the RAF in the Middle East during the war and on his return played for Glasson Dock, Burnley Reserves, Bournemouth and Accrington Stanley before becoming player-coach at Lancaster City. Made one appearance for Morecambe in May, 1955, and another in April, 1958. Became Morecambe Juniors' manager/trainer 1957-58 before taking a similar role with Lancaster City's reserves and then first team 1959-61.

MEE, GEORGE, WILLIAM: 1934-35. Inside-left/Outside-left. 17 (5 cup) apps; 4 (1 cup) goals. Older brother of the famous Arsenal boss Bertie Mee, George had a distinguished career of his own. Signed for Blackpool in July, 1920, and went on to make a record 195 consecutive apps for the club from December, 1920, to September, 1925. Finished with 216 appearances for the Tangerines, scoring 21 goals before a £3,750 move to Derby County in February, 1926. Made 148 appearances for the Rams and scored 21 goals as his side won promotion to Division One in 1926-27 and were Division One runners-up in 1929-30. Moved to Burnley and played for Mansfield Town and Great

Harwood before joining Morecambe as player-coach in January, 1935. Moved to Accrington Stanley in October, 1935, before becoming reserve team coach at Rochdale. Was Blackpool's A team coach during World War II.

MEXBOROUGH TOWN: First opponents on the way to Wembley 1973-74. Morecambe beat them 3-0 on January 12, 1974. Att: 274.

MIDDLEMASS, SCOTT: 1993-94. Defender 16 (2 cup) apps. Well travelled defender who is the son of well-known scout and manager Clive Middlemass. Signed in February 1994 from Bamber Bridge in a swap deal involving David Eaves. Later played for Northampton Town, Sudbury Town, Fulham, Macclesfield Town (trial), Chorley, Foshan (China), Cincinnati Riverhawks (USA), Cambridge Utd and Scarborough.

MIDDLESBROUGH, HENRY: 1951-53 and 1953-54. Centre-forward 16 (4 cup) apps; 5 (1 cup) goals. Ex-Heysham and Morecambe Grammar School player who joined in August, 1951. Rejoined in September, 1953, but only played in one void game.

MIDDLESBROUGH RESERVES: Visited Christie Park for a pre-season friendly on August 2, 2000, winning 3-0.

MIDDLESEX WANDERERS: Played the NPL XI at Christie Park on May 6, 1991, with the NPL winning 1-0.

MIDDLEWOOD ROAD: Home of Guinness Export in Aughton. First visit was in the Combination on November 20, 1965, drawing 2-2.

MILLARD, LANCE: 1966-69. Goalkeeper 119 (53 cup) apps. One of the club's best ever goalkeepers and a real favourite with the long standing supporters. Lance was a giant of a stopper at 6ft 2in tall and 15 stone. Lance played in the league for Aldershot in 1962 and 1963 while in the army before joining Barrow in July, 1964. He made 17 appearances in the 1964-65 season and 36 the following season. He was first spotted playing for Barrow reserves against Morecambe's second string and when released by the Bluebirds was snapped up by Ken Waterhouse. His debut for Morecambe came in a pre-season friendly against Workington on August 6, 1966, with his league debut coming on August 20 – a 2-0 home win over Burscough. Lance was first choice keeper for the next 3 seasons, winning the Lancashire Combination title in 1966-67 and 1967-68 and being a regular in the club's first season in the NPL. His last appearance came in a 1-3 defeat at South Shields on May 10, 1969. Combination League and Cup winner in 1966-67 and 1967-68. Lancashire Senior Cup winner in 1967-68. Lancashire Cup winner in 1968-69.

MILLER, DAVID: 1996-2000. Defender 29+1 (12+2 cup) apps; 1 goal. Experienced defender who joined in July, 1996, from Wigan Athletic. Son of former Burnley boss Brian he made 27+5 appearances for the Clarets, scoring three goals before joining Tranmere Rovers after a spell on loan at Crewe. Moved to Colne Dynamoes before moving back into the league with PNE in December 1986 where he made 49+8 appearances, scoring two goals. Joined Carlisle Utd for £30,000 in September 1989 and made 108+1 appearances, scoring seven goals before a £25,000 switch to Stockport County in March 1992. David *(pictured right)* made 72+9 appearances, scoring one goal before finishing his professional career at Wigan Athletic (35+3 apps; 3 goals). His defensive qualities soon came to the fore but an unfortunate injury picked up against Halifax Town effectively ended his playing career and he retired at the end of the 1997-98 season. Became Morecambe's assistant manager in March, 1999, but was released in May, 2000. Became assistant manager at Leigh RMI before taking over as boss of Stalybridge Celtic in March, 2002.

MILLER, EDDIE: 1951-54. Left-half/Inside-left 112 (18 cup) apps; 25 (2 cup) goals. Former Barrow favourite who also played for Workington. Signed in September 1951 and retired in September 1954 to play for the reserves. Was well known as Carnforth Cricket Club professional. Born in Ulverston on June 21, 1920. Died on September 2, 2002.

MILLER, TOMMY: 1991-92. Defender 10+1 (9+1 cup) apps; 1 (2 cup) goals. Former Runcorn and Altrincham defender who joined in October, 1991. Scorer of the goal that never was in the FA Cup clash with Hull City in 1991 when a superbly struck free kick hit the back of the net and came out without the referee awarding a goal. Left Christie Park in February 1992. Was coach at Cheadle Town 2002-03.

MILLIGAN, LAWRENCE (LARRY): 1980-84. Defender 114 (28 cup) apps; 4 goals. A popular player who went on to have short spell as manager. Started off his paying career by making 19 appearances for Blackpool and seven appearances for Portsmouth while on loan in 1979. After short spells at Barrow, Rochdale and Houston Hurricanes in America joined Morecambe in October, 1980, before being released in October, 1983. Moved to Fleetwood Town where he took over as manager and had great success, taking the team to the FA Vase final at Wembley 1984-85. Returned to Morecambe as manager when Billy Wright was sacked on April 24, 1989, but resigned on October 26, 1989, after some poor results. Coached Wren Rovers and managed Fleetwood again 1992-93.

MILLMOOR: The home of Rotherham Utd and the venue for a 2-0 FA Cup 1st Rd replay defeat on November 27, 1979. Att: 5,671.

MILLS, JOCK: 1929-32. Half-back/Inside-right 102 (11 cup) apps; 12 (1 cup) goals. Ex-Blackpool, Fleetwood, Rochdale and Lancaster Town player who joined in August, 1929. Later played for Standfast and Edmondsons.

MILNE, JIMMY: 1947-48. Left-half. 30 (8 cup) apps; 3 (2 cup) goals. Morecambe's first ever manager when he took over as player-boss in 1947-48 after being in a similar role at Wigan. Moved to become the trainer/coach at Doncaster Rovers before returning to PNE where he became a great servant as trainer before becoming manager between 1961-66. Led PNE to the FA Cup final in 1963-64 and later became general manager and scout. As a player his career started at Dundee Utd before a £900 move to North End where he played from 1932-46, making 233 appearances and scoring nine goals. Along the way he reached the FA Cup final in 1936-37 and won promotion to Division 1 in 1933-34. He was the father of Gordon Milne who played for PNE, Liverpool and England. Jimmy was born in Newtyle, Dundee, on January 24, 1911, and died in Hinckley on December 13, 1997.

MILNER, ANDY: 1997-2000. Forward 24+4 (11+4 cup) apps; 9 (6 cup) goals *(pictured right)*.
Kendal-born player who joined from Chester City on November 15, 1997, for a then record fee of £8,000. Impressed after scoring a hat-trick for Hereford while on loan against the Shrimps a few weeks earlier. Came to the fore while playing for Netherfield, then managed by Dave Edge, and joined Manchester City for £10,250 in January, 1989. A £20,000 move to Rochdale followed in January, 1990, and he made 103+24 appearances, scoring 25 goals there. In August, 1994, he moved to Chester City on a free and scored 24 goals in 106+19 appearances. Unfortunately, his time at Morecambe was cut short by injury and although he had a short spell at Northwhich Victoria in February, 2002, was forced to retire. Spalding Cup winner in 1997-98.

MILNTHORPE CORINTHIANS: Morecambe first met in the North Lancashire League during the 1939-40 season, winning 2-1 at Milnthorpe on February 10, 1940, and 4-2 at Christie Park on March 30. Perhaps Morecambe's worst ever FA Cup defeat was at Milnthorpe on September 24, 1955, when Corinthians won 5-2 in the 1st Qualifying Rd.

MITCHELL, IAN: 1968-70. Defender 42+3 (12+2 cup) apps; 6 (1 cup) goals. Ex-Bolton Wanderers player who joined in August, 1968. Moved to Lancaster City 1970-71.

MITCHELL, RON: 1954-59 and 1960-67. Full-back 216 (62 cup) apps; 4 (1 cup) goals. A local sporting legend, Ron first joined Morecambe in October, 1954, after playing for junior sides such as Red Rose Boys' Club, PNE Juniors and Bolton-le-Sands. His debut came in a reserve team match at Vickers Sports Club which was abandoned. It didn't take long for him to break into the first team however, as his debut came on December 4, 1954, in a 3-1 win at home to Ashton United.
He soon became a first team regular but National Service intervened and he only made two reserve team appearances in 1956-57. He came back stronger than ever and soon became an integral part of the team, starring in the FA Cup run on 1958-59 and making such a good impression that Leeds United paid £1,000 for his services in November, 1958. Unfortunately, Ron made just four first team appearances for Leeds in Division 1 and he returned to Christie Park in 1960, playing his first game back in a 4-2 defeat against Nelson. Amazingly, loss of form saw Mitchell spend the majority of the 1960-61 and 1961-62 seasons in the reserves. His only first team game in 1961/62 came, strangely enough, in the FA Cup, 3rd Rd tie, against Weymouth when he was a late replacement for the injured Don Cubbage. Ron's next game did not come until November 10, 1962, when again he stood in for Cubbage against Lytham and he finished the match as goalkeeper after an injury to Ken Udall. A loyal clubman Ron began to become a regular again in the 1962-63 season, largely as a left-back and played up until he retired 1967 – his last game being a 2-1 defeat against Guinness Export. Even then, Ron stayed loyal to the club serving as reserve team trainer and even caretaker manager along with Gerry Irving in the 1970/71 season. Combination League winner in 1962-63 and 1966-67. Lancashire Cup winner 1962-63. Combination Cup winner in 1964-65.

MITCHINSON, DAVE: 1986-88. Defender 33 (15 cup) apps; 4 (1 cup) goals. Joined from Gretna in October, 1986, and retired in January, 1988. Former Whitley Bay and Gateshead player who helped Blyth Spartans win the Northern League title in 1985-86. Died in 1990.

MOAT GROUND: Home of Gresley Rovers where Morecambe won 3-2 in the FA Trophy, 2nd Rd, on February 11, 1995.

MONK, IAN: 1995-98. Forward 90+9 (29+7 cup) apps; 17 (7 cup) goals *(pictured right)*. A player who tasted success almost everywhere he went. Played for Burnley Belvedere between 1986-92, before moving to Clitheroe where he was the NW Counties

Division 1 player of the year in 1992-93. Moved to Ashton Utd and then Macclesfield, playing 17+8 games and scoring three goals as the Silkmen won the Conference title. Joined Morecambe in December, 1995, after a short loan spell and proved to be one of the best wingers the club has had in recent years. Moved to Leigh RMI in June 1998 and helped them to win the NPL title in 1999-2000. Released by them in 2003-04 and joined Stalybridge Celtic. Lancashire Cup winner in 1995-96. Spalding Cup winner in 1997-98.

MOODY, CHARLIE: 1972-75. Midfield 17+2 (5+1 cup) apps; 1 (1 cup) goals. Ex-Mayfield Utd player, who played for Morecambe reserves.

MOOR LANE: Home of Salford City where Morecambe visited for a pre-season friendly on August 6, 1988, winning 2-1. The ground was the former home of Manchester Rugby Club.

MOOR PARK: Home of Chester-le-Street where Morecambe won a FA Cup, 2nd Qualifying Rd tie, 5-1 on October 2, 1982, with Carpenter, Galley, Brownbill, Halsall and Yates scoring.

MOORBY, JOHN: 1933-37. Right-half 12 (1 cup) apps. Ex-PNE junior who joined Morecambe reserves in February, 1934, and played until the 1937-38 season. Also played in the North Lancashire League 1939-40 and 1940-41.

MORAN, BRIAN: Defender 17 (6 cup) apps; 1 goal. Ex-Blackburn Rovers youngster, who joined in August 1979, aged 18. Moved to Barrow for a 'four-figure fee' in January 1980 and later played for Workington and Great Harwood Town.

MORECAMBE, ERIC: Hugely popular comedian who was born John Eric Bartholomew *(pictured right)* on May 14, 1926, in Morecambe. Became club president in August 1970 for a short period. Died in May, 1984, when he collapsed after coming off stage at a charity show at the Roses Theatre, Tewkesbury.

MORECAMBE RUGBY CLUB: This was the original Morecambe Football Club, being formed in 1876. Their ground was at Moss Lane, near West End Road Bridge, on the site of Battismore and Corringham Roads. In 1895-96 the semi-professional Northern Union (the present Rugby League) was formed. Morecambe remained amateur that season and became Lancashire club champions. In August, 1896, they joined the Northern Union, playing in the Lancashire Senior Competition and were bottom for three seasons. The club was relegated to Division 2 which they won in 1900-01. The Rugby League was reformed into two divisions in 1902-03 and Morecambe finished next to bottom for three seasons. It was back to one division in 1905-06 but Morecambe finished second to bottom again and the club was disbanded.

MORECAMBE POLICE: Met in a friendly at Rosebery Park on April 11, 1923, winning 6-3.

MORECAMBE SERVICES: Morecambe Football Club was closed down after the end of the 1940-41 season because of the war and Christie Park was used by a team called Morecambe Services, mainly made up by RAF members. They played in the wartime Lancashire Combination League finishing 4th in 1941-42 and 5th in 1942-43.

MORGAN, DAVE: 1987-88. Defender 16 (9 cup) apps; 2 (1 cup) goals. Joined in February, 1988, before moving to Colne Dynamoes. Later played for Northwich Victoria, Accrington Stanley, Witton Albion, Guiseley, Lancaster City, Chorley, Ashton Utd and Bradford Park Avenue.

MORLEY, HARVEY: 1962-64. Right-half/Inside-right 69 (13+1 cup); 14 (2 cup) goals. Former PNE junior who joined in August, 1962. Moved to Chorley in 1964 and later played for Netherfield, Fleetwood and Lancaster City.

MOSS LANE: Home of Altrincham with the first visit coming in a North West Floodlit Cup, 1st Rd, match on October 31, 1966, winning 4-2. Att: 3,300.

MOSS ROSE: Home of Macclesfield Town. First visit was on October 18, 1965 for a Macclesfield Floodlit Cup match against Runcorn, winning 1-0. Att: 1,208.

MOSSLEY: First met the Lilywhites in a floodlit friendly at Christie Park on November 23, 1960, drawing 4-4. Att: 900.

MOSSOP, BILL: 1946-49. Right-back 44 (7 cup) apps. Ex-Galgate player who featured in the England v Scotland Junior international at Giant Axe in April, 1939. Local player who joined in November, 1946. Later played for Ingleborough and Williamsons.

MOULE, JAMES: 1951-52 and 1955-56. Inside-forward 27 (4 cup) apps; 10 (1 cup) goals. Ex-Barnoldswick player who joined in August, 1951. Returned to Barnoldswick on 1952-55 and came back for one game in August, 1955. Was a cricket professional with Queensway.

MUTCH, ANDY: Former goalscoring hero for Wolves who became Jim Harvey's assistant manager after Ian Daliziel. Scored 105 goals in 325+13 apps for Wolves after being signed from Southport in February 1986. Formed a deadly partnership with Steve

Bull. Played in the Premiership for Swindon Town after a £250,000 move in 1993 and ended his career at Stockport before playing non-league for Barrow and Southport and Telford where he was assistant manager.

MURPHY, JAMIE: 2000-04. Defender 68+26 (15+9) cup apps; 3 goals. Began his career as a youngster with Blackpool and made 48+7 apps, scoring one goal as the side won promotion to Division Three in 1991-92. Joined Doncaster Rovers on a free in September 1995 and made 47+7 apps. Had a short spell at Cambridge Utd before joining Halifax Town on a free in 1997 and helped them win the Conference title. Made 21+2 apps and scored one goal in Halifax's first season back in the league before being released. A back injury forced him out of the game for almost a full year and he joined Morecambe in July, 2000. Struggled with injury for much of his time at Christie Park and was released in May, 2004. Joined Fleetwood Town in June 2004. Lancashire Cup winner in 2003-04.

MYERSCOUGH, JOE: 1932-33. Inside-right 34 (9 cup) apps; 3 (2 cup) goals. A Galgate-born player who had two spells with Lancaster Town before being signed by Manchester Utd in May, 1920. Went on to make 33 appearances and score eight goals for United and was a member of the side that won the Central League in 1920-21. Joined Bradford Park Avenue for £1,500 on October, 1923, and made 120 appearances for them, scoring 47 goals. Collected a Division Three North runners-up medal with them before rejoining Lancaster Town in July, 1927. Moved to Rossendale before switching to Morecambe in July, 1932. Later played for Fleetwood Town.

Dave McKearney in action versus Yeovil Town, 1998

N

NAIRN, JOHN: 1930-32. Inside-Left 48 (8 cup) apps; 24 (6 cup) goals. Ex-Raith Rovers and Barrow player who joined in September, 1930.

NANSON, ROBERT: 1923-24. Inside-Left/Outside-Left 25 (4 cup) apps; 8 goals. Former New Brighton and Carlisle Utd player who joined in November, 1923.

NATIONAL PARK: Home of Curzon Ashton with the first visit being on September 29, 1992, for a President's Cup, 1st Rd, match with ground-sharing Caernarfon Town, winning 3-1. Att: 66.

NELSON: When Nelson dropped out of the Football League in 1931 they took their reserves' place in the Lancashire Combination. First meeting was at Christie Park on September 5 1931, losing 3-1.

NELSON RESERVES: Joined the Lancashire Combination in 1923-24 with the first meeting being at home on September 15, 1923, winning 4-1.

NENE PARK: Home of Rushden & Diamonds with the first visit being on February 1, 1997 in the Conference, losing 2-1. Att: 2,145.

NETHERFIELD: Renamed Netherfield Kendal in 1999-200 and now Kendal Town. Many meetings in cup and league with the first game being in the North Lancashire League at Christie Park on October 14, 1939, winning 4-3.

NETHERMOOR: Home of Guiseley with the first visit being for a NPL Cup 3rd Rd replay on February 17, 1992, losing 4-2 on penalties after a 3-3 draw. It was the first time Morecambe had been involved in a game which needed penalties to decide the outcome. Att: 821.

NEW BRIGHTON: The original South Liverpool club moved to become New Brighton in June, 1921. First met in the Lancashire Combination at home on October 1, 1921, losing 3-1. Att: 2,000.

NEW BRIGHTON RESERVES: New Brighton joined the Football League in 1923-24, remaining there until 1950-51, when they were voted out and rejoined the Combination. First met New Brighton reserves in the Combination on November 10, 1934 at Christie Park, winning 4-2.

NEW CROSS: Renamed Manchester North in 1923-24.

NEWCASTLE BLUE STAR: One meeting in the FA Cup, 1st Qualifying Rd, away on September 12, 1987, losing 1-0. Att: 177.

NEWLANDS CUP: Began as an end of season match played at Christie Park on FA Cup final evening between Lancaster City and Morecambe to raise funds for the Sailors Children's Society of Newlands, Hull. Frequently guest players appeared, like Ray Charnley after his transfer to Blackpool. Latterly it was a pre-season game between Lancaster City and Netherfield played at Giant Axe. Lancaster City won the first match 2-1 on May 2, 1956. Morecambe's last game in the cup was on February 10, 1970, when City won 2-0 at Christie Park.

NEWTON, KEITH: 1978-79. Defender 27 (6 cup) apps; 1 goal. Former England international *(pictured right)* who signed for the club in 1978. Mick Hogarth was the manager at the time and he pulled off a real coup in bringing the full-back who appeared in the World Cup in Mexico in 1970 to Christie Park. Newton was capped 27 times by England after a successful career at Blackburn Rovers (306 league games), Everton and Burnley (209 league outings). Newton went on to make 33 league and cup appearances for the Shrimps, scoring once, in a 2-2 draw with Gainsborough Trinity. Keith died, aged just 56 in 1998.

NEWTON, WILF: 1932-34. Centre-half 13 (1 cup) apps. Local youngster who joined from Williamsons in April 1933. Returned to Williamsons.

NICHOLSON, HARRY: 1931-32. Outside-right 16 (2 cup) apps; 4 (1 cup) goals. Joined in August 1931 after a successful spell at Lancaster Town (1927-31) where he helped them win the Combination League title and the Lancashire Cup. Suffered a bad injury while at Christie Park before returning to play locally for Williamsons where he worked. Was secretary of Lancaster City for 22 years from 1948-1970. Born in Lancaster in 1906 and died in the city on April 15, 1972.

NORMAN, JOHN: 1994-99 and 1999-2002. Forward 204+47 (72+13 cup) apps; 73 (39 cup) goals. The latest player to score 100 goals for Morecambe was one of Jim Harvey's first signings in July 1994 when he joined for a small fee from Mold. Harvey had spotted his potential as a youngster at Tranmere Rovers. Was released by Rovers in 1990 and had trials at Oldham Athletic and Stockport County before having a short spell at Bury where he made 1+1 first team appearance. His first season at Morecambe was a quiet one and he even spent a time on loan at Chorley in March, 1995, but from then on became a regular goalscorer and creator for the Shrimps. Moved to Hednesford Town in May, 1999, but played just 8+7 games for them, scoring two goals, one of which was against Morecambe. Jim Harvey signed him again in March, 2000, when he went on to score more vital goals, before being released in May, 2002. Moved to Burscough and John *(pictured right)* was part of their FA Trophy winning team along with Paul Burns and later moved to Vauxhall Motors 2003-04. Lancashire Cup winner in 1995-96 and 1998-99. Spalding Cup winner in 1997-98.

NORMANBY ROAD: Ground of the now defunct South Bank where Morecambe lost 1-0 in a FA Cup, 3rd Qualifying Rd, replay on October 20, 1982.

NORTH EUSTON GROUND: Home of Fleetwood Windsor Villa who became the second Fleetwood club. First visit was in the Lancashire Junior Cup 2nd Rd, losing 2-1 to Villa on November 22, 1930.

NORTH LANCASHIRE LEAGUE: At the outbreak of war in 1939 Morecambe resigned from the Combination and took over the reserve team's fixtures in the North Lancashire League, playing in the 1939-40 and 1940-41 seasons before closing down for the duration of the war.

NORTH SHIELDS: In all five meetings with the Robins, all during the 1983-84 season. The first game was in the FA Cup, 2nd Qualifying Rd, at Christie Park on October 1, 1983, drawing 2-2. Att: 292. North Shields won the replay 4-2. They also knocked Morecambe out of the FA Trophy in the same season, winning a 2nd replay 4-1 after drawing 1-1 and 4-4.

NORTH WEST FLOODLIT CUP: Another early effort to unite the best of the Cheshire League and Lancashire Combination in 1966-67. Won 4-2 at Altrincham in Rd 1 on October 31, before losing 5-2 at Northwich Victoria on November 15 in the quarter-final.

NORTH WEST FLOODLIT LEAGUE: The cup gave way to a league in 1967-68. Played home and away in a group with Altrincham, Chorley and Northwich Victoria. Morecambe failed to qualify for the finals.

NORTHALLERTON TOWN: Just one meeting, at Christie Park in the FA Cup, 2nd Qualifying Rd, on October 1, 1988, winning 3-2. Att: 245.

NORTHERN NOMADS: Famous old nomadic club who won the FA Amateur Cup in 1925-26. First met in a friendly at Woodhill Lane on October 9, 1920, winning 1-0. Att: 550. Played against them in the Combination from 1933-34 to 1937-38. The first meeting was at Paticroft on April 18, 1934, losing 4-1. The Nomads reformed after the war and played in Division 2 of the Combination from 1957-58 to 1963-64.

NORTHERN PREMIER LEAGUE

THE Shrimps were founder members of the NPL and played in the competition from 1968/69 to 1994/95 until winning promotion to the Conference.

The full playing record was:

	P	W	D	L	F	A	Pts	Pos
1968/69	38	16	14	8	64	37	46	3rd
1969/70	38	10	13	15	41	51	33	15th
1970/71	42	14	11	17	67	79	39	12th
1971/72	46	15	10	21	51	64	40	17th
1972/73	46	17	11	18	62	49	45	15th
1973/74	46	13	13	20	62	87	39	17th
1974/75	46	14	15	17	71	87	43	13th
1975/76	46	11	11	24	47	67	33	20th
1976/77	44	13	11	20	59	68	37	15th
1977/78	46	11	11	24	67	92	33	21st
1978/79	44	11	13	20	55	50	35	18th
1979/80	42	10	12	20	40	59	32	17th
1980/81	42	11	8	23	42	74	30	21st
1981/82	42	9	11	22	43	86	29	20th
1982/83	42	16	11	15	75	66	59	13th
1983/84	42	11	12	19	59	74	45	19th
1984/85	42	11	14	17	51	67	47	18th
1985/86	42	17	17	8	59	39	68	3rd
1986/87	42	20	12	10	66	49	72	6th
1987/88	42	19	15	8	61	41	72	4th
1988/89	42	13	9	20	55	60	47*	16th
1989/90	42	15	9	18	58	70	37	14th
1990/91	40	19	16	5	72	44	73	3rd
1991/92	42	21	13	8	70	44	76	3rd
1992/93	42	25	11	6	93	51	86	3rd
1994/94	42	29	7	15	90	56	67	7th
1994/95	42	28	10	4	99	34	94	2nd

* 1 point deducted.

Biggest win

Home: 6-1; v Droylsden (May 4, 1991); 5-0;
v Gainsborough (October 26, 1968),
v Kirkby (April 9, 1971),
v Netherfield (April 12, 1971),
v Gainsborough (March 13, 1976),
v Frickley (January 29, 1977).
Away: 6-0; v Matlock (March 27, 1993).

Biggest defeat

Home: 9-0; v Bangor City (Sept 21, 1981).
Away: 7-1;
v South Shields (Nov 17, 1973),
v Goole Town (April 20, 1974),
v Workington (September 29, 1981),
6-0; v Bangor City (November 28, 1970),
v Boston Utd (April 23, 1977).

Most goals in a match

Home: Morecambe 7 Emley 4 (March 30, '93).
Away: Matlock Town 2, Morecambe 7 (April 10, 1975), Mossley 4, Morecambe 5 (March 20, 1978).

NORTHERN PREMIER LEAGUE CUP: Record in this cup is rather dismal. Best effort was to reach the semi-finals in 1989-90, losing both legs to Gateshead, 2-1 at home and 3-1 away.

NORTHOLME: Home of Gainsborough Trinity. First visit was on December 12, 1968, winning 2-1. Att: 1,600.

NORTHWICH VICTORIA: Many meetings in the NPL and more recently in the Conference. A team that Morecambe have never managed to beat on their home pitch. First met at Altrincham in the North West Floodlit Cup Quarter-Final on November 15, 1966, losing 5-2.

NUNEATON BOROUGH: Met the Boro during their spell in the Conference. First meeting was at Manor Park on February 12, 2000, a 1-1 draw with Justin Jackson scoring Morecambe's goal.

John Norman in action versus Doncaster Rovers, 2002

The light at the end of the tunnel

O

O'CONNOR, SEAN: Forward. Born Wolverhampton on August 7, 1981, the striker started his career as a youngster at Hednesford Town in July 1997. Made 12+10 apps, scoring two goals. His form attracted the attention of a number of scouts and he moved to Dundee Utd for £30,000 in February, 2000.
Made 2+1 appearances, scoring one goal and had loan spells at Portadown in Ireland and Morton where he scored eight goals in 20+1 (3 cup) appearances. Joined Queen of the South for £10,000 in March, 2002, and scored 10 goals in 21+9 (3+3 cup) appearances. Helped his side to win the Division Two title in 2001-02 and Bells League Challenge Cup in 2002-03. Joined Morecambe in June, 2004.

O'DOHERTY, EUGENE: 1924-25. Centre-forward 24 (9 cup) apps; 19 (2 cup) goals. Irish-born player who had spells at Fleetwood, Blackpool, Leeds Utd, Ashton National, Halifax Town, Wigan Borough and Walsall before joining in October, 1924. Moved to Clitheroe in September, 1925. Lancashire Combination League winner in 1924-25.

O'DONNELL, CHRIS: 1983-84. Midfield 15+3 (10+2 cup) apps; 4 (2 cup) goals. Former Fleetwood Town, Squires Gate and Wren Rovers player who joined in August, 1983. Moved to Fleetwood Town in February, 1984, and later played for teams including Colne Dynamoes, Wren Rovers and Springfields.

OFFORD, STAN: 1946-48. Left-half 44 (6 cup) apps; 7 (1 cup) goals. Former wartime player with Bradford Park Avenue who had spells with Halifax Town (guest) and Bradford City before joining in August, 1946. Moved to Netherfield and was part of the team that won the Combination title in 1948-49.

OLD EARTH: Home of the former Colne Town with the first visit being on January 23, 1926, losing 3-2.

OLD TRAFFORD: Just one visit which was made by the youth team in Rd 1 of the FA Youth Cup on October 12, 1959. A crowd of 10,882 saw United win 14-0.

OLDEST PLAYER: Morecambe have had many players in their 40s but the oldest was trainer Fred Warburton who in an emergency played one game away against Southport reserves on April 18, 1938. He was aged 57 or 58. Fred had played one game with Bolton Wanderers in 1903-04.

OLDHAM ATHLETIC: A famous meeting came at Boundary Park in the semi-final of the Lancashire Senior Cup on April 22, 1968, when a goal from Arnold Timmins gave the Shrimps a shock 1-0 win.

OLDHAM ATHLETIC RESERVES: Often met the reserves in the Lancashire

---

Combination League. First meeting was at Boundary Park on December 18, 1937 when the game was abandoned because of fog after 70 minutes with Oldham winning 1-0.

OLLERENSHAW, GEORGE: 1946-47 and 1949-51. Left-half 33 (9 cup) apps. Former Bolton-le-Sands player who joined in September, 1946. Returned to Bolton-le-Sands in April, 1947, before having another short spell at Morecambe starting in September, 1949. Captained a Lancashire Amateur XI.

OLLERTON, CHARLES: 1928-30. Goalkeeper 28 (6 cup) apps. Former PNE Reserves team goalkeeper who joined in May, 1928.

ORMEROD, LEWIS: 1920-22. Inside-right 13 (3 cup) apps; 3 goals. Joined in September, 1920, and moved to Burnley in November, 1920.

ORMROD, KEN: A former secretary of the club who gave a lot to the Morecambe cause before retiring through ill health in May, 1991.
A big fan of Albert Dainty, Ken followed him to Christie Park after he joined the Shrimps from Lancaster City. Ken played as a goalkeeper for Skerton School and Lancaster City schoolboys before playing for Skerton Old Boys and Hest Bank in the North Lancashire League. He took over as secretary in June, 1972 and was a popular member of the Shrimps' backroom staff. He received the Visitor 'Local Hero' award in 1992 and was presented with the Lancashire Football Association long service award by LFA secretary Jim Kenyon in May, 1994. He was the man behind the publishing of the comprehensive book on Morecambe Football Club 'Potted Shrimps' which sold out.

Brian Healy (right) v Farnborough Town 1998

The light at the end of the tunnel

Morecambe v Dagenham, 2003/04

OSBORNE, PAUL: 2003-04. Midfield 6+2 (3+1 cup) apps; 1 cup goal. Youngster who progressed through the juniors and reserves team into the first team. Won a Lancashire Cup winners medal in 2003-04 after playing in both legs of the final against Accrington Stanley.

OSWESTRY TOWN: First met in the NPL at the Victoria Ground on March 11, 1980, drawing 0-0.

OTTLEY: 1938-40. Inside-right 39 (5 cup) apps; 12 goals. Joined in September, 1938.

OVAL: Home of Caernarfon Town with the first visit being on November 9, 1982 in the NPL League Cup 1st Rd, 1st leg, drawing 2-2. Att: 116. Thornton and Dean (own goal) scored for Morecambe.

OXFORD UTD: Met the Us at their former home the Manor Ground in the FA Cup 1st Rd on October 30, 1999, losing 3-2.

OXLEY, CYRIL: 1930-31. Outside-right 38 (5 cup) apps; 21 (3 cup) goals. Cyril started his career with Chesterfield making 31 appearances and scoring four goals before a £2,000 move to Liverpool in 1925. Made 31 appearances and scored six goals at Anfield before returning to Chesterfield. Later played for Southend and Kettering Town before joining Morecambe in August, 1930. Returned to Southend 1931-32 and Mansfield Town. Played cricket for Morecambe in 1930. Born in Whitwell on May 2, 1904, he died in 1984.

P

PADIHAM: Met the Storks in the Lancashire Combination in the 1961-62 season, winning 2-0 at the Arbories on November 11, 1961. Won the return game 8-0 at Christie Park on March 31.

PALMER, R: 1933-34. Outside-left 19 (1 cup) apps; 6 goals. Lancaster-born player who joined in August, 1933.

PARILLON, OLLIE: 1991-95. Defender 93+14 (42+6 cup) apps; 4 (1 cup) goals. Ex-Leyland Motors and Horwich RMI player who joined in June 1991. Proved to be an assured defender who was a big crowd favourite, winning the player of the year award in 1991-92. Moved to Barrow in November, 1994, in exchange for Ashley Hoskins and later played for Accrington Stanley. President's Cup winner in 1991-92.

PARK, BRYAN: 1958-61. Right-back/Centre-half 78 (27 cup) apps; 3 goals. Former Blackpool and Wolves defender who had 11 seasons with Netherfield between 1948-58 before joining in August, 1958, at the age of 32. Became Morecambe's trainer for seven seasons before returning to Netherfield as coach in 1968. Became Netherfield's manager in April, 1971, but was sacked in January, 1972.

PARK AVENUE: Former home of the now defunct Bradford Park Avenue. First visit was on October 31, 1970, in the NPL. With the recent death of the club's chairman many thought this could be Bradford's final match and an enthusiastic gate of 2,416 watched an inspired home team win 4-0.

PARK ROAD: Former home of St Helens Town. First visit was on August 18, 1951, with a 3-1 defeat in the Combination League.

PARK VIEW ROAD GROUND: Home of Welling Utd which the home club often referred to as the San Siro Stadium, because of a local sponsor certainly not because of the grandeur of the ground! First visit was in the Conference on March 16, 1966, with Welling winning 1-0. Att: 501.

PARKER, DAVID: 1963-64. Goalkeeper 11 apps. Joined in December, 1963, and moved to Southport in July, 1964. Played a game for Morecambe reserves in December, 1967.

PARKER, GEORGE: 1920-21. Centre-forward 2 (2 cup) apps; 1 cup goal and 1922-23 Inside-left 8 apps. Joined in September, 1920. Moved to Leyland Celtic but returned in March, 1923.

PARKER, PHIL: 1990-91. Midfield 18+2 (5+1 cup) apps; 2 goals. Came on loan from Stockport County from October, 1990, to March, 1991. Later played at Runcorn.

PARKER, ROBERT: 1928-32 and 1933-34. Full-back 96 (12 cup) apps; 2 goals. Former Barrow player who joined in September, 1928, and was a regular before moving to Everton in September, 1932. Returned to Morecambe in September, 1933. Later moved to Chester and Leyland Motors.

PARKINSON, HARRY: 1931-33. Inside-forward/Outside-left 23 apps; 3 goals. Experienced player who had turned out for Altrincham, Oldham Athletic, Macclesfield Town Brentford, Hazel Grove, Lostock Hall and Lytham before signing in December, 1931. Rejoined Lytham 1933-34.

PARKINSON, JOHN: 1977-78. Defender 11 apps. Former PNE junior who signed in November, 1977, from Netherfield. Moved in August, 1978, to work in Newcastle.

PARKINSON CUP: Played 1 tie in this North Lancashire League cup in 1940-41, losing away to King's Own in Rd 2 on February 15, 1941.

PARKSIDE ROAD: Home of Netherfield (now Kendal Town). First visit was on April 13, 1940, for a North Lancashire League game, drawing 2-2.

PARRY, MICK: 1976-82. Forward 215+1 (53 cup) apps; 50 (8 cup) goals. Kendal-born striker who became Morecambe's record signing when he moved from Netherfield for £500 in April, 1976. A good all round player who had a great workrate he was the club's player of the season in 1980-81. Later moved to Workington and Southport before spending 1983-88 at former club Netherfield. Returned to play for Morecambe reserves in the 1988-89 season.

PARRY, STEVE: 1988-89 and 1989-90. Forward 15+2 (14 cup) apps; 6 (3 cup) goals. Rossendale-born striker who had two spells at Accrington Stanley (1981-85 and 1985-88) where he was twice voted player of the year. Joined Morecambe in June, 1988, but left to join Darwen in March, 1989. Returned to play in two pre-season games in August, 1989, but moved to Rossendale Utd. Later played for Lytham St Annes and managed Haslingden and Clitheroe.

PARTON, JAMES: 1930-31. Left-half/Centre-forward 25 (5 cup) apps; 5 goals. Ex-Barrow player who made 45 apps for his home town club before moving to Rochdale and Lancaster Town. Joined in August 1990. Born in Barrow on December 3, 1902, he died in 1981.

PATTON, SANDY: 1932-33. Inside-right 20 (4 cup) apps; 8 (1 cup) goals. Belfast-born player who made 57 apps for Barrow between 1927-30, scoring 10 goals. Joined from Ards in December, 1932. Left to become Barrow's assistant trainer in September, 1933.

PAWSEY, CHARLIE: 1988-89. Defender 13 (8+1 cup) apps; 2 (5 cup) goals. Joined in July, 1988, from Stalybridge Celtic. Other clubs included Irlam Town, Hyde Utd, Horwich RMI, Northwich Victoria and Chorley where he was part of the team that won the NPL title in 1987-88. Moved to Chorley in 1988-89 and later played for Sutton Utd.

PEARSON, DAVE: 1971-76. Full-back 152 (70 cup) apps; 5 goals. One of the players who helped the club lift the FA Trophy at Wembley, Dave was described as *"A cultured and unflappable full-back, a consistent performer who seldom misses the opportunity to link with the forwards."* Dave, real name Aubrey, began his career at Everton before signing for Southport in August, 1967, where he went on to make 91+2 appearances. Had three games on trial at Rochdale before joining Morecambe in July, 1971. Was released in April, 1976, and later played for South Liverpool, Chorley, Burscough and Southport. As a youngster won five Wales Schoolboy caps and also won one Wales Under 23 cap in January, 1970. FA Trophy winner in 1973-74.

PEARSON, GEORGE/GEOFFREY: 1945/46, 1946/47 and 1948/50. Inside-right/Centre-forward 19 (3 cup) apps; 12 (1 cup) goals. Played one game at outside-right in October, 1945, returned in September, 1946 and August, 1948. Played locally for Carnforth Rangers.

PEEL: 1920-22. Right-half 19 (2 cup) apps. Ex-Darwen player who was involved in Morecambe's first game in August, 1920, and became the first player to be sent off when he was dismissed on November 6, 1920, against Dick Kerr's.

PEEL PARK: Former home of Accrington Stanley with the first visit being on February 12, 1921, in a 6-1 defeat. Att: 8,000.

PENRITH: Met the Blues several times in the FA Cup. The first occasion was on September 26, 1953 at Penrith in the 1st Qualifying Rd, winning 6-1.

PERKINS, DAVID: 2000-04. Defender/Midfield 79+6 (25+3 cup) apps. Born in Morecambe on June 21, 1982, David joined the club's academy scheme after being a junior with Blackburn Rovers and Crewe Alexandra. Played for the Reserves and travelled to Trinidad & Tobago with the British Colleges XI. Also captained the English Colleges Under 18s in Italy in 2001. Capped by the England semi-professional team. Was Morecambe's player of the year 2003/04. Collected a Lancashire Cup winner's medal in the same season.

PERKINS, RUSS: 1972-73 and 1974-75. Forward 53 (23 cup) apps; 30 (13 cup) goals. One of the former Morecambe players who went on to manage Lancaster City, Russ had two spells at Christie Park.
A schoolteacher who played for British Colleges, Russ spent his early career at Macclesfield Town and Northwich Victoria before being signed by Dave Roberts in 1972. A striker with a big reputation Russ did not have the best of starts to his Morecambe career. After making his debut in a 4-3 win over Goole Town on August 19, 1972, it took him nine games to score for the Shrimps. It was worth waiting for though by all accounts – an injury time free-kick which gave Morecambe a 1-0 victory over Wigan Athletic. He went on to be top scorer that season with 22 goals but then was forced to move down south with his job as a schoolteacher and played for Walton & Hersham – a season that included a 4-0 FA Cup first round victory over Brian Clough's Brighton & Hove Albion.

Unfortunately – for Russ anyway – the Shrimps went on to win the FA Trophy at Wembley that season.

He was back at the club for the 1974-75 season and managed to score 21 goals in 28 games before his work again took him down south. At the end of the season he was transferred to Northwich Victoria for a small fee. After playing he went on to manage South Liverpool, Witton Albion, Southport, Skelmersdale United, Lancaster City and Burscough. His son Steve has been back to Christie Park with Stevenage, Gravesend and Woking and was a member of the Stevenage team that took Newcastle United to an FA Cup 3rd Rd replay in 1997.

PLAYER OF THE SEASON

1975-76: Peter McLachlan.
1976-77: Geoff Street.
1978-79: Graham Byram.
1979-80: Mick Foster.
1980-81: Mick Parry.
1981-82: Larry Milligan.
1982-83: John McKenna.
1983-84: Mark Baron.
1984-85: Keith Galley.
1985-86: Keith Galley.
1986-87: Vaughan Williams.
1987-88: Dave Lancaster.
1988-89: Graham Jones.
1989-90: Ian Cain.

1990-91: John Coleman.
1991-92: Ollie Parillon.
1992-93: John Coleman.
1993-94: Jim McCluskie.
1994-95: Paul Burns.
1995-96: Ian Monk.
1996-97: Michael Knowles.
1997-98: Kenny Mayers.
1998-99: Stewart Drummond.
1999-2000: Stewart Drummond.
2000-01: Andy Fensome.
2001-02: Robbie Talbot.
2002-03: Craig Mawson.
2003-04: David Perkins.

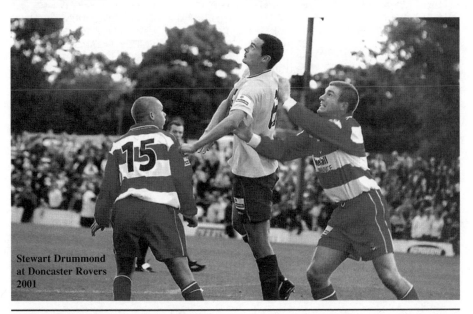

Stewart Drummond at Doncaster Rovers 2001

PLAYERS WITH LESS THAN 10 LEAGUE APPEARANCES;

ABBOTT, BILLY: 2002/03
AITCHISON, IAN: 1979/80.
ALCOCK, GEORGE L. 1933-34.
ALDREN, JACK:1938-39 & 1945-46.
ALFORD, CARL: 1990-91.
ALLINGTON: 1921-22.
ALMOND: 1929-30.
ALTY, STEPHEN: 2000-01.
ANDERSON. 1920-21.
ANDERSON. 1934-35.
ANDERSON. 1939-40
ANGUS, JACKIE:1946-47 &1951-52.
L'ANSON, JIM: 1939-40.
ARMISTEAD, BRIAN: 1952-53.
ARTHUR, IAN: 1984-85.
ASHCROFT, RICHARD: 1960-61.
ASHCROFT, MICK: 1988-89.
ASHTON. 1939-40 & 1940-41.
ASHWORTH, FRANK. 1946-47.
ATHERTON. 1927-28.
ATKINS, ERNEST. 1923-24.
ATKINSON. 1926-27.
ATKINSON, GEORGE 1956-57
AUSTEN. 1940-41
BADGER, TOMMY. 1937-38
BAIRD. 1929-30.
BAKER, STEVE. 1988-89.
BALDWIN, JACKIE. 1960-61
BALDWIN, KEVIN. 2000-02.
BALL, LES. 1989-90
BANKS, ANDREW C. 1998-99
BARGH, E. 1934-35
BARGH. 1950-51
BARLOW, STUART, 1989-90
BARR, JOHNNY. 1954-54
BARRON. 1929-30
BARTHOLOMEW, FRANK. 1920-21
BARTHOLOMEW, REUBEN. 1920-22
BARTLETT, ARTHUR. 1933-34
BASTERFIELD. 1934-35
BATES. 1921-22
BATES. 1927-28
BATES. 1945-46
BATT. 1932-33
BATTERSBY, JOE. 1970-71
BAXTER, JAMES C. 1961-62
BAXTER, STUART. 1975-76
BEARD, GEOFF. 1967-68
BELL, ALEC. 1964-65
BELLAS. 1936-37
BENNETT, CHRIS. 1988-89

BENNETT, H. 1923-24
BENNETT, TOM. 1928-29
BENNIE, STEVE. 1974-75
BENSON, J. 1929-30
BENSON, JACK. 1939-40
BERRY, BRIAN. 1977-78
BIBBY, RICHARD. 1994-95
BILLINGTON, L. 1931-32
BIRCH, RAY. 1987-88
BIRCHALL. 1920-21
BIRNIE. 1923-24
BIRTWISTLE, JIMMY. 1927-28
BLACKBURN, CHRIS. 2003-04
BLACKWELL, ERNEST. 1930-31
BOARNE. 1920-21
BOLTON, PAUL. 1989-90
BOND, ERIC. 1950-51 & 1956-57
BONNICK. 1921-22
BOOTH. 1936-37
BORROWDALE, PETER. 1992-93
BOUSTEAD, STEVEN. 1994-95
BOWERY, JIMMY. 1953-54
BOWEY, KEITH. 1981-82
BOWKER, ROBERT 1945-46
BOWKER. 1964-65
BOWLAND, JIMMY B. 1921-22
BOYD, E. 1933-34
BRABIN, GARY. 1991-92
BRACEWELL, SYDNEY. 1938-39
BRACEWELL, TOM 1935-37 & 1945-46
BRADSHAW, DAVID. 1963-64
BRAGDEN. 1921-22
BRAITHWAITE. 1932-33
BRAYSHAW, JOHN. 1920-21
BRAYSHAW, RON. 1946-47
BRAYSHAW, R. 1930-31
BREAKELL, STEVE. 1982-83
BRENNAN, MARK. 1991-92
BRETHERTON, TOMMY. 1950-51
BRIGHT, EDDIE. 1928-29
BRITTON, IAN. 1989-90
BROAD, JIMMY. 1931-32
BROADBENT. 1927-28
BROADBENT, BILLY, 1936-37
BROADLEY, H. 1921-22
BROADLEY, J. 1921-22
BROMLEY. 1932-33
BROOKBANK, J A.
BROOKFIELD, KEITH. 1962-63
BROWELL, TOMMY. 1933-34
BROWN, CLARENCE. 1932-33

BROWN, DARREN. 1987-88
BROWN, GORDON. 1963-64
BROWN, KEN. 1940-1941
BROWN, NORMAN. 1980-81
BROWN, S. 1937-38
BUCHAN. 1931-32
BUCKLEY, GARY. 1988-89
BUDDEN, JOHN. 1989-90
BULLEN. 1933-34
BURKE, ROBERT. 1955-56
BURNETT, BILLY. 1952-53
BURROWS, BILL. 1920-21 & 1925-30
BURTON, NIGEL. 1979-80
BUSBY. 1928-29
BUSS. 1945-46
BUTLER, GEORGE. 1954-55
BUTLER, JOHN (JAMIE). 1988-89
BUTTERWORTH, JACKIE. 1950-51
BUTTERWORTH, LEE. 1994-95
BYROM, H. 1923-24
CALVER, REGINALD J. 1967-68
CAMPBELL. 1946-47
CANNON. 1945-46
CANTRILL. 1938-39
CAPSTICK. 1938-39
CARBERRY, JIMMY. 1993-94
CARLIN. 1925-26
CARNEY. 1935-37
CARROLL, ALBERT 1938-40
CARRUTHERS, JOHN. 1950-51
CARSWELL, FRED. 1931-32
CARTER, J ALAN. 1938-39
CARTER, JIMMY. 1922-23
CARTNER. 1931-32
CASSON. 1933-34
CASSON, STEPHEN 1984-85
CHAPEL. 1938-39
CHATTERTON. 1921-22
CHESTER, DAVID. 1967-68
CHRISTIE, DAVID. 1927-28
CLARKE, DUNCAN. 1979-80
CLARKE, WILLIAM A. 1928-29
CLAYTON, F. 1938-39
CLAYTON, ROLAND. 1931-32
CLIFFORD. 1931-32
CLUTTERBUCK.1939-40
COATES. 1952-53
COBB, S W. 1933-34 & 1938-39
COLEMAN, GORDON. 1984-85
COLLINS. 1939-40

COLLINS, DAVID. 1989-90
COLLINS, GARY. 1989-90
CONNELL. 1958-59
COOKE, JOHN. 1973-74
COOKSON. 1933-34
COOKSON, IAN. 1978-79
COOPER, W H. 1931-33
COPE, A. 1921-22
COPE, WILLIAM. 1927-28
COPELAND, LEE. 1990-91
CORNTHWAITE, H. 1933-34
COTTAM. 1931-32
COTTAM. 1953-54
COWAN, JACK. 1933-34
COWAN, JIMMY1951-52 & 1956-57
COWLEY, ROB. 1992-94
COWLING, JOSEPH. 1922-23
COWPERTHWAITE, TERRY. 1984-85 & 1986-87
COX. 1945-46
CROOK . 1937-38
CUDSWORTH, NIGEL. 1983-84
CUMMINGS, TOMMY. 1950-51
CURLEY, STEVE. 1990-91
CURWEN, ALAN. 1980-81
CUTTING, JOHN A. 1955-56
DANSON, DICKIE. 1957-58
DANSON, HARVEY. 1984-85
DARGON, JAMES. 1930-31
DAVIDSON. 1931-32
DAVIDSON, DAVID. 1959-60
DAVIES. 1939-40
DAVIES, ANTHONY. 1932-33
DAVIES, GORDON. 1958-59
DAVIES, ROBERT. 1926-27
DAVIES, SYD 1928-29
DAVIES, WILLIAM. 1954-56
DAVIS. 1945-46
DEAN, ALBERT 1928-29
DELL. 1931-32
DEVANEY, PHIL. 1988-89
DEVINE, PETER. 1982-83
DEWHURST, JACK.1921-22
DIAMOND, BARRY. 1987-88
DICKINSON. 1921-22
DICKINSON. 1931-32
DICKINSON, ROBERT. 1973-74
DIGGLE, STUART. 1989-90
DIXON, STEVE. 1987-88
DOCKER, ARTHUR. 1935-36
DODGSON, LEE. 2002-04
DOUTHWAITE, ROBERT. 1946-50

DOWE, JULIAN. 2000-01
DOWNHAM, JIMMY. 1949-50
DRAPER. 1931-32
DRINKWATER, ROY. 1975-76
DRISCOLL, WILLIAM. 1953-54
DUFFY. 1945-46
DUCKSBURY, J. 1920-21
DUNBAVIN, IAN. 2003-2004
DUNDERDALE, S. 1933-34
DYER. 1945-46
EAKINS, DOUGLAS. 1949-50
EASTHAM. 1920-21
EAVES, DAVID. 1993-94
EAVES, ERNEST. 1952-53
EDGE, DAVID JOHN. 1983-84
EDEY, CECIL. 1990-91
ELKIN, BILLY. 1920-22
ELLIOTT, PAUL. 1980-81
ELLIS. 1928-29
EVANS, THOMAS. 1933-34
EWING 1939-49
EYRES, DAVID: 1985-87 *(pictured)*

FAIRCLOUGH, TEDDY. 1949-50
FARRELL, PETER. 1990-91
FARRELLY, STEVE. 1990-91
FAULKNER, MIKE. 1969-71
FAWCETT, STEVE. 1979-80
FIELDS. 1929-30 & 1932-33
FINCH, ERNEST. 1922-23
FIRTH, MALCOLM. 1956-57
FISHER, FRED. 1920-21
FISHER. 1926-27
FISHER, GERRY. 1977-78
FLANAGAN, T. 1924-25
FLANNAGEN, STAN. 1955-56
FLEMING. 1937-38
FLEMING, MIKE. 1971-72
FLETCHER, ALEX. 1950-51

FLYNN, FRANCIS. 1983-84
FOLEY, PETER. 1971-72
FOLEY, STEVEN. 1995-96
FORBES, ANDY. 1986-87
FORROST. 1923-24
FOTHERGILL. 1950-51
FOX. 1962-64
FOXCROFT. 1940-41
FRANCIS, DON. 1955-56
FRETTER. 1920-21
FRYATT, C. 1934-35
GALLAGHER, JASON. 1992-93
GARDNER, STEVEN. 1990-91
GARNETT, C. 1938-39
GASKELL, A. 1920-21
GASKELL, BILLY. 1967-69
GATES, RAY. 1975-76
GEARING. 1933-34
GIBSON, PAUL. 1992-93
GILES, MARTYN. 2003-04
GILL, ANDY. 1994-95
GILLIBRAND, SYDNEY. 1954-55
GILMOUR, A. 1921-22
GILPIN. 1952-54
GORDON 1939-40
GORDON, DALE. 2003-04
GORE, EDDIE. 1938-39
GORST, DAVID. 1975-76
GORST, HARRY. 1922-23 & 1924-28
GORST, PAUL. 1983-88
GORST, WILLIS. 1925-26 & 1927-28
GOUGH, DAVID. 1990-91
GRADWELL, BRIAN. 1954-55
GRAINGER. 1951-53
GRANT, JOHN. 1982-83
GRASS (JUNIOR). 1939-40
GRAY, GARETH. 1992-93
GRAY, LEE. 1991-92
GREEN, ANDY. 1992-93
GREENHOW, TERRY. 1989-90.
GREENWOOD, F. 1930-31
GREGOIRE, MATTHEW. 2002-04
GREGORY. 1953-54
GREGORY, RON. 1961-62 & 1964-65
GREGSON. 1928-29 & 1933-34
GREGSON. 1937-38
GROVER. 1945-46
GUFFOG. 1939-40
HADDOW, PAUL. 1998-99
HAIGH, CHARLES. 1929-30
HALBARD, WALTER. 1957-58
HALL. 1939-1940

HALL, JIMMY. 1982-83
HALLAM, TONY. 2002-2004
HAMILTON, BRIAN. 1976-77
HAMMILL, JIMMY. 1962-64.
HANSON, TREVOR. 1993-94
HARDMAN, JOHN. 1977-78
HARGREAVES, ALEX. 1931-32
HARGREAVES, J. 1924-25
HARRIS, MARTIN. 1984-85
HARRISON. 1921-22
HARRISON, HERBERT. 1947-48
HARRISON, KEVIN. 1983-85
HARRISON, WAYNE. 1987-88
HARROP. 1920-21
HARTLEBURY, KEITH. 1981-82
HARTLEY, DAVID. 1969-70
HARVEY. 1945-46
HARWOOD, CARL. 1991-92
HASTIE, HENRY. 1925-26
HAWLEY, JACK. 1947-48
HAWORTH, JOHN. 1955-56
HAY, ALEX. 2001-02
HAYDOCK. 1928-29
HAYDOCK, STEVE. 1989-90
HAYTON, KYLE. 1997-98
HEALD, ANDY. 1998-2001
HEALD, ROLAND. 1954-55
HEALY. 1945-46
HEATON, E. 1920-21
HEATON. 1945-46
HELM, STEVE. 1989-90
HERRING, MIKE. 1978-79
HESKETH, G. 1921-22
HESKETH, DAVID. 1981-82
HEWITT, HAROLD. 1945-46 & 1946-47
HICKEY, CIARAN. 1998-99
HIGHAM, KENNY 1983-84
HIGHAM, PETER. 1960-61
HIGSON. 1933-34
HILDITCH, MARK. 1994-95
HILL, STEPHEN. 2003-04
HINDLE, GEORGE. 1931-32
HINDLE, J. 1938-39
HIRST. 1926-27
HODGKINSON, DAVID. 1963-64
HODGSON, PHILIP. 1992-95
HOGAN, CHARLIE. 1953-53
HOLCROFT, PETER. 1999-2000
HOLDEN, J. 1931-32
HOLDER, GORDON. 1964-65
HOLGATE, WILLIAM. 1920-21
HOLLAND. 1945-46.

HOLLINGS, CLARRY. 1951-54
HOLMES, DENIS. 1945-46
HOLMES, DEREK. 1954-55
HOLYWELL, JIMMY. 1990-91
HOOLE, WILF. 1949-50
HORRIGAN, IAN. 1995-96
HOSKINS, ASHLEY. 1989-90
HOUGH. 1933-34
HOUGH, GARY. 1983-84
HUDDART. 1924-25
HUGHES. 1939-40
HUGHES, DARREN. 1997-98
HUGHES, J. 1932-33
HUGHES, PAUL. 1980-81
HULL, DAVID. 1977-78
HULLOCK, LAWRENCE. 1929-30
HUNT, STEVE. 1997-98
HUNTER, COLIN. 2000-01
HUNTER. 1926-27
HURST. 1940-41
HURTLEY, BILL. 1950-51
IBBOTSON, DANNY. 1986-87
INGALL. 1939-40
JACKSON, HARRY. 1952-53
JACKSON, REG. 1920-21
JAMES, LEIGHTON: 1993-94
JENKINS, MARK. 1991-92
JOHNS. 1945-46
JOHNSON. 1927-28
JOHNSON, BARRY. 1958-59
JOHNSON, LES. 1932-33
JOHNSON. 1945-46
JOHNSON, STEVE. 1993-94
JOHNSTON, BOB. 1982-83
JONES. 1935-36
JONES. 1940-41
JONES, ALAN. 1958-59
JONES, ALF. 1938-39
JONES, DAVID. 1989-90
JUMP. 195052
KANE. 1929-30
KAY. 1924-25
KAY, JAMES. 1957-58
KEDDY, J. 1923-24
KEEN, PHILIP. 1975-76
KEEN, W. 1922-23
KEIGHAN. 1933-34
KEIGHLEY, JOHN. 1983-84
KELLETT. 1920-21
KELLETT, PETER. 1952-53
KELLY, DAVID. 1986-87
KELLY, TOMMY. 1981-82

KENNEDY, ALAN. 1990-91
KENNEDY, DEAN. 1983-85
KENYON, STEVE. 1986-87
KERR. 1934-35
KERSHAW, RONNIE. 1965-66
KINNEAR, WAYNE. 1994-95
KIRBY. 1932-33
KIRWAN. 1948-49
KITCHEN. 1938-39
KNAPE, JOHN. 1952-53
KNIGHT, FRANK. 1947-49
KNOWLES, GARY. 1984-85
KNOX. 1964-65
LAISBY, JOHN. 1977-78
LAMBERT, MATTHEW. 1993-94
LANCASTER, J M. 1939-40.
LANCASTER, THE REV
WILLIAM JAMES. 1934-35
LANGFORD, JACKY. 1953-54
LAPPER. 1934-35
LAWTON, ALBERT. 1945-46
LEA. 1936-37
LEEMING, MALCOLM. 1983-84
LEIGH, MIKE. 1973-75
LEWIS, P. 1920-21
LEWTHWAITE, 1939-40
LINDSAY. 1957-58
LINES. 1939-40
LINTHWAITE, WILLIAM. 1922-23
LITTLE, JIMMY. 1929-30
LIVESEY, JACK. 1920-21
LIVINGSTONE, ANDY. 1994-95
LIVINGSTONE, RICHARD. 1995-96
LOMAX, GOFFREY. 1989-90
LOMAX, K. 1945-46
LONRIGG, SIMON. 1989-90
LOWE/LAW, D. 1930-32
LOWE, DAVID. 1997-98
LOWE, KENNY. 1987-88
LOWTHER, STUART. 1979-80
LUND, J W. 1931-32 & 1934-35
LYNN, JIMMY. 1969-70
MCBRIDE, PETER. 1967-68
MCCARTHY, DARRYL. 1988-89
MCCARTHY, T. 1922-23
MCCLUGGAGE, ANDY. 1932-33
MCFADDEN. 1930-31
MCFADYEN. 1945-46
MCFALL, ALAN. 1975-76
MCGUIGAN, FRANK. 1962-62
MCHALE. 1957-58
MCLOUGHLIN, GEORGE. 1931-32

MCNALLY, PHIL. 1990-91.
MCNIVEN, DAVID. 1985-86
MCQUEEN, DEREK. 1972-74
MCWHINNIE. 1928-29
MAHON, KEVIN. 1981-82
MAKHZANI. 1952-53
MANSLEY. 1954-55
MARSDEN. 1922-23
MARSDEN, PAUL. 1988-89
MARSDEN, PHIL. 1987-88
MARSHALL. 1955-56
MARTIN. 1930-31
MAUDESLEY. 1949-50
MAY, NICK. 1952-53
MAYO, PETER. 1975-76
MAYOR, COLIN. 1929-30 & 1932-33
MAYOR, JIM. 1940-41
MEADOWS, JOHN. 1938-39, 1954-55 & 1957-58
MEDDICK, GEORDIE. 1951-52
MELLISH, STUART. 1991-92
METCALF, BARRY. 1980-81
MIDDLEBROOK, GARY. 1972-74
MIDDLESBROUGH. 1945-46
MILLER. 1931-32
MITCHELL, NEIL. 1997-98
MOFFATT, GREG. 1985-86
MOORBY, CLIVE. 1980-81
MOORE, PAUL. 1990-91
MOORES, PHILIP. 1988-89
MORGAN, ALAN. 2002-03
MORRIS. 1932-33
MORRIS, BOB. 1921-22
MORRIS. 1945-46
MORRISON. 1945-46
MORTON, NEIL. 1998-2000
MOTT, ASHLEY. 1983-84
MULDOON, JOHN. 1987-88
MULLEN, STEVE. 1982-83
MURPHY, ANDY. 1986-87
MURPHY, IAN. 1991-92
MURRAY. 1933-34
MURRAY, DEREK. 1979-80
MURRAYFIELD, J. 1947-48
MYERS. 1953-54
MYERSCOUGH, R. 1923-24
NAYLOR, FRANK. 1929-30
NECK. 1929-30
NEIL, MELVILLE. 1961-62
NEWBOULT, JACK. 1920-21
NEWMAN, BRIAN. 1982-83
NICHOLLS, PETER. 1988-89

NICHOLS, HARRY. 1930-31
NICHOLSON, 1929-30
NICHOLSON, GRAHAM. 1981-82
NICHOLSON, PAUL. 1980-81
NISBET. 1934-35
NOBLETT, JIMMY. 1922-24
NOBLETT, MIKE. 1983-85
NOON. 1929-30
NORRIS. 1934-35
NORRIS. 1945-46
NUTTALL. 1938-39
NUTTALL MARTIN. 1985-86
O'BRIEN, C. 1920-21
O'CONNOR, PATRICK. 1960-61
O'KEEFE, LEE. 1989-90
OLDRIEVE, PAUL. 1980-81
OLLERTON, ADRIAN. 1976-77
O'NEILL, ALAN. 1969-70
OWENS. 1922-23
OWENS. 1945-46
OWERS, NORMAN. 1978-79
OXLEY, STUART. 1956-57
PALLETT, JOHN. 1963-64
PALMER, ALAN. 1957-58
PARKER, CARL. 1993-94
PARKER, JIM. 1955-57
PARKER. 1950-51
PARKIN, GEORGE. 1930-31
PARKINSON. 1920-21
PARKINSON. 1925-26
PARKINSON, STEVE. 1972-76
PARKINSON, STUART. 1997-98
PARR. 1922-23
PARRY. 1945-46
PEARCE. 1921-22
PEARSON. 1933-34
PEARSON, S. 1946/47
PENNELL, DAVE. 1991-92
PETERS, GRAHAM. 1987-88 & 1989-90
PETLEY. 1945-46
PHILLIPS. 1932-33
PICKERING. 1930-31
PICKLEY. 1929-30
PILKINGTON. 1945-46
POINTON, RAY. 1982-83
PORTER, ALEX. 2001-02
PORTER, KEITH. 1988-89
POTTS, COLIN. 2000-01
POWELL, RICHARD. 1989-90
PRATT, A.S. 1922-23
PRATT, JOHN. 1935-36
PRESTON. 1933-34

PRICE, CHRIS. 2000-01
PRICE, JOHN. 1967-68
PRICKETT, JACKIE. 1954-55 & 1956-57
PRIESTLEY, DEREK. 1957-58
PROUDFOOT. 1921-22
PYE, RON. 1954-55
QUICK, ERIC. 1945-47
RAWLINSON, THOMAS. 1927-28
RAWLINSON. 1946-47
REDSHAW, RAY. 1988-89
REID. 1922-23
REID, DAVID. 1962-63
REYNOLDS. 1920-21
REYNOLDS. 1945-46
RICHARDS, A. 1921-22
RICHARDSON, F. 1930-31
RICHARDSON, I. 1921-24
RICKETTS, PAUL. 1989-90
RIDING, ALAN. 1950-51
ROBERTS. 1945-46
ROBERTS, DONALD. 1959-60
ROBINSON, ALBERT. 1953-54
ROBINSON, CRAIG. 2001-02
ROBINSON, DAVID. 1975-76
ROBINSON, GARY. 1984-85
ROBSON, M. 1934-35
RODWAY, BILLY. 1991-92
ROE, IAN. 1988-92
ROLLINSON. 1946-47
ROSE, J. 1921-22
ROSE, NEIL. 1976-77
ROWE, GEORGE. 1920-21
SANDERSON, ALEC. 1922-23
SANDIFORD, IAN. 1971-72
SANG, RUSSELL. 1988-89
SCHOLES, BOB. 1928-29
SEFTON. 1940-41
SHANNON, DAVE. 1983-84
SHARPLES. 1938-39
SHARRETT, HARRY. 1963-64
SHAW. 1948-49
SHAW, T. 1933-34
SHEARS, BERT. 1933-34
SHENTON. 1939-1940
SHIELDS, VIC.1979-80
SHIRLEY, ALEXANDER. 1952-53.
SHUTTLEWORTH, JOHN. 1953-55
SIDDLE, C. 1940-41
SILCOCK, STEVE. 1982-83
SIMMS, SELDON. 1985-87
SIMPSON. 1933-34
SIMPSON, GARETH. 2002-03

SIMPSON, WALTER. 1922-24
SKINNER, PAUL. 1975-78
SKOCZEN. 1945-46
SLATER. 1951-52
SLATTERY, JOSEPH W. 1954-55
SLOAN, TED. 1952-53
SMITH, ALEX. 1956-58
SMITH, DUNCAN. 1971-72
SMITH, E. 1933-34
SMITH, H. 1921-22
SMITH, JIMMY. 1938-39
SMITH. 1927-28
SMITH. 1933-34
SMITH. 1945-46
SMITHSON. 1931-32
SNOOKES, ERIC. 1989-90
SOUTHERN, MICKY. 1987-88
SOWDEN, PADDY. 1962-63.
SPEIGHT. 1929-30
SPENCER, H. 1933-34
STALKER, J. 1931-32
STALKER, W. 1931-32. 1931-32
STANDING, T. 1920-21
STANFORD, CARL 2001-02
STANLEY, CHRIS. 1989-90
STANTON, BRIAN. 1986-87
STAVELEY. 1945-46
STEPHENSON, A. 1939-40
STEVENS, IAN. 1983-84
STEVENSON, LIONEL. 1951-52
STEVENSON, T. 1920-22
STEWART, JAMES. 1934-35
STONE, DAVID. 1990-91
STRACHAN, DONALD. 1945-46
STRANGEWAY, GEORGE. 1928-29
STRONGE. 1933-34
SUMNER. 1927-28
SUNDERLAND, SEAN. 1990-91
SUTTON. 1921-22
SUTTON. 1933-34
SUTTON, BOB. 1955-56
SUTTON, ROY. 1955-56
SWAIN, JIMMY. 1938-40
SWAIN, SYDNEY. 1954-55
SWAIN, T. 1920-21
SWANNICK, DAVID. 1997-2001
SWITHENBANK, ARTHUR. 1932-33
TAGGART, BOB. 1946-47
TAYLOR. 1924-25
TAYLOR. 1954-55
TAYLOR, ANDY. 1993-95
TAYLOR, DAVID. 1987-88
TAYLOR, PERRY. 2001-03

TAYLOR, SAMMY. 1965-66
TEASDALE. 1945-46
THOMPSON, C. 1965-66
THOMPSON, JOHN. 1933-34
THOMPSON, JIM: 1981-82
THOMSON. 1930-31
THOMSON, BRIAN. 1976-77
THOMSON, PETER. 2001-02
THORNHILL, JACK. 1931-32
THORNTON, CHARLIE. 1922-23
& 1928-29
THORNTON, JOHN. 1946-47 &
1948-49
THORNTON. 1940-41
TIMMS. 1948-49
TOWERS. 1937-39
TOWNSLEY. 1940-41
TRICKETT, RICHARD. 1933-34
TROUGHTON, RAY. 1951-52
TRUEBLOOD. 1952-53
TYRRELL, ALAN. 1988-89
TYSON, 1938-39
TYSON, JACK. 1958-59
UDALL, JAMIE. 1996-97
VALENTINE, TONY. 1986-87
VARLEY. 1946-47
VASCOE, ERIC. 1981-82
VENNAND. 1945-46
VENTRE, FRANNY. 1992-93
VERDIN, GEORGE. 1934-35
WADE. LOFTY. 1927-28
WAKEFIELD, W. 1931-32
WALKER. 1939-1940
WALKER, MARK. 1964-65
WALLACE, BRIAN. 1952-53
WALLBANK, JOHN. 1983-84
WALLER, MICKY. 1998-99
WALMSLEY. 1927-28
WALMSLEY. 1938-39
WALSH. 1920-21
WALSH, ANDY. 1989-90
WALSH, GRAHAM. 1981-82
WALSH, JOHN. 1976-77
WALTERS. 1920-21
WARBURTON, FRED (Jun). 1939-40
WARBURTON, FRED (Sen). 1937-38
WARBURTON, JAMES 1945-47
WARD, FRANK. 1931-32
WARD, PETER. 1999-2000
WARNE. 1951-52
WARNER, ANDY. 1976-77
WEBB. 1946-47

WEBB, CHARLIE. 1923.24
WELSH, PAUL. 1989-90.
WEST, THOMAS. 1950-51
WESTON, HAROLD. 1926-27
WESTON, MIKE. 1983-84
WHARTON, ANDY. 1985-86
WHITE. 1957-58
WHITTINGHAM, KEVIN. 1973-74
WILCOCK, IAN. 2001-02
WILCOCK, STUART. 1988-89
WILCOCK, W. 1930-31 & 1934-35
WILKES, STEPHEN. 1989-90
WILKINSON, GEORGE. 1934-35
WILKINSON, H. 1939-40.
WILKINSON, JACK. 1957-59
WILKINSON, BILL. 1929-30 & 1931-32
WILLACY, JIMMY. 1920-21
WILLIAMS, DAMIEN. 1986-88
WILLIAMS, DAVID. 1923-24
WILLIAMS, GARY. 1989-90
WILLIAMS, JIM. 1987-88
WILLIAMS, N. 1924-25
WILLIAMS, PHILIP. 1987-88
WILLIAMSON. 1931-32
WILLINGHAM, ANDY. 1988-89
WILSON, ARTHUR. 1929-31 &
1933-34
WILSON. 1945-46
WILSON, D. 1961-62
WILSON, J (JUICY). 1922-23
WILSON, KEN. 1982-83
WILSON, MAURICE 1939-40
WILSON, M. 1940-41
WILSON, PHIL. 1988-89
WINGATE, ANDY. 1950-51
WOJCIECHOWICZ, JOE. 1973-74
& 1987-88
WOLSTENHOLME, J. 1931-32
WOLVINE, MARTIN. 1983-84
WOODHOUSE, J. 1923-24
WOODHOUSE. 1945-46
WOODRUFF. 1955-56
WOODS, J. 1923-24
WOODWARD, MALCOLM. 1968-69
WOOLMER. 1934-35 & 1945-46
WORRALL, GARY. 1988-89
WRIGHT. 1937-38
WRIGHT, ANDY. 2000-01
WRIGHT, TERRY. 1964-65
WRIGHT, BILLY. 1988-89
WYNN, DAVID. 1985-86
YATES, ALAN. 1945-46

POCKETT, BILL: 1953-62. Full-back/Half-back 115 (30 cup) apps; 1 goal. A great servant for the club after joining in December, 1953. Amateur player who represented the Lancashire FA in 1957-58 and 1960-61. Had a short spell at Felixstowe before returning to Morecambe in December, 1962.

PORT VALE: Met the Valiants in a pre-season friendly on July 28, 1989 at Christie Park with a Glover own goal giving Morecambe a 1-0 win.

PORTER, DENNIS: 1953-54. Inside-left 17 (2 cup) apps; 1 goal. Joined in September, 1953 and later played for Chorley, Lancaster City and Netherfield. Played cricket for Leyland Motors.

PORTER, J F: 1947-50. Goalkeeper 35 (3 cup) apps. Former PNE and Wigan Athletic keeper who joined in August, 1947.

PORTER, STEVE: 1966-70 and 1971-72. Midfield 131+4 (55+2 cup) apps; 11 (5 cup) goals. A regular member of the Lancashire Combination winning side of 1967-68 Charnock Richard-born Steve was signed from PNE by Ken Waterhouse in the summer of 1966. He made his debut as a substitute against Workington on August 6 but made a somewhat inauspicious start as he had to leave the field with a cut knee. His first team appearances were limited during the season but he obviously made an impact with supporters. The Visitor reported that after a 3-0 reserve team win over Lytham: *"Left-half Steve Porter was mobbed by small boys at the end of the game, he had tackled like a tank and impressed with forceful play."* His full debut came on October 29 in a 2-0 win over Great Harwood but didn't become a first team regular until the 1967-68 season where he starred in the Lancashire Senior Cup victory over Burnley and the Combination Cup triumph over Fleetwood. The next season saw him gain another medal with the Lancashire Junior Cup triumph over Great Harwood on April 23, 1969. A disagreement over his contract saw Steve move to Altrincham for a three figure fee but after a spell at Netherfield he was soon back at Christie Park and after being re-signed made his first appearance in a 1-1 draw with Stafford Rangers on November 20, 1971. His last game was on April 27, 1972, in a 1-2 home defeat by Matlock Town. The Shrimps wanted to retain his services but he moved on to play for clubs such as Leyland Motors and Charnock Richard. Lancashire Combination League winner in 1967-68. Combination Cup winner in 1966-67 and 1967-68. Lancashire Senior Cup winner in 1967-68. Lancashire Cup winner in 1968-69.

PORTLAND PARK: Home of Ashington. Just one visit on March 15, 1969, in the NPL, winning 2-0. Att: 856.

PORTMAN ROAD: Home of Ipswich Town where Morecambe lost 4-0 in the FA Cup 3rd Rd on January 4, 2003.

PORTSMOUTH ROVERS: The team from Portsmouth, a village on the Lancashire/Yorkshire border who Morecambe met in the Preliminary Rd of the FA Cup at home on September 22, 1923, winning 3-0. Att: 2,000.

POSKETT, MALCOLM: 1988-89. Forward 35 (13 cup) apps; 13 (4 cup) goals. Experienced Football League striker who impressed after signing from Carlisle in September, 1988. Began his career with Middlesbrough before moving to Hartlepool Utd who let him go. Realised they made a mistake when he scored 51 goals in a short spell at Whitby Town and signed him back again for £25 in November 1976. Proved to be a good bit of business as he scored 20 goals in 50+1 games and moved to Brighton for £60,000 in February, 1978. Scored 16 goals in 33+12 appearances and was on the move again, this time in a £110,000 deal that took him to Watford in January, 1980. Scored 17 goals in 57+6 appearances and joined Carlisle for the first time for £25,000 in August, 1982, and scored 40 goals in 108+2 appearances before being surprisingly allowed to leave on a free transfer to join Darlington. Had loan spells at Hartlepool and Stockport County before once again joining Carlisle and scoring another 20 goals for them in 67+9 appearances. After a good season for Morecambe joined Workington and also played for Cleator Moor.

POST WAR PLAYERS who have progressed to the Football League:
Stuart Baxter (ex PNE) returned to league football at Stockport County 1975/76.
Stuart Barlow (a game on loan at Morecambe 89/90) from Everton. Later moved to Oldham Athletic for £500,000.
Fred Blondell to Bury 1949/50.
Gary Brabin (played pre-season cup game in 1991/92 while on trial). Later played for Doncaster Rovers, Bury, Blackpool and Hull.
Ray Charnley to Blackpool 1957/58. Moved on to PNE 1967/68, Wrexham 1968/69, Bradford PA 1969/70.
John Coates returned to Southport in 1976.
Malcolm Darling returned to league football with Bury in 1977/78.
Peter Devine played for Morecambe in 1982/83. Moved to Chorley and progressed to Blackburn Rovers and Burnley.
Stewart Drummond moved to Chester City after their promotion from the Conference in 2004.
David Eyres was a youngster at Morecambe but after being released to join Rhyl had a distinguished league career with Blackpool, Burnley, PNE and Oldham Athletic.
Keith Galley moved to Southport in 1975/76.
Steve Gardner returned to league football at Bradford City.
John Hardiker joined Stockport County for £150,000 in January 2002.
Justin Jackson *(right)* after leaving Woking in 1997, played for Notts County, Rotherham, Halifax Town and Rushden & Diamonds.

Jamie McGowan joined Dundee and later played for Falkirk, Motherwell and St Mirren.

Adriano Rigoglioso joined Doncaster in 2003-04 and helped them win the Division Three title.

Alex Russell went on to play for Rochdale, Cambridge United and Torquay.

Geoff Slack joined Stockport County for £750 in 1958.

Alan Taylor joined Rochdale in 1973 and went on to become an FA Cup hero with West Ham Utd.

Brian Thomson signed for West Ham United in 1997.

Jack Trainer joined Rochdale in August, 1982, and made seven apps before returning in October, 1982.

PREMIER INTER-LEAGUE CUP: The GMAC Cup became the Club Call Cup in 1988-89 and finally the Premier Inter-League Cup for its final season in 1990-91 when Morecambe lost 2-1 at Chorley on October 9, 1990. Att: 333.

PRENTON PARK: Home of Tranmere Rovers where the reserves have played in the Lancashire League.

PRESCOT: First met the Tigers in the Lancashire Junior Cup, winning 5-1 at home on November 10, 1924. They became Prescot Cables in 1929-30 and Prescot Town in 1964-65. Returned to being known as Prescot Cables in 1980 with their ground now being known as Valerie Park, Hope Street.

PRESIDENT'S CUP: The top sides in both divisions of the NPL played in the President's Cup from 1986-87 and Morecambe managed to win it in 1991-92 beating Stalybridge Celtic over two legs. It was the only trophy the club had ever won in the NPL.   The first game was at Christie Park on April 14, 1991, with Celtic winning 2-1. Att: 511. The 2nd leg was on April 28 and Morecambe won 2-0. Att: 713.

PRESTON, JOHN: 1967-70. Forward 19+3 (3+2 cup) apps; 2 (1 cup) goals. Former PNE player who made 35 appearances for the reserves joined in March, 1968. Released in April, 1970. Later played for Leyland Motors.

PRESTON NORTH END: Many friendlies but as yet no official first team meetings. First meeting of the first teams came in a pre-season friendly at Christie Park on August 4, 1984, which Morecambe won 3-2.

PRESTON NORTH END 'A': Met PNE's 3rd team in the Lancashire Combination form 1925-26 until 1928-29. First game was at Christie Park on November 7, 1925, with Morecambe winning 3-0.

PRESTON NORTH END RESERVES: First met in a friendly at home on February 4, 1922, winning 3-1. Att: 1,400.

PRESTWICH HEYS: First met the Manchester amateur club in a pre-season friendly on

August 1, 1970, at Christie Park, drawing 2-2. Beat them 5-0 in the Lancashire Junior Cup 1st Rd at Christie Park on November 13, 1973. Also beat them 3-1 in the same competition at Christie Park on February 6, 1975, with Webber, Street and Perkins scoring.

PROCTOR, RENNIE: 1921-23. Outside-left 26 (8 cup) apps; 2 goals. A Caton youngster who played for Lancaster Town before joining in January, 1922. A Rennie Procter also played one game in October, 1937, and came from Caton.

Q

QUAYLE, MARK: 2000-02. Centre-forward 16+4 (9+3 cup) apps; 8 (3 cup) goals. A well travelled striker whose best moment for Morecambe came when he scored the goal that beat Cambridge Utd in the FA Cup 2nd Rd on December 9, 2000. Had been a prolific goalscorer with Everton's junior teams and reserves but was released in1997. Had a year with Notts County making 2+3 appearances before having trials with Grimsby Town and Oldham Athletic. Had short spells with Grantham Town, Ilkeston Town, Altrincham and Halifax before joining Morecambe in July 2000. Joined Telford Utd on loan in September, 2001, and scored 13 goals in 22+2 appearances, before moves to Nuneaton Borough (14 goals in 29 apps), Chester (1 goal in 6+3 apps) and Scarborough. Won one England semi-pro cap v Holland 2001-02.

QUEEN OF THE SOUTH: The Doonhammers visited Christie Park for a pre-season friendly on July 19, 2003, with Morecambe winning 2-1.

QUEENS GROUND: Fleetwood's ground from 1920 until their demise in 1927-28. First visit was on Christmas Day, 1920, for a 2-2 draw.

QUEEN'S PARK: The famous Glasgow amateur club visited Christie Park for a pre-season friendly on July 23, 1999, with Morecambe winning 7-2.

QUEENSGATE: Home of Bridlington Town. First travelled there for a FA Cup 2nd Qualifying Rd tie on September 27, 1986, winning 1-0. Dave Lancaster scored.

QUIGLEY, COLIN: 1981-82. Midfield 25+2 (3 cup) apps; 1 (1 cup) goals. Ex-Tranmere Rovers, Bootle, Oswestry Town and Formby player who joined in October, 1981. Moved to Australia in 1982.

QUIGLEY, GILBERT: 1950-53. Left-back/Left-half 84 (17 cup) apps; 1 goal. Ulverston-born player who signed from Barrow who became a popular regular.

QUINN, TONY: 1983-84 and 1990-91. Forward 15+2 (5+2 cup) apps; 8 (3 cup) goals. A non-league veteran who first joined Morecambe in January, 1984, from Witton Albion after earlier spells at Everton, Wigan and playing in Finland.

Moved to HJK Helsingfors of Finland in the summer of 1984 and on his return played for a host of clubs including Marine, Southport, Caernarfon Town, Mossley, Knowsley Utd and Fleetwood Town. Joined Morecambe again in December, 1990, in an exchange deal involving Colin Russell but was soon on his travels again playing for Lancaster City, Fleetwood Town and Burscough.

R

RACECOURSE GROUND: Home of Wrexham with one visit in the LDV Vans Trophy on October 14, 2003, which ended in a 4-1 defeat. Morgan scored an own goal for the home side. Att: 1,079.

RADCLIFFE BOROUGH: First met in the Lancashire Junior Cup 1st Rd at Christie Park on January 20, 1968, winning 2-1. Att: 1,100.

RAF: Met the Royal Air Force during the war in friendlies, winning 2-0 on January 27, 1940 and losing 5-3 on March 9. In the 1940-41 season the two sides met in the North Lancashire League with a 3-3 draw away on November 23, 1940 and a 5-1 home defeat on March 29, 1941 (Morecambe's last game until the 1945-46 season.).
On October 5, 1940, Morecambe won a friendly at Christie Park 13-1 but the following week the same team lost a North Lancashire League Challenge Cup 2nd Rd tie 10-1, a result which equals the club's worst home defeat.

RAMSBOTTOM UTD: Only one meeting which came in the 1st Rd of the Lancashire Trophy at Christie Park on November 12, 2002. Morecambe won 2-0. Att: 259.

RAWLINGS, O.S: 1923-25. Outside-left 28 (10 cup) apps; 5 goals. Local player who joined in April, 1924. Lancashire Combination League winner in 1924-25.

READ, JOE: 1936-37 and 1938-39. Half-back/Outside-right 36 (8 cup) apps; 7 goals. Former Oldham Athletic player who joined for the first time in August, 1936, before moving to Darwen. Returned to Morecambe in December, 1938. Also played for Morecambe during their two seasons in the North Lancashire League.
Served with the army in Burma during WWII. Played cricket for Royton and Werneth in the 1930s and locally for Trimpell. Born in Oldham 1910, he died in Morecambe on August 18, 1989.

RECREATION GROUND: Home of Aldershot Town with the first visit being a 2-2 draw on November 29, 2003, in the Conference. Att: 2,584.

RED: Has always been Morecambe's colours. Usual strip is red shirts and white shorts although Ken Waterhouse did bring in an all red strip. Since then the club has had red shirts with white sleeves, red and black striped shirts, red and white striped shirts all with black, red or white shorts. Away shirts have seen a variety of colours including purple, yellow, white, amber, green and primrose.

RED LION GROUND: Home of the now defunct Blakenall where Morecambe suffered a shock defeat in the FA Trophy 3rd Rd on January 15, 2000.

REDHEUGH PARK: Former home of the original Gateshead and visited during the club's time in the NPL. First visit on March 22, 1969, ended in a 1-1 draw. Att: 850.

REECE REGIMENT: Met the 26th Training Regiment form Catterick Bridge in a friendly at Christie Park on March 2, 1946, losing 7-2.

REILLY, GEORGE: 1930-31. Goalkeeper 35 (5 cup) apps. Former Blackburn Rovers reserve team player who joined in August, 1930.

RESERVES: When Morecambe FC was formed in 1920/21 the reserve team entered Division One of the North Lancashire League. Five seasons were spent there finishing in 8th, 2nd, 2nd, 3rd and 3rd. The team won the Parkinson Cup in 1922/23 with a 1-0 win over Bolton-le-Sands on April 3 at Giant Axe. They also won the Infirmary Senior Cup in 1923/24 with a 2-1 win over Storeys on April 26 at Quay Meadow. Three seasons were then spent in the West Lancashire League from 1925/26 to 1927/28 before returning to the North Lancashire League again. In 1928/29 they finished fifth and went one place better in the 1929/30 campaign.
Another cup final came in the 1929/30 season but this time the side lost 3-2 to Carnforth Rangers. On the way to the final the Reserves collected a record 16-0 win over Calder Vale at Christie Park with Roland Senior scoring eight goals.
Financial difficulties caused the reserves to be scrapped from 1930/31 to 1932/33. Once up and running again there were two poor seasons in the North Lancashire League before a switch to the West Lancashire League from 1935/36 to 1937/38.
The 1935/36 season saw two greats of the game appear at Christie Park.
Ted Harper was the Blackburn Rovers A team player-coach while on March, 21, a young Tommy Lawton scored two for Burnley A in a 6-5 victory over the reserves.
Another big occasion was when the reserves drew 1-1 with Liverpool A at Anfield in front of a crowd of 6,500. Cup success came again when on April 23, 1938, the reserves beat Bolton Wanderers A 5-2 in the Richardson Cup final at Christie Park. Another financial crisis saw the reserve team scrapped again until reintroduced for the 1939/40 season though only two games were played in the North Lancashire League before war broke out with the first team taking over the reserves' fixtures in the league. The reserves started again in the 1946/47 season in the West Lancashire League, winning the league cup 3-1 against Bury A on June 4, 1947 at Christie Park. Further success came when the reserves lifted the West Lancashire League title in the 1947/48 season with a playing record of P34, W25, D6, L3, F 74, A 33, Pts 56.
They failed to make it a league and cup double however when they lost 2-0 to Hindsford at Atherton in the Richardson Cup final. The club was now getting ambitious and entered Division Two of the Lancashire Combination between 1950/51 and 1952/53 with finishes

of 15th, 17th and 21st. The league proved too strong and costly and the club withdrew to help form a new league, the North West Combination where they finished 6th, 8th, 3rd and 5th. There was one cup final along the way, a 3-2 Shield Final defeat against Windermere at Christie Park. The reserves had a longer and more fruitful spell in the Lancashire Combination from 1957/58 to 1967/68. Playing in Division Two the best season came in the 1961/62 season when they finished runners-up. A cup final was also reached with the reserves losing 1-0 to Chorley on May 7, 1963, in a replay after the first leg was drawn 0-0. A Division Two cup began in 1966/67 and Morecambe lost the final 5-1 at Oldham Athletic reserves on May 9, 1968. In 1968/69 the NPL was formed and the reserves entered Division One of the Lancashire League. Morecambe led the table for a large chunk of the season and were unbeaten until January 11, but some poor results at the end of the campaign saw them finish in second place. Six more seasons were spent in the Lancashire League until 1974/75 finishing 12th, 13th, 17th, 9th, 16th and 13th. The seasons 1975/76 until 1977/78 were spent in the Lancashire Combination with finishes of 14th, 17th and 15th. Then came another change as the club rejoined the Lancashire League until the start of the 1981/82 season when the club withdrew for financial reasons again. When the club was on a sounder financial footing the Reserves re-entered Division Two of the Lancashire League in 1983/84, winning the league title with a final record of P16, W12, D1, L3, F36, A 17. Pts 25.

The reserves were promoted to Division One for the 1984/85 season. The last few seasons have seen the reserves enjoy a string of league titles and under Jeff Udall have won the Lancashire League for the past three seasons with victories in 2001-02, 2002-03 and 2003-04. What's more the reserves has been the breeding ground for a host of current first team players including David Perkins, Garry Thompson, Nick Rogan, Garry Hunter, Michael Stringfellow and Paul Osborne.

Garry Thompson (left) in action versus Doncaster Rovers, 2000

REYNOLDS, FRANK: 1977-78. Forward 14+3 (3 cup) apps; 1 goal. Ex-Netherfield and Leyland Motors player who joined in August, 1977. Released and returned to Leyland Motors in November, 1977.

RHODES, HAROLD: 1936-37 and 1938-39. Centre-half 37 (4 cup) apps; 7 goals. Former Accrington Stanley, Lancaster Town and Nelson player who joined in September, 1936, and played one cup game. Moved to Great Harwood Town before rejoining in August 1938.

RHYL: First met the Beavers at Christie Park in the NPL on February 11, 1984, losing 1-0. Att: 200.

RICHARDSON, ANDY: 1983-85. Midfield 26+2 (10+2 cup) apps; 1 (3 cup) goals. Former Netherfield player who joined in October, 1983. Moved to Penrith and later played for Lancaster City and Barrow.

RICHARDSON, DAVID: 1992-94. Midfield 15+6 (14+3 cup) apps; 1 cup goal. Former Marine player who had a spell in Australia before joining in November, 1992. Moved to Witton Albion in April, 1994 and later played for Holywell, Connahs Quay Nomads and Marine. Played in a five-a-side world student's tournament in Parma, Italy, in 1990.

RICHARDSON, RAY: 1959-63. Left-back 118 (34 cup) apps; 2 goals. An ever present in the Lancashire Combination League winning side of 1961/62 Ray was a strong left-back who had a good turn of pace. Born in Dublin on October 6, 1940, he moved from Northern Ireland to join the ground staff at PNE but made no first team appearances. He joined Morecambe during the 1959/60 season and made his first team debut in a 3-0 win over Fleetwood on February 6, 1960.
He was then almost an ever present until he returned to Ireland at Christmas 1962. His last game was in a 1-1 home draw with Ashton United on December 22, 1962. Lancashire Combination League winner in 1961-62 and 1962-63. Lancashire Cup winner in 1961-62.

RICHMOND, MALCOLM: 1970-75. Forward 120+6 (40 cup) apps; 50 (23 cup) goals. Player who came to the area to teach in Lancaster in September, 1970. Was leading goalscorer in the 1971-72 season with 29 goals but then suffered a broken leg in the last game of the season at Ellesmere Port. Another broken leg in his only first team game during 1972-73 was a huge setback but he made a comeback in October, 1973. Scored the first goal in the FA Trophy victory at Wembley.
Was released in April, 1975, and moved to Skelmersdale Utd. Later played for Horwich RMI and Chorley. FA Trophy winner in 1973-74.

RIGBY, LES: In 1981 the club was in a financial mess after the resignation of boss Jim Thompson after just three days. It was the time for experience and the directors went for one of the best known names on the non league circuit in Les Rigby. A giant character, Les had done the rounds. As a player he made more than 700 appearances for clubs such as Wigan, Netherfield and Lancaster City. He cut his managerial teeth as player boss at Lytham before beginning his managerial career which took him to Fleetwood, Rossendale Utd, Chorley, Great Harwood and Altrincham. It took Les some time to sort out the problems he inherited and results did not go all his own way. Despite the problems, Les did restore some stability to the club but the 1983/84 season was a poor one and after Les said he was not willing to cut his side's wage bill he was sacked in January, 1984. Died on March 6, 1996, aged 61.

RIGOGLIOSO, ADRIANO: 2000-04. Midfield/Forward 83+32 (25+6 cup) apps; 19 (5 cup) goals. Former Liverpool youth team player who was a member of their FA Youth Cup winning team along with Michael Owen. Joined from Marine in July, 2000, and after a time established himself as an important member of the side. Moved to Doncaster Rovers for a fee which rose to £30,000 in November, 2003. Was a substitute for the England semi-professional side against Holland in 2002-03. Adriano helped Doncaster win promotion to Division Two, in their first season back, in the Football League in 2003-04.

RILEY, THOMAS: 1923-24. Right-back 28 (10 cup) apps. Joined in August, 1923. Moved to Lancaster Town in February, 1925.

RIVACRE PARK: Home of Vauxhall Motors and visited for a pre-season friendly on July 29, 2003, drawing 1-1.

ROBERTS, DAVE: 1972-75. Midfield 92+3 (46+3 cup) apps; 6 (3 cup) goals. The man who led Morecambe out at Wembley was manager Dave Roberts.
In 1972 the board of directors were looking for a player manager with a wealth of non-league experience and came across the man who was to make Christie Park history. A midfielder, Dave played as a junior with Liverpool before moving on to Tranmere Rovers, Wigan Athletic, Macclesfield Town, Altrincham and Rossendale United. Already the holder of an FA Trophy winner's medal gained during his spell at Macclesfield. Dave seemed to excel in the competition. Although league form throughout his three year spell was patchy, with mid-table finishes, he enjoyed great cup runs. The 1972/73 season saw the Shrimps reach the quarter finals of the FA Trophy where they lost to Wigan Athletic in a 2nd replay at Ewood Park. The first game ended 1-1 at Christie Park with a Russ Perkins goal earning a replay. The second game at Wigan ended 0-0 in front of 9,349 before Wigan won the third game 1-0 in a game watched by a crowd of 5,693. The Trophy run of 1973/74 was obviously the one that will always remain with the Morecambe fans when he was in charge of the Morecambe team that beat Dartford 2-1 at Wembley. He resigned as manager at the end of the 1974/75 season to take up a post as manager-coach of Kuwait side Kazma. FA Trophy winner in 1973-74.

ROBERTSON, TOMMY: 1932-33. Right-back/Centre-half 38 (9 cup) apps; 9 (3 cup) goals. Former Hartlepool Utd and Bury player who joined in August, 1932, and was the club captain in the 1932-33 season. Moved to Darwen in October, 1933.

ROBERTSON, WILLIE: 1956-59. Left-back 76 (29 cup) apps. Montrose-born defender who was with PNE between 1940-55 and made 52 apps. Also made 45 wartime appearances for PNE and 59 as a guest at Blackburn Rovers. Joined Southport in July, 1955, and played 28 games for them before joining Morecambe in July, 1956, where he stayed until retiring in 1959. Won three Scotland Schoolboy caps in 1937-38 and was described as *"A tough, little sandy-haired scrapper who was strong in the tackle and a tenacious defender."*

ROBINSON, RAY: 1969-70 and 1970-71. Forward 24+1 (3+1 cup) apps; 6 goals. Joined in February, 1970, after being released by PNE where he had played two first team games. Moved to Altrincham at the start of the 1970-71 season but soon returned before leaving for South Shields in November 1970.

ROCHDALE: Beat a 'Dale' side, including many future Morecambe players, 2-1 in a pre-season Marsden Lancashire Cup tie on August 3, 1996. Att: 620.

ROCHDALE RESERVES: Met in the Lancashire Combination in various spells from 1921-22 to 1954-55. The first meeting was at Spotland on April 8, 1922, with Rochdale winning 2-0.

ROCKINGHAM ROAD: Home of Kettering Town with the club's first visit being a successful one on February 27, 1974. On the way to Wembley Morecambe recorded a shock 2-1 victory over Ron Atkinson's side in a 3rd Rd replay. Att: 3,120.

RODWAY, JOE: 1920-22. Centre-half 31 apps; 1 goal. Joined in December, 1920, the son of PNE Left-Back Tommy Rodway (1903-14) later played for Dick Kerr's, Leyland Motors and Horwich RMI.

ROE, STEVE: 1988-90. Forward 22+9 (3+3 cup) apps; 7 (1 cup) goals. Ex-Lancaster City player who like brother Ian joined in August, 1988. Had trials with PNE and Glasgow Rangers before returning to Lancaster City in August, 1989. Later played for Workington, Lancaster City Reserves and Netherfield.

ROGAN, NICK: 2002-04. Forward 3+20 (6+4 cup) apps; 4 (3 cup) goals. Player who made his debut for Netherfield at the age of 16 who has show great promise since making his debut for the reserves in October, 2001. Signed a contract in July, 2002. Scorer of some spectacular goals in the 2003-04 season. Lancashire Cup winner in 2003-04.

RONSON, DEREK: 1950-53. Centre-half 16 (3 cup) apps. Joined in August, 1950. Reserve team captain 1952-53.

ROSEBERY PARK: The original name of Christie Park. A crowd of 200 saw the first game at the new ground on August 3, 1921, a trial between the Reds and the Whites.

ROSS, GEORGE: 1975-77. Full-back 48 (10 cup) apps; 1 (2 cup) goals. A former PNE favourite who made 384+2 apps for the Deepdale club, scoring 3 goals between 1958-73. During his time was a FA Cup finalist, a FA Youth Cup finalist and won the Division Three championship. Left in July, 1973, to join Southport and after a spell playing for Telford and the Washington Diplomats in America joined Morecambe in August, 1975, becoming Reserve team boss in November, 1976.

Moved to BAC Preston as manager in 1977 before joining PNE as reserve team coach until June, 1981. Was caretaker manager and manager at Southport before coaching at Sporting Preston 1992-93.

ROSS, TOMMY: 1924-27 and 1936-38. Centre-forward 95 (17 cup) apps; 97 (17 cup) goals. Perhaps the club's most consistent goalscorer Tommy scored 114 goals in 112 games during two spells, over two decades. A regular scorer in the reserves, Tommy made a stunning debut by scoring all four goals in a 4-2 win over Darwen on October 10, 1925. He scored 10 goals in his first six games for the club but was then amazingly dropped and he struggled to replace the regular centre forward Wagstaffe. When he did get his chance he took it with five goals in two games in February 1926 and most notably a hat-trick in the Lancashire Junior Cup, second replay, win over Chorley at Deepdale on April 21, 1926.

Tommy played the first three matches of the 1926/27 season but was replaced by George Grass and had to be content with a place in the reserves again until George was sold to Blackburn Rovers in April 1927.

This left Tommy free to play in the Combination Cup final against Lancaster Town and he scored one of the goals that helped the side to victory. Unhappy with the way he was being treated, Tommy moved to Lancaster for three seasons but again found it hard to maintain a first team place, despite scoring eight in seven games in the 1928/29 season and chalking up 56 goals in the West Lancashire League for the reserves. Tommy's talent was finally recognised by Fleetwood and in six seasons he scored an amazing 300 goals and was known as the *"Dixie Dean of non-league football"*. In the 1932/33 season he scored a staggering 66 goals.

Lured back to Christie Park for the 1936/37 season Tommy scored a then record 50 goals in the season with six hat-tricks in the process. A financial crisis at the club in 1938/39 saw many good players leave the club including Tommy who rejoined Fleetwood. Lancashire Cup winner in 1925-26. Combination Cup winner in 1926-27.

ROSSENDALE UTD: Morecambe's record win, 14-0, came against the East Lancashire side on September 2, 1967, in a Lancashire Combination League fixture at Christie Park. Arnold Timmins made history on the day with eight goals – a record unlikely to be beaten. The other goals came from Varcoe, Martin (2), Holding (2) and Lea. Att: 1,500.

ROSSETT PARK: The Crosby home of Marine. First visit was in the Lancashire Combination League on April 10, 1936, in a 3-1 defeat. McCormick scored for Morecambe.

ROTHERHAM UTD: Morecambe met the Millers in the FA Cup 1st Rd on November 24, 1979, at Christie Park, drawing 1-1. Att: 4,100. Rotherham won the replay 2-0 on November 27.

ROWBOTHAM, NEIL: 1988-90. Defender 38 (15 cup) apps; 1 goal. Ex-Haslingden, Clitheroe and Accrington Stanley player who joined in June, 1988. Was released in September, 1989, and joined Rossendale Utd. Later played for Horwich RMI, Great Harwood Town and Clitheroe where he was a member of the team that reached the final of the FA Vase in 1995-96.

RUFFER, CARL: Defender. Born in Chester on December 20, 1974 he started his career as a trainee at Everton between 1989-94. Joined Runcorn and made 46+13 apps, scoring one goal before a short spell at Woodley Sports. Joined Chester City in the close season on 2000 and made 56 appearances, scoring four goals. Had a short loan spell at Droylsden before being signed by Jim Harvey in May, 2004. Played for the England semi-pro squad against Holland in 2000-01.

RUGBY LEAGUE: Was played at Christie Park on April 18, 1925, when Morecambe RL team lost 16-3 to Millom in a North Western League match.

RUNCORN: Many meetings with the Linnets in the NPL but the first meeting was a 1-0 win at Macclesfield on October 18, 1965, in the 1st Rd of the Macclesfield Floodlit Cup. Tulloch scored with winner in a game watched by 1,208 people. The team is now known as Runcorn FC Halton.

RUSHDEN & DIAMONDS: Formed in 1992 with the merger of Northants clubs Irthlingborough Diamonds and Rushden Town. First met in the Conference at Christie Park on November 23, 1996, winning 2-0. Att: 1,040.

RUSHTON, JACK: 1930-33. Full-back 72 (10 cup) apps. Joined from Clitheroe in August, 1930. Moved to Barnoldswick Town in the 1933-34 season.

RUSHTON, PAUL: 1994-2000. Defender/Midfield 101+18 (38+6 cup) apps; 1 (1 cup) goals. Former Crewe Alexandra trainee who joined in July, 1994. A versatile player who was distinctive with his mop of ginger hair making him look similar to Arsenal player Ray Parlour. Suffered from ME. Moved to Winsford Utd in the 1999-2000 season and later played for Colwyn Bay. Spalding Cup winner in 1997-98. Lancashire Cup winner in 1989-99.

RUSSELL, COLIN: 1990-91. Forward 10+4 (0+1 cup) apps; 3 goals. Former Liverpool player who made one substitute appearance at Anfield before a £15,000 move to Huddersfield Town in September, 1982, where he made 64+2 appearances and scored 23 goals. After a loan spell with Stoke City he joined AFC Bournemouth for £15,000 in August, 1984, and scored 14 goals from 65+3 appearances. A £5,000 move to Doncaster Rovers followed in July, 1986, and he made 43 appearances, and scored five goals before a £7,000 switch to Scarborough in November 1987 which brought no goals in 12+1 appearances. Had a short spell with Wigan before dropping into non-league with Colne Dynamoes and Bangor City before joining Morecambe in December, 1990, in exchange for Tony Quinn. Moved to Droylsden and later played for Warrington Town.

RUTTER, GEORGE: 1952-60. Full-back/Centre-half 199 (38 cup) apps; 10 (3 cup) goals. A firm favourite with Morecambe fans after joining in September, 1952. The ex-Yorkshire Amateurs player was just one game short of making 200 league appearances before retiring at the end of the 1959-60 season.

RYAN, JOHN: 1972-73. Forward 26 (6+3 cup) apps; 3 (1 cup) goals. Former Football League striker with Tranmere Rovers, Luton Town, and Notts County who joined in August, 1972, from Altrincham. Released in April, 1973, and joined South Liverpool. Later played for Netherfield. Made one appearance for Morecambe reserves in April, 1975.

RYDER, ALBERT: 1946-47 and 1949-52. Left-back/Centre-half 90 (13 cup) apps; 3 goals. Joined in August, 1946. Moved to Lancaster City 1947-48 before returning to Morecambe in August, 1949. Later played for Carnforth Rangers.

RYEDALE PARK: Home of Gretna who now play in Scotland. First venture north came in the FA Cup, 3rd Qualifying Rd, on October 12, 1985, winning 2-0.
Returned in the same season for an FA Trophy, 3rd Qualifying Rd tie, on December 3, 1985, winning 2-1 with goals from Thornton and Galley.
The first game was drawn 1-1 at Christie Park with Wynn scoring. Att: 481.

S

ST DOMINICS: Met the Liverpool side in a friendly on January 15, 1991, winning 2-1.

ST HELENS TOWN: First met the 'Town' in the Lancashire Combination at Park Road on August 18, 1951, losing 3-1. Meddick scored for Morecambe.

ST JAMES' PARK: Home of Exeter City. First meeting was a 4-0 defeat in the Conference on November 15, 2003. Att: 2,993.

ST JAMES' PARK: Home of Wigan Rovers in Poolstock. Met in the Lancashire Combination during 1966-67 and 1967-68. First visit was on April 25, 1967, with a 2-0 victory.

SALFORD CITY: Met the 'Ammies' at Moor Lane in a pre-season friendly on August 6, 1988, winning 2-1, Att: 50. Goals from Parry and Steve Roe.

SALISBURY, IAN: 1973-77. Defender 27+5 (6+2 cup) apps; 1 cup goal. Joined in August 1973 as a 19-year-old. Switched to rugby union 1977-78 before returning to football and playing for Lancaster City, 1980-81, and then Netherfield in 1987-89. Has coached locally and in America for a number of years.

SALTERGATE: Home of Chesterfield who Morecambe beat 2-1 in the FA Cup 1st Rd on November 16, 2002. Lee Elam and Garry Thompson scored.

SANDALLS, HAROLD: 1989-90. Midfield player who was an unused sub in one game. Later played for Bamber Bridge, Clitheroe and Longridge Town.

SANDHEYS PARK: The pre-war home of New Brighton. First visit was in the Lancashire Combination on March 29, 1922, and ended in a 3-0 defeat.

SANDY LANE: Former home of Skelmersdale Utd. First visit on March 25, 1922, ended in a 3-1 defeat.

SANDY LANE: Former home of Tooting & Mitcham where Morecambe lost 2-0 in the FA Trophy 3rd Rd on February 21, 1976. Att: 1,500. They now play at Imperial Fields.

SANG, NEIL: 1995-97. Defender/Midfield 11+4 (1+3 cup) apps. Well travelled former Everton trainee who signed for a short spell in February, 1996, after playing for Torquay, Runcorn, Stalybridge Celtic, Caernarfon Town, Macclesfield, Netherfield and Ilkeston Town. After a loan spell at Gretna moved to Chorley in February 1997. Later played for Bangor City and Marine before retiring to become a football agent.

SATTERTHWAITE, JACK: 1921-23. Left-half 57 (9 cup) apps; 2 goals. Joined from Barrow in December, 1921, and had two good seasons. Moved to Morecambe Victoria and later played for Lancaster Town, Barrow, Morecambe Park Villa, Skerton Athletic and Edmondsons. After two years out of football returned to play for Edmondsons in 1935-36.

SAUNDERS LANE: The Lancashire Constabulary ground at police HQ in Hutton. First visit in a pre-season friendly on August 15, 1989 ended in a 3-2 defeat. Steve Holden scored both Morecambe's goals.

SAYER, PETER: 1985-87 and 1988-89. (on loan from Northwich Victoria). Midfield 71+1 (45 cup) apps; 3 (10 cup) goals. A real crowd favourite after being signed by Joe Wojciechowicz in the summer of 1985. Born in Cardiff in 1955 he was a Welsh international, making his debut at the age of 22 in a 3-0 victory over Czechoslovakia, the then European Champions in a World Cup qualifier. The midfielder really came to the fore with a starring role in Wales's 1-0 victory over England at Wembley and Brighton boss Alan Mullery paid £100,000 for his services from Cardiff in February, 1978. Two years later PNE boss Nobby Stiles paid £85,000 for him but unfortunately for all parties it was a bad time for the club. Sayer himself suffered from injury problems and he eventually moved to Chester City before being released in 1985. Peter spent two years at the club making 71 league and 44 cup appearances scoring three league and 10 cup goals before moving to Chorley and Northwich Victoria. He returned to Christie Park in November, 1988, on loan from Northwich but made just one appearance. Lancashire Cup winner in 1985-86 and 1986-87.

SCARBOROUGH: Many meetings with the Seadogs in the NPL and Conference. First game between the two sides was a 1-1 draw at Christie Park in the NPL on November 23, 1968. Att: 1,510.

SCHOFIELD, COLIN: 1971-74. Midfield 38+5 (26 cup) apps; 3 goals. Ex-PNE apprentice who had spells with Aldershot, Crewe Alexandra and Northwich Victoria before joining in October, 1971. Later played for Bacup Borough. His son David played for Morecambe in a couple of pre-season friendlies in 2003-04 while on a break during a football scholarship in America. Young David played in the same England Schoolboys squad as Nick Coyle.

SCOTT, BRIAN: 1960-61. Goalkeeper 12 (5 cup) apps. Former Fleetwood and Rossendale Utd player who joined in August, 1960. Returned to Fleetwood in January, 1962, and later played for Darwen.

SCOTT, MIKE: 1976-77. Midfield/Forward 22+4 (14+1 cup) apps; 1 (1 cup) goals. Ex-Everton youngster who had trials with Arsenal and Wigan Athletic before joining Morecambe in October, 1976. Moved to Wigan and had a trial with Plymouth before settling down at Runcorn from 1977-82 and helping them win the NPL in 1980-81 and the Conference 1981-82. Joined Marine at Christmas 1982 and ended his playing career at South Liverpool 1985-87. Managed Bursough between 1988-89 and has had a long spell as assistant manager at Formby.

SCOTT, PAUL: 1961-67. Defender 212 (66 cup) apps; 5 (3 goals). A player who made close to 300 appearances for the club between 1961 and 1967 after joining from Queen of the South. Born in Wisbech on June 6, 1940, Paul was spotted playing for Wisbech Town by Blackpool and joined their grounds staff in 1959. Things did not work out and after a move to Scotland, Paul was asked to fill the gap left by Harry Mattinson. He made his debut in a 3-2 defeat at Rossendale on October 14, 1961, and was a virtual ever present until 1967. His six seasons at Christie Park brought three Lancashire Combination Championships (1961-62, 1962-63 and 1966-67), two Lancashire Cup wins (1961-62 and 1962-6) and two Combination Cup wins (1964-65 and 1966-67). His importance to the side was stressed by a report in the Lancaster Guardian in 1962/63 which read: *"The main reason for the successful season has been the strength of Morecambe's half-back line. Scott has rarely been mastered while Dunn and Keen as attacking half backs have been the downfall of many teams. This formidable trio was the key to victory in many games."* Paul's last appearance came in a 2-0 defeat at Wigan Athletic in the 2nd leg of the Lancashire Floodlit Cup final on May 12, 1967.

SCUNTHORPE UTD: The Iron. The club's youth team played at Glanford Park in 2002-03 in the FA Youth Cup, losing 5-2.

SEALAND ROAD: Chester City's old ground and the scene of the club's great FA Cup, 2nd Rd, win on November 25, 1961.

SEAMER ROAD: Former name of Scarborough's McCain Stadium with the first visit being a 0-0 draw in the NPL on January 18, 1969. Att: 1,600.

SEASIDERS: Former nickname of the club. When Morecambe joined the NPL in 1968-69 a competition was held to find a new nickname with the Shrimps being the winner.

SECRETARIES: L B Brookfield was the first secretary in 1920-21 but he was replaced after a month by W R Bradbury. Later secretaries have been F J Sibbald, R C Quick, M Holmes, G Newsham, K D Ormrod, B Cowburn, D Smith, D Cooke, N Marsdin.

SEED, TERENCE: 1951-52. Left-back 20 (4 cup) apps. Former PNE player who made 81 apps for Carlisle who joined from Accrington Stanley in August, 1951. Had his contract cancelled in January, 1952. Born in Preston on September 3, 1923. Died in December, 1994.

SEEDHILL: Former home of Nelson with the first visit being a 2-0 win against their reserves in the Lancashire Combination on February 9, 1924.

SEEL PARK: Home of Mossley with the first visit being a 2-1 win in the FA Cup, 4th Qualifying Rd, on November 2, 1968. Att: 2,000.

SEMI-FINALS of the CONFERENCE PLAY-OFFS: There were two epic games with Dagenham & Redbridge in 2002-03 in the first of the league's play-offs. The tie ended 3-3 on aggregate with Dagenham winning 3-2 on penalties. The first tie was on May 1, 2003, with Dagenham winning 2-1. Att: 3,447. The second leg saw Morecambe win 2-1 after extra time. Att: 5,405. Dagenham went into the final where they were beaten by Doncaster Rovers.

SENIOR, ROLAND: 1929-30 and 1931-32. Inside-right/Centre-forward 21 (9 cup) apps; 7 (3 cup) goals. Ex-Morecambe Central School and Morecambe Victoria who played for the Reserves in 1923-24. Played for Carnforth Rangers 1924-29 and rejoined Morecambe in August, 1929. Scored eight goals for the reserves in their record 16-0 win over Calder Vale in the North Lancashire League Challenge Cup on September 28, 1929. Had another spell at Morecambe in August, 1931, before moving back to Carnforth Rangers.

SHARPLES, DAVID: 1988-91. Midfield/Forward 73+4 (32+3 cup) apps; 4 (2 cup) goals. Former Blackburn Rovers trainee who played for Padiham, Clitheroe, Chorley and Accrington Stanley before joining in August 1988. Moved to Darwen in November 1990 and later played for Great Harwood Town, Lancaster City and Clitheroe. During his spell was described as *"the Shrimps' midfield mainstay, a very busy and constructive player."*

SHAW, FRED: 1933-34. Right-back/Right-half 37 (4 cup) apps; 3 goals. Ex-Barrow and Lancaster Town player who joined in August, 1933. Later played for Milnthorpe Corinthians.

SHAW, KEVIN: 1975-77 and 1983-85. Defender 27+1 (12+1 cup) apps; 2 cup goals. Lancaster-born player who joined in August, 1975 as a 17-year-old. Had trials with PNE before moving to Lancaster City in September, 1977. Moved to Workington and played for Netherfield and Middleton before moving back to Morecambe in February, 1984. Joined Lancaster City again in October, 1984.

SHAW, STUART: 1970-71. Forward 23+1 (7 cup) apps. A player who made three first team appearances for Everton before a £12,000 move to Crystal Palace in December, 1966. Moved to Southport for £3,000 in March, 1967, and scored six goals in 66+1 appearances. Joined Morecambe in August, 1970, after a short spell with Port Vale. Released in May, 1971, and later played for Skelmersdale Utd, South Liverpool, Howard Sports and Fleetwood Hesketh.

SHAWBRIDGE: Home of Clitheroe with the first visit being a 2-2 draw in the FA Cup on September 5, 1925. Clitheroe had just moved to Shawbridge when they entered the Lancashire Combination in 1925-26.

THE SHAY: Home of Halifax Town and now called the Shay Stadium. Drew 1-1 on the first visit in the Conference on September 26, 1995. Att: 919.

SHEFFIELD: Met the world's oldest club in the FA Cup, 1st Qualifying Rd, at Christie Park on September 9, 1995, winning 7-0. Att: 467.

SHEFFIELD LEAGUE: Met in a friendly at Woodhill Lane on March 26, 1921, winning 3-2. Gradwell (2) and Aldred scored.

SHEFFIELD UTD: Morecambe beat a Utd XI 4-1 at Christie Park in a pre-season friendly on July 21, 2001.

SHEPSHED CHARTERHOUSE: Met the Raiders in the NPL from 1988 to 1992. In the 1991-92 season they were renamed Shepshead Albion (their name from 1890 to 1975) and then renamed again to Shepshed Dynamoes when reformed in 1994.
The first meeting was at the Dovecote on October 8, 1988, a 2-2 draw. Steve Parry and Malcolm Poskett scored.

SHILDON: Met the Railwaymen in the FA Cup, 1st Qualifying Rd, at Dean Street, on October 20, 1984, winning 5-3. Att: 97. Goals came from Baron, Grimshaw, Barnes, Grant and Leaver. Also met in the FA Trophy, 2nd Qualifying Rd, on October 20, 1990, winning 3-0. Att: 160. Brown, Cain and Windridge scored.

SHIRLEY, JIMMY: 1952-53. Centre-half 35 (6 cup) apps. Joined in August, 1952, from Wigan Athletic where he made 188 apps, scoring 14 goals as they won the Combination title in 1947-48 and 1950-51. Captained Morecambe in 1952-53 with some sources referring to Jimmy as being the player-manager. Moved to Crompton Recs and had a short spell as manager at Wigan Athletic in January, 1959.

SHIRLEY, MARK: 1996-2000. Forward 82+8 (24+2 cup) apps; 13 (2 cup) goals. Former Nottingham Forest trainee who played for Southport, Caernarfon Town, Ashton Utd and Lancaster City before joining Morecambe in November, 1996.
A stylish winger who turned down a £15,000 move to Rushden & Diamonds during his spell at the club. Joined Accrington Stanley in May, 1999, and helped them win the NPL Division One title in 1999-2000. Was Stanley's player of the year in the same season. Lancashire Cup winner in 1989-99.

SHOREFIELDS GROUND: Former home of the original South Liverpool. First visit was on January 29, 1921, losing 3-2.

SHOWGROUND: Home of Great Harwood and now known as the Sportsman Ground. In 1929-30 the ground was known as the Lidgett Ground.
First visit was in the Combination on September 18, 1920, losing 2-1. At: 2,000. Thompson scored for the Shrimps.

SHREWSBURY TOWN: First met in the LDV Vans Trophy at Gay Meadow, losing 3-0 on October 22, 2002. Att: 1,602.

SIGNINGS: Record signing is £25,000 which Jim Harvey paid Northwich Victoria for Steve Walters on May 30, 2000. **Record sale** is £175,000 when Justin Jackson moved to Rushden & Diamonds on June 16, 2000.

SILVERLANDS: Home of Buxton where Morecambe won 4-1 on their first visit in the NPL on August 11, 1973.

SIMMS, DICK: 1934-36. Right-back 74 (12 cup) apps. A player who spent seven years at Lancaster Town before joining in August 1934. Moved to Clitheroe 1936-37.

SIMONSIDE HALL: South Shields' home from 1949 to 1974 when they moved to Gateshead. First visit was for the final game of the 1968-69 NPL season on May 10, 1969, losing 3-1. Att: 1,080.

SIMONSWOOD LANE: Home of the now defunct Kirkby Town. First visit was in the Lancashire Combination on October 20, 1967, winning 4-0 with goals from Holding (2), Borrowdale and Timmins.

SINCIL BANK: Home of Lincoln City with the first visit being in the FA Cup, 1st Rd, losing 1-0 on November 20, 1976.

SKELMERSDALE UTD: First met in the second game at Christie Park on September 3, 1921 in the Combination, losing 1-0. Att: 1,500.

SLACK, GEOFF: 1956-59. Right-half/Forward 75 (31 cup) apps; 7 (6 cup) goals. Morecambe-born player who joined in August, 1956, and impressed a host of scouts.

Stockport County paid £750 for his services on November 24, 1958, and he went on to make eight appearances and scored one goal for them. Moved to Netherfield in January, 1960, and later played for Horwich RMI and Lancaster City (1966-68).

SLATER, JOHN: 1953-54 and 1955-56. Goalkeeper 10 apps. Joined in August, 1953, as a 17-year-old from Ulverston. Left to do his National Service and returned to play for the Reserves in 1955-56. Joined Netherfield in 1959.

SLATER, ROY: 1955-56. Inside-forward 11 (1 cup) apps; 1 goal. Joined in August 1955.

SLOAN, TED: 1952-53. Outside-right/Inside-right 13 (1 cup) apps; 2 goals. Joined in October, 1952.

SLOANE, JOE (JACK): 1920-22 and 1924-28. Goalkeeper 117 (28 cup) apps; 1 goal. Ex-PNE amateur who joined in January, 1921. Moved to Accrington Stanley where he made 33 appearances before returning to Morecambe in September, 1924. Combination League title winner in 1924-25. Lancashire Cup winner in 1925-26 and 1926-27.

SLOUGH TOWN: First met the Rebels in the FA Trophy, 4th Rd, at Wexham Park on March 19, 1977, losing 2-0. Att: 1,500.

SMALLEY, LESLIE: 1935-36. Outside-right 15 apps. Former Oldham Athletic, Hereford Utd and Clitheroe player who joined in August, 1935. Later played for Moffats Works. Born in Blackburn on September 10, 1911. Died in Southampton on March 1983.

SMELT, TOM: 1926-27. Inside-right 33 (10 cup) apps; 20 (8 cup) goals. Tom was a well-travelled player who had spells with Mexborough Town, Chesterfield Municipal, Rotherham Town, Wombwell, Accrington Stanley, Exeter City and Chesterfield before joining in August 1926.
Moved to Manchester City in April 1927 where he made two appearances and scored one goal. Joined Oldham Athletic in April 1928 and later played for Crewe Alexandra, Scunthorpe Utd and Rotherham Utd. Tom was also a good all-round cricketer who was a professional for Crompton Cricket Club in the Central Lancashire League in 1930. Lancashire Cup winner in 1926-27.

SMITH, GARY: 1984-86. Midfield 20 (7 cup) apps; 1 goal. Ex-Prescot Town player who joined in October, 1984.

SMITH, J: 1920-21. Inside-right 11 apps; 1 goal. Played in Morecambe's first game in August, 1920.

SMITH, KEN: 1953-55. Outside-left 32 (2 cup) aps; 6 goals. Ex-Blackburn Rovers amateur.

SMITH, LEON: 1998-2001. Midfield 10+11 (4+3 cup) apps; 1 goal. Signed a contract in May, 1999, after impressing in the reserves. Was loaned to Bamber Bridge in September 2000 and was released in May, 2001. Signed for Stevenage Borough in June, 2001, and made five substitute appearances before being released in October, 2001. Had a loan spell at Altrincham and played for Atherton LR and Hyde Utd.

SMITH, MARK: 2000-02. Goalkeeper 36 (13 cup) apps. Ex-Nottingham Forest trainee who joined Crewe where he made 61+2 apps. Helped them win promotion to Division Two in 1993-94. Moved to Walsall in August, 1996, and then Rushden & Diamonds where he made 50 appearances before joining Morecambe in the close season of 2000. Released and later played for Eastwood Town, Scarborough and Ilkeston Town.

SMITH, ROY: 1958-59 Centre-forward 10 apps; 1 goal. Former Wigan Athletic player who scored 54 goals in 99 Combination games for the Latics between 1955-58. Joined Southport for £300 in September 1958 but after scoring just four goals in 23 appearances joined Morecambe in March, 1959. Tragically died in an underground accident in Wood Pit, Haydock, on June 3, 1959.

SMITH, BILLY: 1950-54. Centre-forward 78 (15 cup) apps; 33 (7 cup) goals. Joined in August, 1950, and moved to Lancaster City in November, 1953. Later played for Clitheroe.

SMITH: 1929-30. Outside-left 11 apps; 2 goals. Former Clitheroe player who joined in February, 1930.

SNASDELL, BILL: 1967-70. Goalkeeper 14 (12 cup) apps. Former Chelsea junior who played for Fleetwood before joining in June 1967. Later played for Clitheroe. A well-known Northern League cricketer and character in local sport he sadly died in October, 1985, aged just 37.

SOLIHULL BOROUGH: Beat the West Midlands club 3-2 in the FA Trophy, 1st Rd, on January 10, 1998, at Christie Park. Att: 766.

SOLLITT, ADAM: Goalkeeper. Former Barnsley trainee (1991-97) who had a spell at Gainsborough Trinity before moving to Kettering Town in 1998. Helped Kettering finish as runners-up in the Conference and reach an FA Trophy final at Wembley. Voted Conference goalkeeper of the year in 1999-2000. His form was so good Northampton Town paid £30,000 for his services on July 25, 2000. Made 14+2 (4 cup) appearances for the Cobblers before being released in the close season of 2002. Had spells at Rushden & Diamonds and Scarborough before joining Morecambe in May 2004. Won three England semi-pro caps in 1999-2000 v Italy, Holland and Wales.

SOUTH BANK: First met the now defunct club in the FA Cup 3rd Qualifying Rd at Christie Park on October 16, 1982, drawing 1-1. Att: 414. South Bank won the replay 1-0.

SOUTH LIVERPOOL: Met the original South Liverpool club in 1920-21 and 1921-22 seasons. They then moved to become New Brighton. First meeting was Morecambe's second ever home game with a 4-3 defeat on September 4, 1920. Att: 1,000.
The club was reformed in 1935-36 and played at Holly Park. First meeting came in the Lancashire Combination on September 7, 1935, losing 1-0. The club has now reformed again and is playing in the Liverpool County Football Combination.

SOUTH SHIELDS: First meeting was a 2-1 win at Christie Park in the FA Cup 1st Rd on November 4, 1961. Att: 6,100.

SOUTHAMPTON: Met the Saints in a friendly at Christie Park on September 2, 1998, to mark the opening of the new North Stand by Sir Bobby Charlton. A crowd of more than 3,000 watched the Saints, managed by former Morecambe assistant boss David Jones, win 3-0.

SOUTHEND PARK GROUND: Home of Penrith with the first visit being on September 26, 1953, in an FA Cup, 1st Qualifying Rd, tie. Morecambe won 6-1 with goals from Johnstone (4), W J Smith and Miller.

SOUTHERN MAIDS XI: A Morecambe XI played a friendly with the theatrical company who were appearing in Lancaster at Woodhill Lane on March 10, 1921, losing 4-3.

SOUTHPORT: Many meetings with the Sandgrounders in the NPL and the Conference with numerous cup clashes. The first senior meeting was a 2-2 draw in the 1st Rd of the Lancashire Senior Cup at Christie Park on October 9, 1973. Att: 515. Morecambe beat the then Football League side in a 2nd replay.

SOUTHPORT RESERVES: During Southport's Football League days the Reserves were regular opponents in the Lancashire Combination League.
The first meeting was a 1-1 draw at home on February 2, 1924. Att: 1,500.

SPALDING CUP: The Conference League Cup which Morecambe won in the 1997-98 season. After a couple of 1-1 draws in the two-legged final against Woking the Shrimps won 4-3 on penalties. The 1st leg was at home on March 25, 1998, and ended 1-1. Att: 782. The 2nd leg at Kingfield on May 4, 1998, also finished 1-1 after extra time. Att: 2.045.

SPAVIN, ALAN: 1975-76. Midfield/Inside-left 22 (8 cup) apps; 1 goals. The 70s was an era where the club went for player managers and the Lancaster-born former PNE favourite was no different, taking over from Dave Roberts in 1975.
Alan played as a junior with Carnforth Rangers before going on to enjoy an excellent career at Deepdale. He had two spells at North End 1958-74 and 1977-79 and made 414 league apps, scoring 26 goals before joining Telford United as player-coach.
After Dave Roberts resigned Spavin took control for the 1975-76 season but after a promising start the club struggled in the league. There were some good cup results

however with what had become a rare FA Cup win, the first since 1971. The club reached the 3rd Rd of the FA Trophy where they lost 3-0 at Tooting & Mitcham. Spavin's reign was cut short as he resigned in March, 1976, to take over as assistant manager of American club Washington Diplomats. He still lives in the States.

SPEAKMAN, SAM: 1959-61. Outside-left 60 (18 cup) apps; 39 (18 cup) goals. Former Bolton Wanderers and Middlesbrough junior who made 68 appearances and scored nine goals for Tranmere Rovers between 1954-56. Moved to Wigan and then Horwich before joining Morecambe in August 1958. Moved to Earlestown 1961-62 and later played for South Liverpool.

SPENCER, RONNIE: 1933-35 and 1936-38. Centre-forward 85 (15 cup) apps; 35 (9 cup) goals. Young amateur who joined in April, 1934. Moved to Lancaster Town in March, 1935, and played in their Combination title-winning side of 1935-36. Rejoined Morecambe in August, 1936, and later played for Clitheroe and Darwen.

SPENNYMOOR UTD: First met the Moors in the FA Cup, 4th Qualifying Rd, at the Brewery Field on October 28, 1967, losing 1-0. Att: 2,500.

SPOTLAND: Home of Rochdale. First visit was to play Rochdale reserves in the Combination, losing 2-0 on April 8, 1922.

SPRINGFIELD PARK: Former home of Wigan Athletic and the defunct Wigan Borough. First visit was to play Wigan Borough in the Combination on March 16, 1921, losing 3-1. Morecambe never managed to win a league match against Wigan Athletic at Springfield Park but did manage a 2-1 victory in the Lancashire Junior Cup semi-final on April 29, 1963. Armstrong and Fawcett scored. Att: 5,158.

SQUIRES, ALAN: 1948-50. Right-back/Left-half 49 (6 cup) apps. Fleetwood-born player who made wartime guest apps for PNE, Fulham, Southend Utd, Plymouth Argyle and Bournemouth. Moved from PNE to Carlisle in December, 1946, and made 25 appearances for the Cumbrians before joining Morecambe in August, 1948. Joined Netherfield in the 1951-52 season.

SQUIRES GATE: Ground used by Blackpool B for their games in the Lancashire Combination in the early 1950s. First visit was on September 23, 1950, losing 3-1.

SQUIRES GATE FC: First met in a friendly at Christie Park on September 30, 1989, winning 6-0.

STADIUM, THE: Billingham Synthonia's ground on Central Avenue in Cleveland. Met in the FA Trophy on November 2, 1985, winning 2-0. Gordon and Sayer scored. Att: 116.

STAFFORD RANGERS: First met in the NPL on October 18, 1969, at Marston Road, drawing 1-1. Att: 2,027. Wroth scored.

STAINES TOWN: Morecambe first met the Swans in the FA Trophy, 2nd Rd, at Christie Park on February 5, 1977, drawing 2-2. Att: 818. Drew the replay 0-0 before winning the 2nd replay 2-1 at Stafford.

STAINTON PARK: Home of Radcliffe Borough with the first being a pre-season friendly on August 13, 1988, winning 2-0.

STALYBRIDGE CELTIC: Visited Christie Park for their first ever game in the NPL on August 20, 1988, winning 2-1. Att: 484.

STANDFAST: Met in the North Lancashire League at Christie Park on October 19, 1940.

STANLEY, RON: 1978-80. Defender 33+1 (5+1 cup) apps; 1 goal. Former Wolves apprentice who joined in September, 1978. Moved to Wren Rovers 1981-82.

STATION VIEW: Home of Harrogate Railway Athletic with the first meeting being a 3-2 victory in the FA Cup, 4th Qualifying Rd, on October 27, 2001. Chris Lightfoot scored two with Wayne Curtis grabbing a late winner.

STENHOUSEMUIR: Met the Warriors in a pre-season friendly at Christie Park on July 25, 1999, drawing 1-1.

STENSON, GED: 1981-82. Midfield/Forward 10+1 (2 cup) apps. Former Everton apprentice who played for Port Vale, Bury, Hyde Utd, Prescot Town, Oswestry Town, and Formby before joining in October, 1981. Moved to Prescot Town in February, 1982. Later played for Winsford and Witton Albion.

STEVENAGE BOROUGH: First met the Boro in the Conference at Christie Park on April 6, 1996, winning 1-0. Att: 1,227.

Robbie Talbot in action versus Stevenage Borough

STIMPSON, BARRY: 1986-88 and 1995-96. Defender 83+1 (38 cup) apps; 12 (5 cup) goals. One of the most popular players to appear for Morecambe in recent years. Came to the club as the then record signing when he joined from Gateshead for £2,250 in August, 1986. Also became the club's record sale for a time when he moved to Colne Dynamoes for £6,000 in November 1988.
As a Football League player made 66+2 appearances and scored two goals for Hartlepool Utd between 1980-83 before a move to Chesterfield in November, 1983. Made 27 appearances before a move back to Hartlepool in December, 1984, where he made another 18 appearances before being released and joining Gateshead.
After a successful spell at Colne where he helped them win the NPL title he played for Northwich Victoria, Chorley and Barrow before having a good spell at Lancaster City. Came back to Morecambe for a short spell in September, 1995, but returned to Lancaster City in December, 1995. Managed Middleton locally and became assistant boss at Workington before becoming player-coach and assistant manager to Tony Hesketh at Lancaster City between 1998-2002. Lancashire Cup winner in 1986-87.

STOCKPORT COUNTY: The Shrimps first met in the FA Cup, 1st Rd, on November 25, 1978, at Edgeley Park, losing 5-1. Att: 3,294.

STOCKPORT COUNTY RES: Met in the Lancashire Combination during 1921-22. Lost 2-0 at Edgeley Park on January 7, but won the home game on February 11, 3-0. Farnworth, Walker and Manley scored in a game watched by 1,700.

STONEBRIDGE ROAD: Home of Gravesend & Northfleet with the first visit being a 3-2 defeat in the Conference on March 22, 2003. Att: 1,040. The next visit was a 6-0 defeat in 2003-04.

STONES, W: 1949-51. Inside-right 33 (3 cup) apps; 4 goals. Ex-Leeds Utd and Normanton player who joined in August, 1949.

STOTT, ERIC: 1946-50. Goalkeeper 34 (5 cup) apps. Former Blackburn Rovers player who retired after breaking his neck in a game at Wigan Athletic on January 15, 1949. Did return for one game in September 1949. Was a Morecambe director from July 1971 to March 1978. Born in Lancaster he died in Southport on August 16, 1978, aged 52.

STOURBRIDGE: Met the Glassboys in the FA Trophy 3rd Rd at the War Memorial Athletic Ground on February 10, 1973, drawing 1-1. Att: 766. Won the replay 3-1 on February 13 with goals from Russ Perkins (2) and Alan Taylor. Att: 875.

STRANDS LANE: Home of Milnthorpe Corinthians with the first visit being in the North Lancashire League on February 10, 1940, winning 2-1.

STRAUGHTON, PETER: 1929-30. Inside-left 34 (7 cup) apps; 22 (1 cup) goals. Joined from Workington in August, 1929. Had a good spell but returned to his former club in July, 1930.

STREET, GEOFF: 1970-81. Centre-half 326 (111 cup) apps; 18 (10 cup) goals. A stalwart centre-half during the 1970s, Geoff is without doubt one of the most popular Morecambe players of all time. Born in Manchester he joined Manchester City as a junior and signed as a professional in August, 1965, but failed to make a first team appearance and was released, signing for Southport in August, 1967. Made just nine league appearances for the Sandgrounders before moving to Plymouth Argyle in July, 1968 – a far from fruitful move as he failed to make an appearance in a first team shirt. He returned north to Altrincham and Barrow (14 apps, 1 goal) before moving into non-league football. Geoff was Ken Waterhouse's first signing as manager in December, 1970, and after a period of moving up and down the country he became a Morecambe regular for the next 10 years. His debut came in a 3-1 home defeat by Scarborough on December 19, 1970, and went on to make 437 appearances for the club scoring 28 goals. He was an important member of the FA Trophy wining side and also played in the Lancashire Senior Cup defeat by Manchester City in the same season. Moved to Lancaster City in December, 1980. FA Trophy winner in 1973-74.

STRINGFELLOW, MICHAEL: 2000-04. Midfield 65+16 (12+6 cup) apps; 3 goals. Former Morecambe Youth team player who joined the club's Academy after a spell at Blackburn Rovers' School of Excellence. Signed for the club in December, 2000, and produced some excellent performances in big games. Was the reserves' team player of the year in 2000-01.

SUGDEN, RYAN: 2003-04. Centre-forward 13+20 (5+2 cup) apps; 6 (3 cup) goals. Former Oldham Athletic player who was with the Boundary Park club from the age of nine. Signed professional forms in November, 1998, and made 4+17 first team apps, scoring one goal. Had a loan spell with Burton Albion before signing for Scarborough in February, 2002. Joined Chester City and scored 12 goals in 26+7 apps before a move to Burton Albion in 2003. Joined Morecambe in September, 2003. England semi-pro international. Ironically was sent off playing against Morecambe for both Scarborough and Chester City. Lancashire Cup winner in 2003-04.

SUTTON, JIMMY: 1971-76. Midfield 183+5 (68+2 cup) apps; 12 (8 cup) goals. Another Glaswegian who became a Morecambe favourite. Jimmy was a junior with Newcastle United before joining Mansfield Town in July, 1970, where he made 15 starts and had the distinction of scoring in a League Cup game against Liverpool at Anfield. After being released by the Stags Jimmy signed for Morecambe in the summer of 1971 and made his debut in a 3-1 defeat in a pre-season friendly against Burnley reserves. His league debut was more memorable however, as the Shrimps beat Scarborough 1-0 away. Jimmy will always be remembered for scoring the goal that helped Morecambe win the FA Trophy in 1974. He was a regular for the Shrimps for six seasons scoring a total of 20 goals before becoming player manager of Wren Rovers in May, 1976, where he replaced another former Morecambe favourite Keith Borrowdale. Became player-coach and then player-manager at Lytham before returning to Wren Rovers in December, 1982. FA Trophy winner in 1973-74.

SUTTON UTD: Met the U's in the Conference during the 1999-2000 season with the first game being at Christie Park on December 4, 1999, winning 6-2. Att: 1,460.

SWAN, IAIN: 2002-04. Defender 53+7 (12 cup) apps; 1 goal. Former Oldham Athletic trainee who made one first team appearance. Had a loan spell at Leigh RMI and Partick Thistle (0+2 apps) before signing for Leigh in the close season 2000. Made 63+3 apps, scoring one goal at Hilton Park before joining in July, 2002. Lancashire Cup winner in 2003-04.

SWAN, JOCK: 1934-39. Goalkeeper 175 (31 cup) apps. Consistent goalkeeper who had five excellent seasons at Christie Park before the war. Moved to Netherfield in February, 1939, and later played for Lancaster City.

SWANSEA CITY: Met the Swans in a pre-season friendly at Christie Park on July 21, 1997, drawing 1-1.

SWINDLEHURST, JAMES: 1923-25. Half-back/Forward (Goalkeeper for 1 game) 13 (9 cup) aps; 1 goal. Joined in September, 1923.

SZABO, TIBOR: 1985-87. Forward 32+7 (12+1 cup) apps; 18 (6 cup) goals. Bradford-born player with Hungarian parents who made 8+5 first team apps, scoring one goal for his home town team. He was released in 1979 and joined Macclesfield Town. Moved to Mossley for £2,000 in August, 1980, before joining Gainsborough Trinity in 1984 and Goole Town in January, 1985. Had another short spell at Mossley before joining Morecambe in January, 1986, where he proved to be a regular goalscorer.
Moved to Buxton and later played for Accrington Stanley, Droylsden and Atherton LR.

T

TABERNER, FRED: 1963-65. Inside-right 38 (6 cup) apps; 20 (5 cup) goals. Joined from Altrincham in March, 1964, for a small fee after spells at Leeds Utd, Wigan Athletic, Horwich RMI. Moved to Witton Albion and scored 65 goals in two seasons before a move to Macclesfield Town. Fred was player manager at Chorley 1968-72 and Radcliffe Borough. Combination Cup winner in 1964-65.

TAKANO, KEISUKE (KENNY): 1995-2000 and 2000-01. Defender/Forward 54+24 (15+7 cup) apps; 2 (1 cup) goals *(pictured right)*. First Japanese player to score in the FA Cup when he recorded an unforgettable goal against Emley on November 25, 1997. Born in Tokyo he played some games for Tranmere Rovers reserves before joining Morecambe in November, 1995. Impressed in the reserves before making his first team debut. He was briefly banned by the FA from playing in any games where money was taken through the turnstiles but the rule was soon changed. Moved to Southport in February, 2000, for a small fee but made just 2+2 appearances. Returned to Morecambe before moving back to Japan after his university course finished. Helped Morecambe win the ATS Lancashire Trophy in 1998-99.

TALBOT, ROBBIE: 2000-03. Forward 41+22 (7+6 cup) apps; 25 (4 cup) goals. Former Everton junior, Blackpool trainee, Rochdale and Marine player who was signed for £9,000 from Burscough on February 8, 2002. Impressed Jim Harvey after playing against Morecambe in the FA Trophy and he made the step up to the Conference with ease. Scored four goals on his full debut against Leigh RMI in the Conference's League Cup competition. Unfortunately an injury gained while playing against Chester City hindered his career at Christie Park significantly. Struggled to come back to full fitness and moved to Burton Albion for £7,000 in July, 2003. Player of the season 2001-02.

TAMWORTH: First met the Lambs in the FA Trophy 1st Rd at the Lamb Ground on January 22, 1972, winning 4-1. Att: 999. Richmond (2), Lea and Lancaster scored.

TATE, JEFF: 1980-81. Midfield 17 (3 cup) apps; 1 goal. Former England U18 Schoolboy international who made five appearances for Burnley between 1978-80. Joined in August, 1980, but broke his leg while playing for the Shrimps. Moved to Mossley and later played for Whitley Bay.

TAYLOR, ALAN: 1972-73. Forward 27+3 (13+1 cup) apps; 7 (4 cup) goals. A local player who became the most famous player in the country on a special day in May 1975 when he scored both the goals as West Ham beat Fulham to win the FA Cup final at Wembley. Was born in Hinckley on November 14, 1953, before moving to the area and attending Carnforth High School. Played for the local schoolboy's team, Carnforth Rangers, Lancaster Boys Club, Lancaster City Juniors and Mayfield Utd before joining Morecambe in August, 1971. Made a real impression in the reserves before breaking into the first team and showing his undoubted potential. Had a trial with Everton before being transferred to Rochdale for £2,500 on May 15, 1973. Made 55 appearances, scoring seven goals before joining West Ham for £45,000 on November 23, 1974. As a Hammer he picked up an FA Cup winners medal, played in the Charity Shield defeat by Derby and in the European Cup Winners Cup final v Anderlecht in 1975-76. After 88+10 appearances and 25 goals he moved to Norwich City for £90,000 in August, 1979, but made just 20+4 appearances, scoring five goals before another £90,000 move to Vancouver Whitecaps in Canada. Moved again in October, 1980, when Cambridge Utd paid £130,000 for his services but scored just four goals in 17+1 appearances and had his contract cancelled in March, 1981. Had a spell at Hull City and then joined Burnley in August, 1984, and made 60+4 appearances, scoring 22 goals until being released in the close season of 1986. Bury was the next port of call with 55+7 appearances and 10 goals between 1986-88, followed by a short second spell at Norwich scoring one goal in one full start. Dropped into non-league with Thetford Town in July, 1989, and had a short spell as player and assistant manager.

TAYLOR, FRANK: Reserves team manager for three seasons. Took over as first team boss for seven games between October, 28, and December 6, 1988, after Larry Milligan was sacked.

TAYLOR, HAROLD: 1932-33 and 1933-34. Left-back 44 (9 cup) apps. Joined in August, 1932. Moved to Chorley but returned to Morecambe in November, 1933. Later played for Leyland Motors.

TAYLOR, HARRY: 1937-39. Inside-right/Centre-forward 11 (2 cup) apps; 2 goals. Joined in December 1937, mainly playing for the reserves.

TAYLOR, KEN: 1964-65. Left-back 18 (5 cup) apps. Player who made 200 appearances for Blackburn Rovers between 1950-63. Joined in August 1964.

TAYLOR, MICKY: 1976-78. Midfield 86+1 (26 cup) apps; 6 (2 cup) goals. Former PNE and Blackburn Rovers amateur who had long spells at Southport (1962-68) and Netherfield (1968-72) before a £1,500 move to Wigan Athletic. Helped them reach the FA Trophy final in 1972-73 when they lost to Scarborough and was also a regular as Wigan finished as runners-up in the NPL in 1973-74. Joined Morecambe from Lancaster City in June, 1976, but left to become player-coach of California Sunshine. Took a similar role at Barrow in October, 1978, and became manager in December, 1979, before being sacked in May, 1983. Had spells managing Workington, Southport, Fleetwood Town and Fulwood Amateurs.

TAYLOR, PAUL: 1993-96. Defender 18+6 (7+2 cup) apps. He played locally for Carnforth Grasshoppers, Lancaster City and Morecambe Youths before progressing into the first team via the Reserves. Moved to Netherfield in 1996 and later played for Gretna and Carnforth Rangers.

TAYLOR, DICK: 1936-39. Left-back 102 (16 cup) apps; 12 (1 cup) goals. Former Chorley and Fleetwood player who joined in June, 1936.

TELFORD UTD: First met the Bucks at Christie Park in the FA Trophy, 2nd Rd, on February 1, 1975. Morecambe were defending their trophy but were knocked out after losing 3-2. Att: 1,836.

THOMAS, ROB: 1976-77 and 1982-83. Forward 62+1 (23+1 cup) apps; 17 (9 cup) goals. Former Blackpool player who joined for the first time in June, 1976, from Lancaster City where he was a prolific striker. Scored 49 goals in the 1972-73 season and 29 in the 1974-75 campaign. Moved to Barrow in August, 1977, and scored 37 goals from 145 appearances before becoming player-coach and then player-manager at

Fleetwood Town. Returned to Christie Park in August, 1982, but was released in February, 1983, and joined Lancaster again. Later he was the player-manager at Wren Rovers and played for Fleetwood, Blackpool Mechanics and Poulton Town.

THOMPSON, GARRY: 1999-2004. Forward 112+27 (29+8 cup) apps; 23 (6 cup) goals Born in Kendal on November 24, 1980 this winger with electrifying pace came through the Academy to become a first team regular and England semi-pro international. Signed for the first team in July, 1999, and has scored some vital goals. Lancashire Cup winner in 2003-04.

THOMPSON, GEORGE: 1962-64. Goalkeeper 31 (7 cup) apps. Ex-Huddersfield, Chesterfield and Scunthorpe keeper who joined PNE for £4,400 in October 1952. Made 140 appearances at Deepdale and played in the FA Cup final in 1953-54. Moved to Manchester City for £7,500 in July, 1956, but made just two appearances before moving to Carlisle and becoming a regular for five seasons and chalking up 203 appearances. Joined in May, 1962, and retired in March 1964. Won one England B cap. Born in September, 1926, he died in March 2004.

THOMPSON, HARRY: 1934-36 and 1936-40. Forward 25 (9 cup) apps; 4 (2 cup) goals. Joined in September, 1934, but moved to Heysham LMS in 1936-37. Returned in January, 1937.

THOMPSON, JIM: 1981-82. Defender 8 (3 cup) apps. Has the distinction of being Morecambe's shortest serving manager, lasting just three days in 1981.
The Glasgow-born defender began his professional career with Chelsea making 33 appearances and scoring one goal before spending 14 successful years with Burnley from 1967 to 1981, making 294 appearances, scoring three goals. He began the 1981/82 season as a Morecambe player but after Don Cubbage resigned took over as player manager. Within three days however he resigned for business reasons.

THOMPSON, JOHN: 1920-21. Outside-right/Inside-left 22 (3 cup) apps; 4 goals. Played in Morecambe's first game in August, 1920, and was one of the club's first professionals. Moved to play for Derby County reserves in November, 1920.

THOMPSON, JOHN: 1923-24. Goalkeeper 32 (6 cup) apps. Former Southport stopper who played for Barrow in their first ever game in the Football League on August 27, 1921, against Stockport County. Joined Morecambe in November, 1923, and moved to Morecambe Park Villa in 1924-25. Emigrated to Canada in March, 1928, but returned in 1931. Was Carnforth Cricket Club's professional and also played for Morecambe.

THOMSON, ARTHUR: 1927-28 and 1934-39. Forward/Right-half. 201 (37 cup) apps; 18 (2 cup) goals. Player originated from County Durham who signed in October, 1927. Had a trial with Huddersfield Town in November, 1927, before moving to Manchester United in May, 1928, for a modest fee. Made just three appearances, scoring one goal in a 4-1 defeat by Arsenal at Highbury in February, 1931.

Moved to Southend Utd in August, 1931, where he made 14 appearances and in May, 1932, joined Coventry City, making just one appearance before a move to Tranmere Rovers. Rejoined in August, 1934, and became a real favourite.

THOMSON, BRIAN: 1976-77. Forward 6+1 (4 cup) apps; 1 (1 cup) goals. Made his debut as a youngster for the reserves in March, 1976, and signed first team forms in November. Made a great impression and was transferred to West Ham United for £2,750 on December 17, 1976, after a trial. Failed to make a first team app however and moved to Mansfield, making 54+9 appearances and scoring one goal between 1979-81. Later played for Corby Town, Kings Lynn and Boston Utd where he was a member of their FA Trophy final team of 1984-85.

THORNLEY, MARK: 1993-95. Goalkeeper 32 (13 cup) apps. Popular keeper who played for Alfreton Town, Belper Town, Sutton Town, Stafford Rangers, Worksop Town and Fleetwood Town before joining in June, 1993. Unfortunately, a broken leg delayed his debut until November, 1993. Moved to Lancaster City in exchange for Glenn Johnstone in October, 1994, and became almost an ever present for the next nine seasons. Made more than 400 appearances at Giant Axe before retiring in July, 2003. Made a brief comeback in September, 2003, and had a few games for Kendal Town in January, 2004.

THORNTON, GEOFF: 1989-92. Goalkeeper 60 (24 cup) apps. Joined Morecambe in November, 1989, and proved to be a reliable keeper. Previously had played for Southport, Prescot Cables, Bangor City, Burscough and Runcorn.

THORNTON, JIM: 1984-86. Forward 34+6 (20 cup) apps; 16 (13 cup) goals. Impressive front runner who joined from Marine in March, 1985. Moved to Southport in August, 1986, and back to South Liverpool 1986-87. Lancashire Cup winner in 1985-86.

THORNTON, NORMAN: 1920-21 and 1921-26. Full-back/Forward 18 (7 cup) apps; 1 goal. Had one game in August, 1920, before moving to Glasson Dock and later Bare Utd and Skerton Athletic. Rejoined in the 1921-22 season.

THORNTON STADIUM: Home of the now defunct Ellesmere Port Town. First visit ended with a 2-1 NPL defeat on September 25, 1971. Richmond scored. Att: 600.

THRELFALL, JACK: 1939-40. Forward in the North Lancashire League scoring three goals in 11 appearances.

THRELFALL, WILFRED: 1925-26, 1927-28 and 1929-30. Outside-left 41 (12 cup) apps; 3 (1 cup) goal. Joined in December, 1925, and moved to Sunderland in May, 1926, for a fee in the region of £350. Joined Birmingham and had a trial with Bournemouth before returning to Morecambe in March, 1928. Moved to Lancaster Town but returned for a third spell in August, 1929. Moved to Rossendale Utd 1930-31 and later played for Morecambe Victoria and the reserves. Born in Morecambe on October 15, 1906, he died on February 13, 1988. Lancashire Cup winner in 1925-26.

THURSTON ROAD: Home of Leyland Motors. The first visit was a 3-1 defeat by the then West Lancashire League side in the 1st Rd of the Lancashire Junior Cup on October 15, 1921. Att: 200. Gornall scored. The ground is now the headquarters of the Lancashire FA.

TICKHILL SQUARE: Former home of Denaby Utd from 1912 until they were forced to withdraw from the Northern Counties East League in 2002. Just one visit for an FA Cup, 1st Qualifying Rd, tie on September 11, 1993, which Morecambe won 4-0. Att: 124.

TIMMINS, ARNOLD: 1964-70. Inside-forward 185+12 (75+2 cup) apps. One of the club's legends Arnold made 260 starts for the Shrimps in six seasons scoring 133 goals. He was signed from Workington, then a Football League Division Four side, by new player manager Geoff Twentyman at the start of the 1964/65 season. He started the season at left-half and made his league debut in a 4-2 home defeat by Netherfield on August 27, 1964. As the season progressed he moved into a more forward role and the goals started to come. His legendary status was assured when he was the leading scorer in both Lancashire Combination title winning sides in 1966/67 and 1967/68, scoring 22 and 20 league goals in respective seasons. The highlight of his career was the eight goals he scored in the club's record 14-0 win over Rossendale Utd on September 2, 1967, a feat that equalled the eight goals scored by Jimmy Ashworth in a 12-0 victory over Great Harwood Town on December 28, 1946. After the club joined the NPL, Arnold dropped back into midfield and struggled to get his place. His final game for the Shrimps was on April 25, 1970, in a 3-1 home defeat by Scarborough when he came on as a substitute. Timmins joined Chorley in the 1970/71 season and went on to play in the Preston & District League. Arnold was born in Whitehaven on January 29, 1940 and died on Chorley on May 14, 1994.
Combination League winner in 1966-67 and 1967-68. Combination Cup winner in 1964-65 and 1967-68. Lancashire Senior Cup winner in 1967-68. Lancashire Cup winner in 1968-69.

TITTERINGTON, HARRY: 1926-28. Outside-right 23 (3 cup) apps; 5 (2 cup) goals. Played one game for the reserves in 1922, but joined in October, 1926.

TODHUNTER, PETER: 1982-87. Goalkeeper 12 (5 cup) apps. Joined in April 1983 and largely played for the reserves, helping them win the Lancashire League Division Two title in 1983-84. Moved to Lancaster City in October, 1987, an later played for Netherfield and Blackpool Mechanics.

TOMLINSON, JIM: 1929-30. Right-half 33 (6 cup) apps. Player who made 20 appearances for Accrington Stanley before joining in August, 1929.

TOMLINSON, NEIL: 1969-71. Centre-half 30 (7 cup) apps; 2 (2 cup) goals. Local player who joined in July, 1969, and was released in May, 1971. Later played for Carnforth Rangers and Mayfield Utd. Had a spell with Lancaster City and Netherfield.

TOMLINSON, PAUL: 1989-96. Defender *(pictured right with the ATS Trophy)* 195+2 (86+3 cup) apps; 18 (8 cup) goals. Former Burscough and Mossley defender who joined in December, 1989. Proved to be an influential signing who helped the team win promotion to the Conference with some reliable performances and vital goals. Moved to Lancaster City for £3,000 in July, 1996, and later played for Caernarfon Town, Accrington Stanley and Darwen. President's Cup winner in 1991-92. Lancashire Cup winner in 1993-94 and 1995-96.

TOOTING & MITCHAM: First met the Terrors at Sandy Lane in the FA Trophy 3rd Rd on February 21, 1976, losing 2-0. Att: 1,500. Met the following season in the same round at Christie Park and own 3-2. Att: 1,138. In an attempt to confuse their opponents Morecambe turned out with their usual numbers reversed with the Right-back given the number 11 shirt and so on.

TOW LAW TOWN: First met the Lawyers in a pre-season friendly at Christie Park on August 2, 1975, winning 3-2.

TOWERS GROUNDS: The second home of New Brighton from 1946-47 although the ground had been used by the former New Brighton Tower from 1897-1901. First visit saw a 2-0 win over their reserves on May 17, 1947 in the Lancashire Combination.

TOWERS, FRANK: 1976-78, 1978-79 and 1982-83. Forward 69+1 (24+1 cup) apps; 20 (7 cup) goals. Former Blackburn Rovers reserves and Leyland Motors player who joined in September, 1976. Moved to Los Angeles Lazers in April, 1978, before returning in September, 1978. Moved to Southport and played for Barrow and Netherfield before rejoining again in July, 1982, but was only an unused sub in one league and one cup game before moving on to Lytham.

TRACEY, CHARLES: 1928-29, 1932-34 and 1934-35. Forward 45 (8 cup) apps; 24 (3 cup) goals. Former Fleetwood player who joined in November 1928. Moved to Great Harwood, Watford and Morton before returning to Morecambe in April, 1933. Joined Lancaster Town in February, 1934, and returned for a third spell in August, 1934, before moving to Fleetwood.

TRAINER, JACK: 1981-82 and 1982-84. Defender 67 (15 cup) apps; 6 (1 cup) goals. Glasgow-born player who made 101+4 appearances, scoring five goals for Halifax Town between 1976-79. Played one game and scored one goal for Bury in 1980 and played for Waterford before joining Morecambe in March 1982.
Returned to the Football League with Rochdale in August 1982 and made seven appearances before returning to Christie Park in October, 1982. Left to join the prison service and later played for Witton Albion.

TRAINOR, STEVE: 1989-90. Midfield/Forward 10 (3 cup) apps; 2 goals. Former Blackpool, Runcorn and Fleetwood Town player who joined in August, 1989, but moved to Wren Rovers in November, 1989. Had a third spell at Fleetwood before becoming a regular at Lancaster City between 1993-97, winning their player of the year award on two occasions. Had a brief spell at Bamber Bridge before returning to Lancaster for two more seasons. Ended his playing career at Fleetwood Freeport and retired in Summer 2001.

TRANMERE ROVERS: First met in a pre-season friendly at Christie Park on July 18, 1995, losing 6-0.

TRANMERE ROVERS RES: Met in the Lancashire Combination & Cheshire League Inter-League Cup 1st Rd at Christie Park on September 2, 1961, winning 4-1. Att: 1,800.

TRAYNOR, JAMES: 1946-48 and 1949-50. Outside-left 28 (2 cup) apps; 11 (1 cup) goals. Ex-Everton junior who joined from Heysham LMS in January, 1947. Returned for a second spell in January, 1950. Later played for Trimpell until aged 54.
Born in Liverpool in 1919 he died on October 17, 2000, aged 81.

TRENTMILL ROAD: Home of the now defunct Eastwood Hanley with the first visit being in the NPL League Cup 2nd Rd on January 30, 1989, losing 2-1. Att: 215. McCarthy scored.

TRODDEN, JOHN: 1935-37. Inside-left 44 (10 cup) apps; 8 goals. Former PNE amateur who joined in December, 1935. Moved to Lancaster City 1937-39 and later played for Clitheroe.

TROTTER, ALAN: 1935-36. Inside-right 24 (2 cup) apps; 4 goals. Former Carlisle amateur from September, 1928, to May, 1935, but made only two first team appearances. Also had as short spell at Arsenal.

TROTTER, HARRY: 1948-50 and 1953-56. Forward 96 (12 cup) apps; 21 (2 cup) goals. Ex-PNE reserves team player who joined in August 1948. Moved to Clitheroe but returned in November 1953.

TULLOCH, RON: 1965-66. Inside-right 20 (5 cup) apps; 5 (2 cup) goals. Ex-Hearts and Southend player who made 73 appearances for Carlisle between 1957-60, scoring 22 goals. Moved to Netherfield and helped them win the Combination Cup in 1960-61 before joining Morecambe in August, 1965. Returned to Netherfield as player-manager in 1966-67.

TULLY, KEVIN: 1981-83. Forward/Midfield 15 (4 cup) apps; 1 goal. Ex-Football League player with Blackpool, Cambridge Utd, Crewe Alexandra, Port Vale and Bury who joined from Barrow in March 1982. Moved to Glossop and became player coach and assistant manager at Witton Albion before leaving in December, 1984. Managed Droylsden 1984-85, Witton Albion 1996-99 and Winsford Utd 1999-2000.

TWENTYMAN, GEOFF: 1964-65. Centre-half 20 (12 cup) apps; 1 cup goal. A man who later became known for his work as Liverpool's chief scout during their glory years in the 1980s Geoff cut his managerial teeth at Christie Park. Carlisle-born Geoff was a centre-half with Carlisle United between 1946 and 1953 making 149 appearances before joining Liverpool with whom he played 170 games, scoring 18 league goals, mainly in the old second division. A spell in Ireland with Ballymena followed before a return to Carlisle where he made 10 more appearances before replacing Joe Dunn as Morecambe boss in 1964. As player-manager Geoff made 20 league and 12 cup appearances for the Shrimps. His season in charge saw the club finish third in the Lancashire Combination and win the Combination Cup. He left in 1965 to embark on his successful scouting career at Liverpool.

TWERTON PARK: Home of Bath City. First visit was a 3-2 defeat in the Conference on March 9, 1996. Att: 511.

TWISS, MICHAEL: Born in Salford in December, 1977, he began his career as a trainee at Manchester Utd and made one League Cup app. Had a loan spell at Sheffield Utd in 1998-99 and scored one goal in 2+10 (2+2 cup) appearances before a move to Port Vale where he made 15+3 (3+3 cup) appearances, scoring 3 (2 cup) goals. Dropped into the Conference with Leigh RMI in 2001 and enjoyed a good season with 15 goals in 29+4 appearances. Moved to Chester in 2002 and in two seasons made 21+16 appearances, scoring six goals. Helped Chester win the Conference title in 2003-04. Joined Morecambe in May, 2004.

TYM, KENNY: 1983-84. Defender 37 (15 cup) apps. Former St Helens Town player who made more than 250 appearances for Marine between 1978-83 before joining in September, 1983. Moved to Chorley in the 1984 close season and later played for Southport and Skelmersdale Utd before retiring in January, 1986.

TYSON, BILLY: 1933-34. Winger 14 (1 cup) apps; 5 goals. Lancaster-born player who joined in January, 1934. Moved to Glentoran and helped them win the Irish Cup in 1934-35 before joining Lancaster Town in October, 1935. Moved to Accrington Stanley in September, 1936, before a £1,200 switch to Blackburn Rovers in October, 1937. Made just six appearances, scoring two goals before joining Boston Utd in August, 1938. Later played for Accrington Stanley and Southport and was a wartime guest player with Newcastle Utd and Lincoln City. After the war played for Lancaster Moor Hospital. Born in Skerton, Lancaster in 1916 he died in February, 1987.

U

UBERSCHAR, NEIL: 2000-03. Defender 15+10 (4+3 cup) apps. Morecambe-born player who progressed through the Youth team and Reserves into the first team. Captained the reserves in 2001-02. Played in some big games before being released in July 2003, joining Lancaster City.

UDALL, JEFF: 1963-66, 1966-68 and 1969-72. Midfield/Forward 50+6 (15+3 cup) apps; 4 (1 cup) goals. Played for Morecambe reserves in 1962-63 but moved to Lancaster City in December 1965. Returned to Morecambe in October 1966, moving to Chorley in October 1968 for a short spell before returning to Christie Park again. Was released by Morecambe in May, 1972, and moved to Trimpell. Managed Morecambe reserves from February, 1980, until the team was disbanded in October, 1981. Coached Lancaster Under 18s from 1990-92 before returning to manage Morecambe Youths in the North Lancs League and take over the reserves again helping them win a string of league titles. A great servant of the club.

UDALL, KEN: 1963-64. Goalkeeper 302 (82 cup) apps. A highly respected goalkeeper Ken made almost 400 appearances for the Shrimps between 1954 and 1964.
Born in Lancaster on May 25, 1936, Ken played for Greaves School and Lancaster Schoolboys at left-half before switching to goalkeeper and playing for Lancaster Youth Club. Another product of Morecambe's youth policy in the 50s Ken made his debut on March 27, 1954, at home to Darwen in a 4-4 draw. He played 24 games in the 1954/55 season but only made five appearances in 1955/56. A season later though he was the Shrimps' first choice stopper from 1956/57 until February 1963 and went on to win two league championship winner's medals and a Lancashire Junior Cup winner's medal in 1961/62. Although shorter than many goalkeepers he had great agility and many say he could have played in the league had he been a couple of inches taller. His greatest moment came with a superb performance in the FA Cup victory over Chester City in 1961/62. He made his last appearance for Morecambe in a 4-0 win at home to Prescot Cables in December 1963 and moved to Lancaster City where he enjoyed three good years. Ken was well known in local sporting circles as during the summer he was a wicketkeeper for Lancaster Cricket Club. He died on July 11, 1986, aged 50. Lancashire Combination League winner in 1961-62 and 1962-63. Lancashire Cup winner in 1961-62.

ULVERSTON TOWN: Played Ulverston in the Lancashire Junior Cup 1st Rd on November 20, 1926, winning 6-3. Att: 2,500.

UNDERHILL STADIUM: Home of Barnet with the first visit being a 1-0 defeat in the Conference on March 9, 2000. Att: 1,316.

V

VALLEY PARADE: Home of Bradford City and now known as the Bradford & Bingley Stadium. Only visit was on December 22, 1973, to play Bradford Park Avenue who were using the ground in their final season in the NPL. Morecambe won 1-0. Att: 648.

VARCOE, DEREK: 1962-71. Defender 236 (85+1 cup) apps; 6 (3 cup) goals. A local sporting legend who was as well known on the cricket field as he was on the football field. Milnthorpe-based Derek was signed in the 1964/65 season by Geoff Twentyman, making his debut in a pre-season friendly against Burnley reserves on August 12, 1964. His league debut came in a 6-1 defeat at Horwich RMI on September 3, 1964 but things did get a lot better. In his first season he made 20 league and 4 cup apps. He made his mark as an ever present in the Lancashire Combination title winning sides of 1966/67 and 1967/68. He also played in the sides which won the Lancashire Senior Cup in 1966-67 and the Lancashire Combination Cup in 1966-67 and 1967-68. An experienced defender who had a touch of quality Derek was also an ever present in the club's first season in the NPL. His last season with the Shrimps was in the 1970/71 campaign, playing his final game on April 27, 1971 – a 3-2 win at Chorley. Moved back to Milnthorpe Corinthians and later played for Lancaster City and Netherfield. Derek sadly died of Motor Neurone Disease on October 12, 2003, aged 58.

VAUXHALL MOTORS: Met the Motormen in a pre-season friendly at Rivacre Park on July 29. 2003, drawing 1-1.

VICKERS, MAURICE: 1946-49. Forward 53 (8 cup) apps; 14 (2 cup) goals. Striker who played for Lancaster City before and after the war. Joined Morecambe in November, 1946, and started a long association with the club. Coached the Reserves and Junior sides between 1955-57 and 1959-61 and was a club director 1967-68. Was a scout and coach for the first team and later became a director of Lancaster City.

VICKERS SPORTS CLUB: Met in a friendly at Christie Park on February 6, 1990, winning 3-0.

VICTORIA GROUND: Home of Bromsgrove Rovers with the first visit being a 1-0 defeat on April 30, 1996. Att: 626.

VICTORIA PARK: Home of Burscough with the first visit being a 2-1 win over Burscough Rovers in the Lancashire Combination on September 14, 1927. Luty and Walmsley scored.

VICTORIA PARK: The second home of Nelson with the first visit being a 1-0 win in the Lancashire Junior Cup, 2nd Rd, on January 24, 1982.

VICTORIA PLEASURE GROUNDS: Former home of Goole Town with the first visit being a 5-0 win in the NPL on May 3, 1969. Att: 1,000.

VICTORIA ROAD: Home of Dagenham & Redbridge with the first visit being a 2-2 draw on September 16, 1995, in the Conference. Att: 834. Burns and Grimshaw scored. Became known as the Glyn Hopkins Stadium in 2003-04.

VICTORIA ROAD (PARK): Former home of Oswestry Town with the first visit being a 0-0 draw in the NPL on March 11, 1980.

VICTORY PARK: Home of Barnoldswick Town with the first visit being a 2-0 defeat in the Lancashire Combination on November 1, 1924. Att: 2,000.

VICTORY PARK: Home of Chorley with the first visit being a 2-1 win on December 4, 1920 in the Lancashire Combination.

VISTA PARK: Home of Earlestown with the first visit being a 2-1 win in a Lancashire Junior Cup semi-final replay tie on April 26, 1951.
Earlestown were reformed in 1945-46 and continued until disbanding in December 1963. The ground was then used by Newton FC in the North West Counties League until 1990. Wilf Mannion was Earlestown manager from November 1960 until being sacked in October 1962.

VIZARD, COLIN: 1959-61. Inside-left 50 (13 cup) apps; 18 (6 cup) goals. Former Everton, Rochdale, Horwich RMI, Prescot Cables and Wigan Athletic player who joined in November, 1959. Moved to Prescot Cables in December, 1961. Played for Earlestown and Burscough.

VOTES: Morecambe applied 11 times to join the Football League but were always unsuccessful. Got no votes in 1957, 1958, 1959 and 1961. One vote was obtained in 1960, 1962, 1964, 1965, 1966 and 1970. The best year was 1963 when two votes were gained. Morecambe had to apply for re-election on 1 occasion to both the Lancashire Combination and the NPL and were successful.

VS RUGBY: Met Valley Sports Rugby in a pre-season friendly at Christie Park on August 12, 1995, winning 4-2.

W

WADDINGTON, PADDY: 1952-53. Inside-left 19 (4 cup) apps; 1 goal. Joined Morecambe in July 1952 after five seasons at Chorley.

WADE, PHILIP: 1973-76. Defender 17 (1 cup) apps. Local player with Woodhill Rangers, Ryelands/St Chads, Morecambe reserves and Lancaster Celtic. Had trials with Manchester City and also played with York City reserves.

WAGSTAFF, TOM: 1925-26. Centre-forward 25 (14 cup) apps; 21 (7 cup) goals. Ex-Fleetwood and Wigan Athletic player who made two appearances for Sunderland in 1922-23. Joined in August, 1925, and was a prolific scorer before joining Crewe Alexandra 1926-27.

WAITE: 1946-47. Left-back 12 (3 cup) apps. Joined in September, 1946.

WAKEFIELD, JOE: 1931-32. Right-half 13 (3 cup) apps. Ex-Barrow and Ulverston Town player who joined in September, 1931.

WALKER, GEORGE: 1964-65. Inside-left 31 (10 cup) apps; 13 (6 cup) goals. Sunderland-born player who turned out for Chippenham Town and Bristol City before making 164 appearances, scoring 52 goals for Carlisle between 1959-62. Joined in August, 1964, and moved to Netherfield. Combination Cup winner in 1964-65.

WALKER, SAMUEL: 1921-23. Outside-right/Inside-right 21 (5 cup) apps; 2 (3 cup) goals. Joined in January 1922. Released in May 1923.

WALKS STADIUM: Home of Kings Lynn with the first visit being a 0-0 draw in the NPL on Sunday, March 29, 1981. Att: 326.

WALMSLEY, KEIRAN: 2002-04. Defender 27 (6+2 cup) apps; 2 goals. Longridge-based Right-back who broke into the first team in the 2003-04 season. Another player who progressed through the reserves. Lancashire Cup winner in 2003-04.

WALSH, JOHN: 1981-82. Forward 32+1 (4 cup) apps; 10 goals. Ex-PNE, Southport and Chorley player who made his debut in the 9-0 home defeat by Bangor City on September 21, 1981. Moved to Leyland Motors in the 1982-83 season. Had a spell in Australia and also had a second spell at Chorley in 1988-89.

WALSH, LAURIE: 1977-78, 1978-81 and 1989-91. Defender 147+2 (41+2 cup) apps; 12 (3 cup) goals. Ex-PNE apprentice who joined for his first spell from Wren Rovers in August 1977, aged 19. Moved back to Wren Rovers in January, 1978, but rejoined Morecambe in July, 1978. Released in April, 1981, he moved to Southport and played for

Workington, Lancaster City, Penrith and Fleetwood Town before returning for a third time in August, 1989. Later moved to Wren Rovers and Fleetwood Town.

WALSH, MARK: 1985-86. Midfield/Forward 10+1 (9+1 cup) apps; 2 goals. A professional who made 56+6 apps for PNE, scoring two goals between 1979-85. Had a short spell with Auckland in New Zealand and Exeter City before joining in September, 1985. Moved to Chorley in January, 1986, and later played for Workington, Accrington Stanley, Clitheroe, Darwen and Great Harwood Town.

WALSH, STEVE: 1977-78. Forward 11+2 (2 cup) apps; 3 (1 cup) goals. Former Blackpool reserves, Chorley and Netherfield player who joined in August, 1977. Released in November, 1977, and joined Heskin. Later played for Southport and Leyland Motors.

WALTERS, STEVE: 2000-01. Midfield 20+2 (9 cup) apps; 1 (2 cup) goals. Still the club's record signing after joining from Northwich Victoria on May 20, 2000, for £25,000. A player who made a name for himself as a junior when he was capped by England at Under 15, Under 16 and Under 18 levels. Broke into the Crewe Alexandra team at an early age and made 135+11 appearances, scoring 10 goals between 1988-94. Joined Northwich Victoria on a free transfer in December, 1994, and was a vital member of their side for five seasons, making 176+2 appearances and scoring 35 goals. Unfortunately, his spell at Morecambe was a disappointing one by his previous high standards and he was sold to Stevenage Borough for £17,000 in March 2001. Made just 17 appearances, scoring two goals before a £10,000 move to Kidsgrove Athletic in November, 2001. Later moved to Rhyl where they won the League of Wales title in 2003-04.

WAR MEMORIAL ATHLETIC GROUND: Home of West Midlands club Stourbridge with the first visit being a 1-1 draw in the FA Trophy, 3rd Rd, on February 10, 1973.

WARBURTON, FRED (JUNIOR): Outside-right who made one appearance and scored one goal in the North Lancashire League during 1939-40 season.

WARBURTON, FRED (SENIOR): 1937-38. Outside-right 1 app. Perhaps the most famous name ever to be associated with the club. Began his playing career with one appearance for Bolton Wanderers in 1903-04 and later played for Bryn Central (Bury), Swindon Town, Plymouth Argyle and Accrington. It was as a coach that he came to the fore as he was in charge of the Dutch national side between 1911-21 and then Den Haag from 1921 until his retirement in 1935. He and his family returned to England and he became Morecambe's coach between 1935-39. In an emergency he played one game for Morecambe on April 18, 1938, in a 3-2 defeat at Southport reserves, aged 57 or 58 and became the club's oldest player. His sons, Fred junior, George and James all played for Morecambe. Fred died on November 29, 1948, aged 68.

WARBURTON, GEORGE: 1936-37, 1939-40 and 1945-48. Winger 52 (23 cup) apps; 17 (8 cup) goals. Born in the Netherlands in 1916 the son of another Morecambe player Fred, George was one of the first Shrimps stars to move into league football when he was signed by Aston Villa in November 1937. Unfortunately he never really made the grade and failed to grace the first team at either Villa Park or PNE, where he moved on to. He finally made his Football League debut for Chester City in the 1938-39 season, making 10 appearances and scoring once. During the war he guested for Chester, Notts County, Leeds United, Middlesbrough and Darlington. Rejoined Morecambe in February, 1946, and helped the club win the Combination Cup in 1945-46. Later played for Netherfield, Lancaster City, Ingleborough and Trimpell. Combination Cup winner in 1945-46.

WARBURTON, JAMES: 1945-47. Right-half 9 (11 cup) apps; 2 (2 cup) goals. Ex-Sparta Rotterdam player who joined in February, 1946. Helped the club win the Combination Cup in 1945-46. Moved to Lancaster City and later played for Ingleborough. Combination Cup winner in 1945-46.

WATERHOUSE, KEN: 1965-66. and 1970-72. Inside-forward 76 (33 cup) apps; 2 (1 cup) goals. One of the club's most successful managers, who, legend has it, was given the Morecambe job in preference to Brian Clough. Ken had two spells at the Christie Park helm with his first term of office beginning in 1965. Born in Ormskirk Ken played for Burscough before joining PNE where he made 22 appearances and scored five league goals. From there he moved to Rotherham and between 1958 and 1963 made 115 league appearances, chalking up 11 league goals before joining Bristol City and finally Darlington. He enjoyed unrivalled success as boss winning the Lancashire Combination twice, the Lancashire Combination Cup twice, the Lancashire Senior Cup and the Lancashire Junior Cup. It was a great blow to the club when Ken left to become the trainer at Blackburn Rovers at the end of the 1968-69 season. Ken was reappointed boss in December, 1970, but he failed to lift to the club to the heights of his former reign and was sacked in May, 1972, and was replaced by player-manager Dave Roberts.

WEBB, BILL: 1959-61. Centre-forward 10 (6 cup) apps; 6 (1 cup) goals. Lancaster-born player who had trials with Wolves. Played a handful of games with Morecambe reserves aged just 14. Signed for the first team in August, 1958, and moved to Wigan Athletic for £15 in November, 1960. Made 19 appearances, scoring seven goals for them before moving to Netherfield 1961-63. Emigrated to Australia in 1964.

WEBB, TREVOR: 1963-67. Forward 37+1 (16+2 cup) apps; 35 (6 goals). A prolific goalscorer whose apps were limited by the form of Keith Borrowdale.
Joined in December, 1963, and moved to Chorley in May, 1967. Later played for Lancaster City and Carnforth Rangers. Managed locally with College Wanderers and Lancaster City reserves and also had a spell as assistant manager of Morecambe reserves. Made one appearance for the reserves in 1970-71. Later became a director of Lancaster City. Combination Cup winner in 1964-65 and 1966-67.

WEBBER, TONY: 1973-77. Forward 124+3 (38 cup) apps; 53 (24 cup) goals. A striker who carved his name into Morecambe folklore with a superb performance in the FA Trophy triumph in 1974. It was he who set up the goals for Mal Richmond and Jimmy Sutton and was described as a *"lethal striker"* in the People's report of the match.

A Wigan-born schoolteacher Tony was released by Bolton Wanderers and joined Skelmersdale United before joining the Shrimps for £250 in the summer of 1973 to replace Russ Perkins. He scored on his debut in a 4-1 win a Buxton on August 11, and went on to become a regular in the FA Trophy winning side, scoring 2 goals in the superb replay win at Kettering. He finished the 1974-75 season as top scorer with 22 goals and repeated the feat in the 1975-76 season with 29 goals including four in consecutive games – a 5-3 win at Radcliffe Borough in the Lancashire Junior Cup and in a 5-2 FA Trophy success at Crook Town. His last game was on October 5, 1976 when he was a substitute in a 1-0 home defeat by Great Harwood. He was transferred to Altrincham for a fee approaching £1,000. He went on to play for Lancaster City before managing several clubs including Rossendale United, South Liverpool and Horwich RMI. FA Trophy winner in 1973-74.

WEBSTER, JACK: 1931-33 and 1934-35. Centre-forward 41 (7 cup) apps; 12 (4 cup) goals. Former Blackpool, Fleetwood and Lancaster Town player who signed in January, 1932. Returned to Lancaster Town 1934-35 but came back to Morecambe for a second spell in December, 1934.

WELFARE GROUND: Home of Durham club Brandon Utd with the only visit being a 6-0 win in the FA Cup 1st Qualifying Rd on September 14, 1996. Goals came from Ceraolo (2), Leaver (2), Grimshaw and Norman. Att: 267.

WELFARE PARK: Home of Bedlington Terriers with the only visit being a 3-1 win in the FA Cup, 4th Qualifying Rd, on October 28, 2000. Black, Hardiker and Thompson scored.

WELFARE PARK: Home of Horden Colliery Welfare with the only visit being on January 12, 1980, in the FA Trophy, 1st Rd. Morecambe won 2-1 with Nick Jones scoring both goals. Att: 381.

WELFARE SPORTS GROUND: Former home of Emley with the first visit being a 2-1 win in an NPL League Cup 4th Rd reply on March 15, 1990. Att: 458.

WELLING UTD: First met the Wings at Christie Park on February 4, 1992, in the FA Trophy, 2nd Rd, winning 2-1. Att: 883.

WEST, PAUL: 1995-97. Defender 24+6 (5+3 cup) apps; 1 goal *(pictured right)*. Extremely popular individual who was at Port Vale, Bradford City and Wigan Athletic (where he made 2+1 apps), before joining in January, 1996. Unfortunately, suffered from niggling injuries and was released in May, 1997. Had a short spell with Bradford Park Avenue before moving to Evesham Utd in the Midlands where he was player coach 1997-2002. Came up against the Shrimps in the FA Trophy.

WEST HAM UTD: The Hammers visited Christie Park for a friendly on April 22, 1976, winning 9-1. Att: 4,000. The Visitor report read: *"The elegant Trevor Brooking's artistry was a privilege to watch."*

WEST HAM UTD U23 XI: After the transfer of Brain Thomson to West Ham they brought a young side down to Christie Park for an end of season friendly on May 24, 1977. West Ham won 4-2 with Alan Taylor scoring a hat-trick and Anton Otulakowski also scoring. Att: 723.

WEST LANCASHIRE LEAGUE XI: Played a friendly against the select XI on January 25, 1983, drawing 3-3.

WEST VIEW: Home of Bacup Borough with the first visit being on August 31, 1920, in the Lancashire Combination, winning 2-1.

WESTFIELD LANE: Home of Frickley Athletic with the first visit being in the NPL on March 30, 1977, winning 2-0. Att: 246.

WESTMORLAND COUNTY FA XI: Met in friendlies at Christie Park on November 9, 1983, drawing 1-1 and on February 19, 1985, winning 1-0 with a goal from Barnes.

WESTON, JIMMY: 1983-85. Midfield 80 (22 cup) apps; 4 goals. Ex-Skelmersdale Utd player who joined Blackpool for £2,500 in January, 1974, and made 97+8 apps, scoring eight goals for the Bloomfield Road club. In June, 1980, joined Torquay Utd for £5,000 and made 38 appearances, scoring one goal before a £7,500 move to Wigan Athletic in September, 1981. In two seasons made 63+3 appearances, scoring two goals before being released in the close season of 1983. Joined Morecambe in July, 1983, and released in May, 1985. Player of the year 1982-83.

WETHERBY ROAD: Home of Harrogate Town with the first visit being a 2-0 win in the FA Cup, 1st Qualifying Rd, on September 7, 1985. Galley and Thornton scored. Att: 266.

WEXHAM PARK STADIUM: Home of Berkshire club Slough Town with the first visit being a 2-0 defeat in the FA Trophy, 4th Rd, on March 19, 1977. Att: 1,500.

WEYMOUTH: First met the Terras in the FA Cup 3rd Rd on a famous afternoon at Christie Park on January 6, 1962. Lost 1-0 in a game in front of a record crowd of 9,383.

WHADDON ROAD: Home of Cheltenham Town with the first visit being a 2-1 defeat in the Conference on December 13, 1997. Att: 1,717. Healy scored.

WHALLEY, ERIC: The current Accrington Stanley chairman had a disappointing spell as boss at Christie Park. He had a big act to follow when taking over the reins from the popular Joe Wojciechowicz and was not helped by the mass exodus of the club's best players to Colne Dynamoes. Eric, a former reserve team player with Accrington Stanley in their Football League days, took over in June, 1988. A self-made businessman he had a great deal of experience as a non-league manager at places such as Great Harwood, Clitheroe and Accrington Stanley. Unfortunately, for Eric his spell as boss was something of a disaster and he resigned five months after taking over. The end came on November 8 when his side slumped to their 10th defeat in a row at Mossley.

WHEATSHEAF PARK: Home of Staines Town with the only visit being for a FA Trophy, 2nd Rd replay, on February 8, 1977, drawing 0-0 after extra time.

WHEATSHEAF SPORTS GROUND: Home of Newcastle Blue Star with the only visit being a 1-0 defeat in the FA Cup, 1st Qualifying Rd, on September 12, 1987. Att: 177.

WHIPP, HARRY: 1922-24 and 1927-28. Centre-forward 32 (5 cup) apps; 16 (1 cup) goals. Ex-Stoke City and Carlisle Utd player who played for Lancaster Town 1918-21 and Scotforth 1921-22 before joining in September, 1922. Moved to Lancaster Town but returned to Morecambe in August, 1927.

WHITBY TOWN: Met the Seasiders at Christie Park in the FA Cup, Preliminary Rd, on September 4, 1982, winning 2-0. Att: 234.

WHITE, JOHN: 1986-88. Midfield 28+1 (14+2 cup) apps; 3 (2 cup) goals. Ex-Wren Rovers player who joined in January, 1987. Released in April, 1988. Moved to Wren Rovers and later played for Colne Dynamoes. The son of Tom White who played for Crystal Palace, Blackpool, Bury and Crewe Alexandra. Was the nephew of the legendary John White who was a member of Spurs' double-winning side and a Scotland international.

WHITE MOSS PARK: Second ground of Skelmersdale Utd with the first visit being in the Lancashire Combination on December 6, 1958, winning 2-1. Skelmersdale are now sharing Burscough's ground.

WHITEHEAD, IAN: 1960-64 and 1965-66. Inside-left 96 (27 cup) apps; 91 (25 cup) goals. A prolific goalscorer in the early 1960s, Ian was another to join the club after being released by PNE. After playing for North End reserves he was released in June, 1960, and made his debut for the Shrimps in a 4-1 home win against Bacup Borough on August 20, 1960. Dropped after a 7-0 defeat at Netherfield he became a prolific goalscorer with the reserves for most of the season but only ended up playing 11 league and one cup game in his first season at Christie Park, scoring four goals. He started the 1961/62 campaign in the reserves but after Jimmy Baxter retired after three games he was given his chance to shine again and took it with both hands, scoring 48 goals in 32 league and 13 cup appearances as Morecambe won the league and Junior Cup. Amazingly he was only the second top scorer behind Keith Borrowdale. He went one better the season after however with a club record 45 league goals from 39 games as the Shrimps retained the championship. He also chipped in with four cup goals to make it 49 for the season. The next season was a real anti-climax however as he, and the team, struggled for form and he was transferred to Horwich RMI after eight league games. He was brought back to Christie Park by new manager Ken Waterhouse in the 1965/66 season but despite scoring six league goals in six games was not retained. His last game was in a 3-1 home defeat to Fleetwood in the Combination Cup on October 5, 1965. Ian scored four goals in a game on three occasions against Burscough in 1961, Lytham in 1963 and Bacup Borough in 1965. Lancashire Combination League winner in 1961-62 and 1962-63. Lancashire Cup winner 1962-63.

WHITLEY BAY: First meeting was a 1-1 draw in the NPL at Hillheads on September 24, 1991. Att: 401. Ian Cain scored.

WHITTAKER: 1931-32. Inside-right 15 apps; 2 goals. Joined in January, 1932.

WHITTAKER, HARRY: 1934-35. Outside-left 11 (3 cup) apps; 2 goals. Ex-Burnley A team player who had spells with Rossendale Utd, Accrington Stanley Reserves and Rawtenstall Star before joining in October, 1934.

WHITTAKER, NORMAN: 1920-22 and 1924-27. Half-back/Forward 26 (5 cup) apps; 5 (1 cup) goals. Former Lancaster Town player who was in Morecambe's first ever line up in August, 1920. Played for the YMCA in 1924-25 and returned to Morecambe in September, 1924. Combination Cup winner 1926-27.

WHITTAKER, WILLIAM: 1922-23. Inside-forward 25 apps; 3 goals. Ex-Portsmouth player who joined in August, 1922. Released in May, 1923, and later played for Ulverston Town.

WHITTINGHAM, PAUL: 1975-79. Defender 54+5 (6 cup) apps; 2 goals. Paul made his debut for the reserves at the age of 15. Made his first team debut at the age of 16 on January 17, 1976, against South Liverpool. Later played for Lansil and Morecambe Reserves.

WIGAN ATHLETIC: With the demise of Wigan Borough during the 1931-32 season a new club was formed for the 1932-33 season. Wigan joined the Cheshire League and were champions in 1933-34. First meeting was a 4-1 defeat on February 10, 1934, at Christie Park in the 2nd Rd of the Lancashire Junior Cup.

WIGAN BOROUGH: Formed in 1920-21 with the first meeting between the clubs coming in the Lancashire Combination on March 5, 1921. Wigan won 2-1. Att: 1,200.

WIGAN BOROUGH RESERVES: Wigan Borough joined the Football League in 1921-22 and their Reserves entered the Lancashire Combination in 1923-24. First meeting was at Rosebery Park on October 27, 1923, with a 2-2 draw.

WIGAN ROVERS: An attempt to form another club in Wigan. Formed in 1959 they joined the Lancashire Combination League in 1961-62 and had two seasons in Division One in 1966-67 and 1967-68. First meeting was at Christie Park on April 15, 1967 with Morecambe winning 2-0. Lea and Martin scored.

WIGNALL, MARK: 1982-84. Midfield 18+1 (2 cup) apps. Former Wigan Athletic player who made 34 apps for the Latics between 1980-82. Joined Morecambe in December, 1982. Later played for Fulwood West End and Bamber Bridge.

WILCOCK, T: 1922-23. Goalkeeper 28 (9 cup) apps. Joined in August, 1922, after eight seasons at Chorley. Released in May, 1923, and moved to Great Harwood. Later played for Fleetwood.

WILD, HARRY: 1932-33. Centre-half 11 (4 cup) apps. Joined in January, 1933.

WILDE: 1952-53. Outside-left 14 (1 cup) apps; 1 goals. Joined in December, 1952.

WILKINSON, T W: 1938-40. Outside-left 15 apps; 1 goals. Joined after playing locally with the Technical College in the North Lancashire League.

WILKINSON, RAY: 1976-77. Forward 10 (1 cup) apps; 1 goal. Former Skelmersdale Utd player who joined Wigan for £800 in January, 1975, and helped them win the NPL title in 1974-75. Returned to Skelmersdale Utd and Bootle before joining in June, 1976. Returned to Bootle in November, 1976.

WILLIAMS, CHRIS: 1965-67. Goalkeeper 24 (8 cup) apps. Ex-PNE player who joined in August, 1965. Joined Chorley in May, 1967.

WILLIAMS, VAUGHAN: 1985-88. Midfield 89 (42 cup) apps; 3 (1 cup) goals. Local-born player who was on Everton's books as a junior after having trials with Bolton Wanderers and PNE. Played for Skerton Athletic before joining Lancaster City for the first of two successful spells at Giant Axe in the 1974-75 season. Was there until joining Workington for £5,000 in the 1980-81 season, signing for Morecambe in February, 1986, for £900, being the club's player of the year in the 1986-87 season. Was one of a number of players to join Colne Dynamoes in 1988-89 before returning to Lancaster City between 1989-97. Made more than 450 apps for City in his career and later managed the reserves. Lancashire Cup winner in 1985-86 and 1986-87.

WILLIAMSON, JOHNNY: 1933-34. Inside-right 15 (1 cup) apps. Player of vast experience who joined Morecambe in his 40s in August 1933. Was a member of PNE's FA Cup final side of 1921-22 and made 63 apps, scoring two goals, for the Deepdale club before moving to Grimsby Town where he played just once. Later played for Doncaster Rovers and had two spells at Lancaster Town before joining Darwen and Barrow. Became PNE's kitman before retiring in October, 1960.

WILLIAMSON, JOHN: 1975-77 and 1977-79. Forward 46+9 (19+3 cup) apps; 14 (6 cup) goals. Joined for the first time in August, 1975, and had a trial with Wrexham before moving to Atherton Collieries in the 1977-78 season. Returned to Morecambe in March 1978 before moving to Macclesfield Town in February, 1979.

WILLINGTON: Met the 'Blue & Whites' in the FA Cup, 4th Qualifying Rd, on November 1, 1975, drawing 2-2. Grundy and Webber scored for the Shrimps who won the replay 4-1 after extra time on November 4. Kershaw (2), Ross and Webber scored.

WILLOW FARM: PNE's old training ground where Morecambe met a PNE XI for a friendly during the Arctic winter of 1963. A game on January 19, ended in a 6-1 defeat.

WILSON, ALBERT (DERBY): 1925-27. Outside-left 22 (12 cup) apps; 3 goals. Lancaster-born player who played for his home town team before and after WWI, helping them win the Combination title in 1921-22. Made 17 appearances for Barrow in 1923-24 before returning to Lancaster. Joined Morecambe in August, 1925, but had to retire after a knee injury in 1927. He successfully sued the Morecambe FC committee for an industrial injury in a case that must have been one of the first of its kind. Born in Lancaster in 1897 he died on July 22, 1977.

WILSON, GEORGE: 1949-51. Centre-forward 36 (4 cup) apps; 22 (1 cup) goals. Former Fleetwood player who joined in September, 1949, for £50. Moved to Wigan Athletic in November, 1950, for a small fee and later played for St Helen's Town.

WILSON, G B: 1933-36. Inside-right/Centre-forward 14 apps; 7 goals. Lancaster-based player who joined in September 1933.

WINCHAM PARK: Now known as the Bargain Booze Stadium and the second home of Witton Albion and temporary home of Northwich Victoria 2002-04. First visit was a 2-0 defeat in the NPL on May 1, 1999. Att: 412.

WINDRIDGE, DAVID: 1990-91. Forward 26+3 (6 cup) apps; 5 (1 cup) goals. Experienced Football League player who joined in July, 1990. Began his career as a junior with Sheffield Utd before a move to Chesterfield where he made 66+12 appearances, scoring 14 goals between 1979-83.
A free transfer to Blackpool followed and between 1983-87 he scored 18 goals in 87+12 apps. After being released in May, 1987, he had short spells at several clubs including Galatasaray in Turkey, Northwich Victoria, Cork City, Bury, Rochdale and Colne Dynamoes before coming to Christie Park. Moved to Wren Rovers in the close season on 1991 and later played for Fleetwood Town.

WINN, NORMAN: 1920-21 and 1926-27. Outside-left 27 (1 cup) apps; 4 (1 cup) goals. Former Lancaster Town and Lancaster Discharged player who joined in November, 1920. Moved to Bradford City for £150 at the end of the 1920-21 season and made 85 appearances for them between 1921-26, scoring 10 goals. Had spells with Chorley and

Lancaster Town before returning to Morecambe in April, 1927. Born in Lancaster on August 24, 1900, he died in Morecambe in May 21, 1972.

WINS, RECORDS: Record win is 14-0 v Rossendale in the Lancashire Combination at Christie Park on September 2, 1967. Att: 1,500. Timmins scored four goals in eight minutes. Morecambe won 32 of the 42 matches played in the 1961-62 season to win the Lancashire Combination. In the 1962-63 season the club won 20 of their 21 home league games as they lifted the title.

WINSFORD UTD: First met the Blues in a 2-0 defeat in the NPL at the Barton Stadium on September 26, 1992. Att: 541.

WISEMAN, W: 1931-32. Centre-forward/Inside-left 12 apps; 9 goals. Former Clitheroe player who joined in January, 1932. Later played for Settle.

WITHERS, PETER: 1994-96. Forward 10+6 (0+1 cup) apps; 2 goals. Skilful player who began his career with South Liverpool before a £5,000 move to Runcorn in October 1989. In three seasons made 78+29 appearances, scoring 16 goals before a four-figure fee took him to Southport in 1992. Helped them to win the NPL title in 1992-93 before moving to Chorley in the close season of 1994. Joined Morecambe in March, 1995, and moved to Marine in October, 1995.

WITTON ALBION: First met the Albion in a 1-0 defeat at Christie Park in the NPL on September 22, 1979. Att: 399.

WOJCIECHOWICZ, JOE: 1973-74 and 1985-88. Midfield 7 apps. The former Blackpool apprentice only made a handful of appearances for Morecambe in the 1973/74 season and also turned out for Barrow and Lancaster but really made his mark as a coach and a manager. After a successful spell as boss at Workington Joe, a Morecambe man, took charge in February, 1985, and had three very successful seasons, especially in the Lancashire Cup.
Morecambe reached the final of the competition for three years in succession beating Chorley 3-2 in the 1986/87 season and the same team again 2-0 the season after. The only defeat came in the 1987/88 season with a 2-0 reverse against Marine at Burnden Park. In the league the Shrimps finished 3rd, 6th and 4th. There was a general feeling of disappointment when Joe resigned as manager in May, 1988, to become full-time coach of Colne Dynamoes, taking a number of top players with him.

WOKING: First met the Cards in a 3-0 defeat at the Kingfield Stadium in the Conference on November 4, 1995. Att: 2,679.

WOLVERHAMPTON WANDERERS: First visited Christie Park for a pre-season friendly on July 13, 2002, in an exciting 3-3 draw. The Premiership new boys returned on July 26, 2003, and were crushed 6-1 by an inspired Morecambe. Att: 1,521.

WOODBURN, DAVID: 1984-88. Midfield 34+2 (15 cup) apps; 5 goals. One of the most committed midfield players you could wish to see. Joined in April, 1985, after playing for Dalton Utd, Barrow and Vickers Sports. Moved to Barrow and later had a long spell at Lancaster City 1988-94 where he had a brief period as caretaker manager in October, 1992. Lancashire Cup winner in 1985-86.

WOODHILL LANE: Used the cricket field for the first season in 1920-21 with the first trial match being on August 7, 1920. Opening league game was a 4-1 defeat against Fleetwood on August 28, 1920. Att: 3,000.

WOODHOUSE, DICK: 1920-24 and 1925-32. Right-half/Left-half 134 (35 cup). Ex-Morecambe Central School, White Lund, Poulton Athletic and Bare Utd who joined in November 1920. Became the club's first real legend as apart from a short spell at Skerton Athletic in 1924-25 he spent 18 seasons with the club. A loyal and devoted servant he won the Lancashire Junior Cup in 1925-26 and was a member of the Combination runners-up team of 1925-26. Was the reserve team trainer from 1933 to 1938 and made his last app for the Reserves on Christmas Day, 1937. Was trainer for Brook & Kershaws 1938-39, playing an occasional game. Born in Morecambe in 1901, he died on January 21, 1983.

WOODWORTH, TONY: 1988-89. Goalkeeper 13 (6 cup) apps. Ex-Burnley apprentice who made one first team app who joined in July, 1988. Moved to Great Harwood 1988-89 and later Darwen.

WOOF, CLIFFORD: 1981-82. Defender 20 (5+1 cup) apps; 1 cup goal. Ex-Everton apprentice and Liverpool professional (no first team appearance), who played non-league for Southport and Oswestry Town and helped Liverpool Sunday League side Fantail win the 1980-81 FA Sunday Cup. Joined Morecambe in August, 1981, and later played for Irlam Town, Netherfield, Prescot Cables, Saffron Walden and Newmarket Town.

WOOLERSON, SIMON: 1989-90. Defender 22+1 (7 cup) apps; 1 goal. Former Blackpool Rangers player who joined from Fleetwood Town in August, 1989. Moved to Wren Rovers and then Fleetwood Town before joining Lancaster City in July, 1993.

WORKINGTON: Met the former Football League club in the NPL but the first meeting was in a friendly at their former ground Lonsdale Park on December 10, 1921, losing 5-4. Aldred, Bateson, Emmison and Hampson scored.

WORKSOP TOWN: First met the Tigers in the NPL at Christie Park on September 7, 1968, drawing 0-0. Att: 1, 650.

WORLD WAR TWO: Started the 1939-40 season in the Lancashire Combination but resigned after three games and took over the reserves teams fixtures in the North Lancashire League. The annual meeting at the end of the 1940-41 season reports that after defaulting one game, the last five matches were unplayed. The club lost £98 on the season, raising the debt to £303. One game saw gate receipts as low as 31/2d. In the previous season £81 was raised from rent from travelling people but after damage was caused they were evicted so income from that source was wiped out. No season tickets were sold, donations were down and gate receipts were down £70. As a result the club was closed down for the rest of the war. A team called Morecambe Services, mainly the RAF, continued to use Christie Park for the 1941-42 and 1942-43 seasons, playing in a wartime Lancashire Combination. Many players with Football League experience played for this side. No football was played at Christie Park during the 1943-44 and 1944-45 seasons.

WREN ROVERS: First met the club now known as Blackpool Wren Rovers in a Lancashire Junior Cup 2nd Rd tie which ended 0-0 at Christie Park on January 5, 1980. Att: 191.

WRESTLING: Bouts were held on the Christie Park pitch in July, 1953. Top of the bill was Jackie Pye who beat Mike Marino.

WREXHAM: Met just once, in an LDV Vans Trophy tie, at the Racecourse Ground on October 14, 2003, losing 4-1. Att: 1,079.

WRIGHT, BILLY: . 1988-89. Defender 6 (6 cup) apps; 1 goal. Billy was a giant of a defender who had a very successful career with Everton, Birmingham and Carlisle before a short spell as Morecambe's boss covering parts of 1988 and 1989. Billy was born in Liverpool and signed for Everton as a schoolboy. He made 166 league and 26 cup appearances scoring 10 goals for the Toffeemen before joining Birmingham where he started 111 league and 26 cup games. He finished his career at Carlisle with 41 league and 6 cup appearances before joining the Shrimps on October 6, 1988. After Eric Whalley resigned on November 8, Wright, who was forced to stop playing because of injury, was asked to take over as caretaker manager. He held the position for six games before being asked to take over full-time. His spell was not exactly successful however and he parted company with the club on April 22, 1989 after a 2-0 defeat at Bangor City.

WRIGHT, MARK: 1999-2001. Defender 22 (2+1 cup) apps; 1 cup goal. Ex-Everton schoolboy who made one first team app between 1988-91. After a loan spell at Blackpool joined Huddersfield Town and made 25+7 appearances, scoring one goal. Moved to Wigan in November, 1993, and made 27+2 appearances, scoring two goals. Played for Chorley, Witton Albion and Droylsden before joining in June, 1999. Was released in December, 2000.

WROTH, CHARLIE: 1967-70. Forward 62+10 (25 cup) apps; 20 (6 cup) goals. Ex-Bolton Wanderers and Chorley player who joined in August, 1967. A respected marksman he moved to Betherfield in the 1970-71 season and later played for Clitheroe.

WYCOMBE WANDERERS: Met the Chairboys in the FA Trophy 2nd Rd at Christie Park on January 30, 1993, drawing 1-1. Att: 2,196. Wycombe, then managed by Celtic manager Martin O'Neill, won the replay 2-0 and went on to win the Trophy final and Conference title.

Y

YATES, STEVE: 1981-82 and 1983-84. Midfield 37+2 (12+1 cup) apps; 3 cup goals. Ex-Chorley and Wigan Athletic. Joined Morecambe in December, 1981, but emigrated to South Africa in November, 1982. Returned to the country and joined Morecambe again in September, 1983. Later played for Chorley.

YEOVIL YOWN: Morecambe first met the Glovers in the Conference at Christie Park on January 17, 1998, winning 1-0. Att: 1,219.

YOUNG, JERRY: 1933-34. Outside-right 29 (3 cup) apps; 6 goals. Joined Morecambe in October, 1933, for a season. After spells at Horwich RMI and Accrington Stanley played some games for Morecambe in the North Lancashire League in 1940-41. Also known as a cricketer with Farnworth in the Bolton League.

YOUNG, JOSEPH: 1925-31. Right-Back 165 (41 cup) apps; 22 (7 cup) goals. Joined Morecambe in September, 1925, after playing for PNE 1920-21, Barrow 1921-22, Lancaster Town 1922-23, Kendal Town and Lancaster Town 1924-25. Lancashire Cup winner in 1925-26 and 1926-27. Combination Cup winner in 1926-27.

YORK CITY: Morecambe have met York City three times in the FA Cup proper rounds with the most recent coming in the 1985/86 season. The first meeting came in the 1966/67 campaign and was a real titanic struggle. After beating Milnthorpe Corinthians, Nelson, Netherfield and South Liverpool in the qualifying stages the teams met at Bootham Crescent and fought out a tough 0-0 draw. The replay at Christie Park also ended all square (1-1). As a result the tie needed a second replay which took part at Manchester City's Maine Road. A crowd of 4,283 saw York steal a narrow 1-0 win. The next meeting came just a couple of seasons later, with a 2nd Rd tie in the 1968/69 season, that unfortunately ended in a 2-0 defeat. The final meeting came in the 1985/86 season in a 1st Rd tie won by the Shrimps, after victories over Harrogate Town, Billingham Town, Gretna and St Helens Town in the earlier stages. Drawn to travel to Bootham Crescent again the Shrimps had much the better of the tie but unfortunately could not find the scoresheet and had to settle for a 0-0 draw and another replay. The club chose Maine Road as the venue for the second time and in front of just 1,305 people the Shrimps went down 2-0.

YORK STREET: Home of Boston United. The club's first visit there ended in a 2-0 defeat in the Northern Premier League Cup 1st Rd on August 31, 1968. Att: 2,179.

YOUNGEST PLAYER: Reported to be Simon Longrigg who came on as a substitute at Bishop Auckland in a NPL game on September 13, 1989 after just turning 16.

YOUTHS: The club first ran a youth team from 1955-1961 playing in the North Lancashire League Under 18s division. Coach Maurice Vickers and trainer Ronnie Meadows led the team to the league title in 1955-56 and 1956-57 and runners-up spot in 1958-59 and 1959-60. The R L Dilworth Cup was won in 1956-57 and in 1959-60 after victories over Red Rose on both occasions. The same team were also beaten in the Junior Challenge Cup final of 1957-58. A famous moment came in the 1959-60 season when the club entered the FA Youth Cup, bowing out 14-0 to Manchester United at Old Trafford. Director Ben Birchall started an 'A' team in 1963-64 which won the North Lancashire League Division Three title and came second in Division Two the following season. The 1965-66 season was played in the West Lancashire League. Another director, Mike Easthope, ran an Under 16s team in the Service of Youth League with the team including Jamie McGowan. In 1992-93 the club took over the running of Hawk Rovers and became Morecambe Hawk, the forerunners of today's comprehensive Morecambe Youth set up. A Morecambe Youth side entered the North Lancashire League again in 1992-93 under Jeff Udall. With players such as Stewart Drummond, Jamie Udall, Andy and Paul Taylor in the side they won the Lancashire Youth Cup with a 4-0 win over Burscough and the Lancashire Floodlit League with a two-legged victory over Southport. The team won the North Lancashire League Division Three championship and Parkinson Cup in the 1993-94 season. Other honours won by the youths include the Lancashire U16s Youth Cup in 1999-2000, the North West Alliance Premier Division 200-02 and the North West Alliance Premier Cup 2001-02. The club were also finalists in the Lancashire Youth Cup U12s 2000-01 and U18s 2001-02.

YZENDOORN, JOHN: 1976-78. Defender 70+2 (25 cup) apps; 9 (1 cup) goals. His name may have been a bit of a mouthful but he could certainly play. After signing from Lancaster City in July 1976 he gained a reputation as an excellent full back. John made 41 appearances for the Shrimps in the 1977-78 season before emigrating to Australia where he quickly made his name playing for Prahran Slavia (Melbourne) and became an Australian international.

Z

ZOLOTARCZUK, RAYMOND. 1977-78 and 1981-82. Forward/Midfield 6+5 (0+1 cup) apps. First signed in November, 1977, and returned in February, 1982. Former junior with Lincoln City and played for Toronto in Canada.

*Morecambe players and staff celebrate winning promotion
to the Nationwide Conference.*

The light at the end of the tunnel